"Whenever I sit at Joey's feet in a circle of people to sing, his sparse but powerful words in between each *nigun* are as delicious as the music itself. This book is a collection of those deep insights, rooted in Jewish text and tradition, given wings by Joey's unique spiritual genius. I always regretted not being able to write down every word in those sacred circles—thank God he has done it for me! This book is a treasure for anyone who leads or participates in Jewish prayer—indeed, for anyone with a spiritual bone in their body."

Rabbi Lizzi Heydemann, Mishkan Chicago

"It's no wonder that Joey Weisenberg has the following that he does. He manages to honor Judaism's musical canon while taking it roaring into the future in ways that are rousing, haunting, heartrending and exciting. His book, *The Torah of Music*, weaves the stories, liturgy, history, and poetry that make music such a primary, powerful source of spiritual transformation. This book will make you want to sing."

Abby Pogrebin, *My Amazing Jewish Year*

"Like in Rabbi Nahman's description of prayer, Joey Weisenberg wanders through the field of Jewish writing and gathers beautiful flowers, short texts on music and song, to create a bouquet for the practitioner. In the process, he reflects on his own experience as a song and prayer leader, offering a model for the important process of connecting practice to text for any practitioner who attempts to bring together prayer and song."

Rabbi Ebn Leader, Hebrew College

"Joey's readings of Jewish sources are fresh, spiritually awake and grounded in lived experience. Texts and prayers that I have read a hundred times come alive with new meanings and creative possibilities through Joey's scholarly wisdom and keen observation. His reflections, at times humorous, at times uplifting, are drawn from years of experience studying music, leading prayer and teaching communities to open their mouths and hearts to breath together and listen. Each time I look up from the page, I find myself sitting quietly or walking through the streets and suddenly I am hearing everything around me and within me, singing. This book is itself a prayersong—elegant and earthy, inspiring and thought-provoking, evocative and soul-stirring."

Rabbi Miriam Margles, Danforth Jewish Center

The Torah of Music

For Josh
Enjoy!

Joey

The Torah of Music

Reflections on a Tradition of Singing and Song

JOEY WEISENBERG

Translations by

JOSHUA SCHWARTZ

with Foreword by

RABBI ELIE KAUNFER

Hadar Press
New York
2017

Design by David Zvi Kalman

Hadar Press
190 Amsterdam Avenue
New York, NY 10023
www.hadarpress.org

ISBN-10: 1-946611-02-6
ISBN-13: 987-1-946611-02-4
2017930747

Printed in the United States of America
1 3 5 7 9 10 8 6 4 2

In memory of my father-in-law, Steven Weingrod (1950–2017)

Foreword   *xi*

Preface   *xv*

Translator's Note   *xix*

Acknowledgements   *xxi*

INTRODUCTION   *1*

PART ONE: STUDIES AND STORIES

1. Songs of Prophecy and Torah   *17*

2. Songs of Ascent   *27*

3. Quieting   *37*

4. Listening   *47*

5. Joining Together Through Song   *59*

6. Holy Instruments   *77*

7. Songs of Struggle   *89*

8. Brokenness and Wholeness   *94*

9. Praise and Gratitude   *107*

10. Renewing the Songs of Life   *115*

Contents

PART TWO: OPEN LIBRARY

Torah   122

Prophets   125

Writings   130

Mishnah   136

Talmud   139

Midrash   167

Medieval   183

Mystical   193

Halakhic   207

Hasidic   212

Siddur/Mahzor   248

Twentieth Century   250

The Piezetzner's Essay on *Nigun*   258

SELECTED BIBLIOGRAPHY   267

Foreword

I learned to play piano as a child, and I have prayed daily for most of my life, but I never really understood music or prayer until Joey Weisenberg taught me. In this book, Joey teaches me—and all readers—about music, prayer, and Torah. Perhaps most importantly and most uniquely, he skillfully integrates all three.

I have sat with Joey countless times over the past twelve years as he led groups large and small in singing. I watched him win over the hardened skeptics, the people who like to sit in the back and roll their eyes at song (I was one of those people). I watched him introduce original melodies: first one, then a second, then dozens and dozens—drawn from traditional sources, but, over time, infused with an American style. All of us were beginners in learning the music, no one with a head start. I clapped, stomped, slapped my knee, all at the direction of Joey, working hard to absorb that concept foreign to so many of us—rhythm.

All along, I thought I knew the purpose of all this singing: the goal was to create music. To really learn the melody, to sing something over and over again until it entered into "your *kishkes*," as Joey would say. Twenty times in a row—minimum. This was a radical practice—a shift to focus and repetition in a world that favors channel surfing.

And Joey's music has made a tremendous impact. This month alone I heard his songs in a sixth grade classroom in St. Louis, a rabbinical seminary in New York, and a Hillel conference in Orlando. Tens of thousands of people have played Joey's music; it has gone "mainstream" in the wider Jewish world.

And not just the sound of the music, but the way we can sing the music. Closer together, everyone contributing, regardless of skill or experience. When he was 28, Joey wrote a book, *Building Singing Communities*—he has done that in dozens of communities across the country.

Then, one day, Joey changed his tune. He explained that singing is not really about singing, ultimately. It is about listening. Only when we are close together can we really listen to each other. I can't hear your voice and stay on track with your beat if you are far away from me.

But it isn't just about listening to each other. It is about listening to everything that surrounds us. The distant car honking, the hum of the air conditioner, the out-of-tune doorbell. Even more: the sounds of nature, the stillness of the air, the "subtleties of all creation," as Joey says.

Perhaps at best it is listening to the silence that follows the beautiful song. The song is not the point; the song—and its end—allow us to finally listen to that silence that we all ignore in our busy, noisy lives.

There is a moment at the end of one of Joey's singing circles when everyone is up on their feet, singing loudly a melody they learned for the first time an hour earlier, a melody that has finally entered their souls. Joey is in the middle—not because he wants to be, but because he knows that he has to be, at least in the beginning. He slows down the tempo a touch, and wraps his fist on itself signaling us all to stop—in unison. And then Joey cocks his ear, and listens. And we all listen as well. I have heard the most beautiful sounds in that moment of full silence.

A midrash teaches that before God gave the Torah on Mount Sinai the entire world was silent. Every living being, all of nature, stopped its gurgling, murmuring, rustling, and speaking. Then God's voice broke forth.

This book is the Torah of music that follows the silence. Joey has collected in these pages the highlights of the Jewish textual tradition's lessons about music. The research alone is an impressive achievement, and the masterful translations by Joshua Schwartz allow all readers to sense their beauty. Joey is not the first to highlight the connection between Torah and music; the Talmud itself draws those connections clearly. But the framing and life lessons that accompany these texts allow, for the first time, Joey's voice as a teacher of Torah to be clearly heard. This is important because Joey is not only a musician; he is a lover of Torah, in the deepest and broadest sense of that word, and he has taken that love and transmitted it in these pages.

Joey is a sensitive and creative interpreter of texts. I saw him working on those skills a decade ago when he studied Talmud in my class at Yeshivat Hadar every morning. He moved slowly, asking questions, taking it in. In short, he listened. And because he has been listening very carefully to Torah for years, he now has something to say about it. This is good news for all of us because we need to hear the Torah that Joey can teach us.

I once asked Joey why he changed the formula of his successful song-leading sessions, why he started to teach from the Talmud instead of just leading us in song. He said he can't always do the same thing forever, and the next frontier of his own learning and growth was delving into the sources of our heritage, to uncover the deeper meaning that lies between Torah and song. Joey sang, he listened, he heard the voice of Torah calling, and he recognized that Torah and song cannot be forever kept apart. This book is the fusion of those passions that Joey combines at an expert level.

Music is infinite and the Torah is infinite. I am grateful to learn from Joey the beginning of the ways in which these infinite forces can intertwine, integrate, and, ultimately, return to what they always were: one unified whole. In this book, Joey shows all of us the beginnings of that process.

Enjoy the process and don't forget to listen closely.

Rabbi Elie Kaunfer
February, 2017

Preface: Why this book?

Dear friend,

Thank you for picking up this book.

I wrote this book as a *chizuk*, or strengthening of the spirit, for musicians, community leaders, prayer leaders, and others who, like myself, would like to learn more about the story of music as a Jewish spiritual practice, and play some part in its unfolding narrative. "Torah" means teaching. In this book, we'll look not only at teachings from the Jewish tradition that involve music but also at what music itself has to teach us. I hope that this book will help deepen the musical and spiritual culture of twenty-first-century Jewish life, and ideally find use outside the Jewish world as well.

I've found that singing has transcended barriers in the Jewish world, and increasingly outside of the Jewish world as well. While it certainly helps that I am able to wear a beard and brandish a smile, I have found that, with only a few exceptions, almost all distinctions of orthodoxy or denomination seem to melt away when the singing begins. I've opened my eyes in various cities around the world to find myself leading and singing *nigunim*[1] with many thousands of people, representing very different groups of people:

Hasidim in Milwaukee and Brooklyn,
transgender grandfathers in Miami,
reconverted Marranos in Houston,
a cowboy in a ten gallon hat in Dallas,
four-hundred Seventh Day Adventist, evangelical Christians in Chattanooga,
the "Frozen Chosen" Jews in Anchorage, Alaska,
Catholics and Muslims in Ontario,
young Orthodox Jews in London,
top-hatted Spanish-Portuguese Jews in New York,
hippie Jews in Berkeley,
farming Jews in Connecticut,

---

[1] *Nigun* (pl. *nigunim*), in contemporary Jewish circles, means a wordless melody. However, it can also mean a melody, whether wordless or not, especially in older sources. You will thus find the words nigun and melody used interchangeably throughout this book.

Baptist preachers in Detroit,
klezmer revivalists in Montreal and Toronto,
Gypsy grandmothers in the Ukrainian Carpathians,
a man *davening* with a white dog in his armpit in Louisville,
philosemites in Weimar, Germany, and Krakow, Poland,
mystics in Jerusalem,
Holocaust survivors in the Bronx,
Jewish Socialists in Paris,
Reform Cantors in Philadelphia,
Yiddishists in Vilna,
youth leaders in London…
…and I'm just getting started.

Across all lines, music speaks and resonates and connects and deepens our human experience. Still, we still have a long way to go towards fully hearing each other's songs and prayers, towards fully realizing music's potential. Can we allow melody to connect us with our neighbors, with our enemies and our friends? Can we allow music to transcend the barriers we've constructed between Jews? Can music overcome divisions between all peoples? Can we learn to hear the music being sung by all of creation?

This book is not intended to be an academic or historical study of Jewish music, a scientific study of music's affects on a person, or a timeless traditional *sefer* (holy book). Rather, this book is a collection of musical hopes and dreams that seeks to reignite the musical-spiritual imagination in the particular time we find ourselves living in. As such, in addition to the many dozens of quotes from traditional Jewish sources, I have also peppered the book with stories from my own experience as a musician, *ba'al tefillah* (prayer leader), and teacher.

There are three sections to this book:

The first is an introduction, describing, in very broad strokes, how music has been a fundamental player in Jewish spiritual life throughout the ages.

The second section is a series of studies and stories related to song and music, showing how Jewish texts might talk to each other and to us, across time.

The third section is a chronological collection of musically-oriented texts from the Jewish tradition, arranged as if you were walking into a traditional Jewish library in which all of the old books had miraculously been opened to their most musical passages, and also translated! If you enjoy browsing in a traditional library and experiencing texts directly on your own, you may prefer to skip to this section to glance directly at the sources. For a more curated experience that includes more of my own interpretations of this material, please read on.

The texts and teachings in this book are drawn from the full range of Jewish experience, up through the middle of the twentieth-century. I believe that they represent a corpus of traditional ideas about music that we can use to encourage and support musical movements in this present moment.

I hope that you will use these texts to teach others and to continue to expand and develop the musical traditions that have been so transformational for all of us. More than that, I hope you will use these ideas as a rooted basis for inventing your own ideas, your own musical midrash, and most importantly, your own music!

With appreciation,
Joey Weisenberg
November 2016

Translator's Note

How to Make Words Sing

> May my words be sweet before You;
> it is for You my soul thirsts.
>
> —*Anim Z'mirot*

Elemental in music is its ability to move us, to move something within us, to capture a feeling and impart it to its listeners. Music is able to bring us from one state to another, invoking the original meaning of the word "translation," a change in position, to literally be moved. It is in our ability to grow, to become something else, that we partake of the Infinite; the Torah, after all, was given to us, not to the angels, who are perfect and static. Perhaps less than music changes us, music makes us aware of how we change, that we change, that time passes, that we are in movement. Music itself is a translation: a change in state over time.

There is more to language than just the words. So much of how language works involves time, velocity, pacing, force, even the haunt of absence, of empty space. To translate requires attention, not just to what is being said, but to what is happening—in the text, and in us. Language, in this way, is always already musical.

Every selection in this book is like a prayer. More than it says anything, it expresses desire, articulating the distance between what is and what could be. The texts in this books are not merely descriptive of music's power, its genius, its beauty; they are prescriptive, voicing a theory of what music is, what music could be; they are evocative, attempting not merely to speak about music, but recreate what it is and what it does.

In translating, I drew from musical concepts as a guide: rhythm, metre, dynamics, and, most of all, harmony. Writing about music requires a kind of expression and mode of creation, whose unique quality inheres in its ability to slip and slide, to break and mend, to evoke and impose, to burrow and ascend, to infuse and transcend. I tried to ensure a resonance the words, that they would reverberate when read out loud, or merely when they ring in one's mind. These words about music cannot merely be about music; they must sing, too. In these prayers, I pray that they move.

Joshua Schwartz

Acknowledgements

This book is a collection not only of ancient texts about music, but also of ideas and worldviews that I've absorbed through years of musical-spiritual exploration with a wide variety of musicians, teachers, and friends. Thank you to the people, in large cities and small towns around the world, that I've had the privilege to sing and talk with. You have all shown that it's possible to create amazing collective musical-spiritual artistry when we set ourselves to the task.

In particular, I'd like to thank Rabbi Michel Twerski of Milwaukee, whose sweet singing and seemingly endless wellspring of Torah teaching deeply affected me as a teenager, and Cantor Noach Schall, who taught me the ins and outs of *nusah* (traditional prayer chant) over the course of three years of serious study. Thank you also to Dr. Chaim Kranzler and Rabbi Simkha Weintraub for their ongoing mentorship, friendship, and life-curiosity.

Many others have provided critical inspiration and partnership over the years: Michael Alpert, Cantor Carey Cohen, Rabbi Eliezer Diamond, Rabbi Nancy Flam, Eric Gold, Rabbi Yosef Goldman, Rabbi Shai Held, Rabbi David Ingber, Rabbi Ebn Leader, Dr. Elli Kranzler, Chazan Jack Kessler, Rabbi Miriam Margles, Rabbi Marcia Praeger, Rabbi Aviva Richman, Rabbi Dorothy Richman, Lani Santo, Rabbi Jonathan Slater, Andy Statman, Rabbi Ethan Tucker, Rabbi Ben Zion Twerski, Cantor Jeff Warschauer, Rabbi Arthur Waskow, Rabbi Sam Weintraub, Michael Winograd, and Rabbi Adam Zeff all shared critical teachings, inspiration, and thought partnership over the years. Rabbi DovBer Pinson's book *Inner Rhythms*, as well as Moshe Idel's various articles on Jewish musical mysticism were particularly valuable for me in opening up Jewish spiritual traditions around music.

Thank you to the staff, students, and faculty at Mechon Hadar. Jeremy Tabick and Anna Leah Berstein Simpson cleaned up and copy-edited this book and helped it to flow. Rebecca Cushman helped with layouts and edits in early drafts. Rabbi Elie Kaunfer, in particular, has been a major mentor to me and a shepherd of these ideas. It's a privilege to have colleagues who make each other better at what they do—as in when Elie and the Hadar team read part of an early draft and then told me, "Make no mistake about it, this draft doesn't just need-copy editing, it needs GLOBAL REVISION."

Zachary Anziska, Aryeh Bernstein, Nancy Ettenheim, David Ferleger, Rabbi Elie Kaunfer, Dr. Chaim Kranzler, Rabbi Miriam Margles, Deborah Sacks Mintz, Rabbi Aviva Richman, Jeremy Tabick, Molly Weingrod, Bob Weisenberg, Dena Weiss and others carefully read early drafts of this book and offered important feedback and encouraged me to rewrite it altogether. My brother Sam Weisenberg offered his usual honest perspective (i.e. "This book would be much better if it was interesting").

Thank you to David Zvi Kalman who designed the layout of this book, and to Andrew Benincasa for his work on the beautiful paper cut illustrations. Most of all, I couldn't have done this project without Josh Schwartz's skills in research, his valuable insights, and his beautiful translations, which he has created with poetry and precision. His enthusiasm for this project has been very encouraging to me throughout. Thanks for the partnership in creating this work, Josh!

Thank you to my family. My mother Nancy Ettenheim taught me my first major and minor chords and corrected my writing, always laughing because I couldn't even pronounce the word "English" correctly. My father, Bob Weisenberg, a phenomenal and passionate musician, has always encouraged the type of musical dreaming that's in these pages, and has been the only person in the world with whom I can freely talk about music for hours with no embarrassment. Above all, this book would not have been possible without the inspiration, patience, and encouragement from my partner Molly Weingrod, and for the constant sounds and songs of our children, Lev, Mozi, Bina, and Manu.

Introduction

Music: Ubiquitous in the Jewish Story

Music occupies a central role in many of the stories of our tradition. Many, if not most, of the great leaders, visionaries, and spiritual leaders of our ancient tradition relied on music as heavily as Jews do today. Music was born into the Torah's record of human history with the birth of the first musician, Yuval.[1] In the midrashic tradition, Abraham and Isaac were associated with the first shofar,[2] Jacob with singing,[3] Serah with the harp,[4] Joseph with the symphony,[5] Moses with the flute,[6] Miriam with the tambourine,[7] David with the harp,[8] Solomon with the Song of Songs,[9] Assaf with the cymbal,[10] Hannah and Deborah with their famous songs,[11] and those just get us started.

---

[1] Genesis 4:20–21 (#1 in the Open Library. I will refer to sources I've cited in the Open Library throughout the text in this form).

[2] Pirkei D'Rabbi Eliezer 21 (#85). In addition, Isaac was known for singing—see Shabbat Minhah *Amidah* prayer, "*Avraham yagel, Yitzhak y'ranen…*"

[3] Talmud Bavli Hullin 91b (#69); *Sefer HaYashar*, Parshat VaYigash (#96); Nahman of Breslov, *Likkutei Moharan* II, 63 (#150); *Sefat Emet*, Leviticus, Passover, 5658 (#156).

[4] Sefer HaYashar, Parshat VaYigash (#96).

[5] Louis Ginsburg, "The Ruler of Egypt" in *Legends of the Jews* (Philadelphia: Jewish Publication Society, 1955), p. 74.

[6] Talmud Bavli Arakhin 10b (#71).

[7] Exodus 15:20–21 (#3).

[8] 1 Samuel 16:23 (#10), Talmud Bavli Berakhot 3b (#39).

[9] Song of Songs 1:1. Some important texts like the Song of Songs and other texts that support but do not directly address musical-spiritual concepts, are not included in the Open Library. The texts selected for the Open Library are texts that (for the most part) directly mention music or a musical process.

[10] 1 Chronicles 16:5–9 (#33), Talmud Bavli Arakhin 13a (#75)

[11] 1 Samuel 2:1, Judges 5:1.

The entire people of Israel, whose name hints at "Singing to God (*Shir El*),"[12] are depicted as singing a collective song of freedom,[13] which we reenact every day. Many, if not all, of the prophets required music in order to make their prophecies,[14] the Levites sang and performed music constantly to accompany the Temple sacrifices,[15] and the angels had one main occupation—to sing.[16]

Everyone and everything sings. Our ancient stories describe that music was sung by men and women, children and adults, slaves and rulers, professionals and laymen, Jews and gentiles, refugees and settled folks, by the brilliant and the simple. All of the creatures of the land continue to sing their songs, too, from the birds to the beasts and from the trees to the grasses. Music even goes beyond life—inanimate objects sing, from the mountains to the rivers to the seas![17]

The Tanakh, the Talmud, and the Midrash refer many hundreds of times to music,[18] the Zohar writes of music over and over,[19] and the Hasidic Masters were awash in song, writing about music frequently, and singing all the time. Indeed, the Torah and its commentaries are nothing but an attempt to articulate in words what the divine Song says directly to our hearts, and that's why the Torah itself is called a Song.[20]

And yet, given the fundamental place of music in the stories of Jewish tradition, what is the story that is told by music itself? Is music a kind of story, or does music transcend story? Can music ever be fully defined by the words of a story? Is there any story that can capture the beauty and power of music? How do the stories that are told about music, such as the stories in this book, compare to the stories that music itself tells?

Music Signifies Life

Music has been included in every stage of the Jewish story since the very beginning because it is a fundamental sign of life.

---

[12] *Sefat Emet*, Leviticus, Passover, 5658 (#156).

[13] Exodus 15:1–2 (#2).

[14] Meir ibn Gabbai, *Avodat HaKodesh* Part 4, ch. 23 (#124).

[15] 1 Kings 10:12 (#13); 1 Chronicles 16:5–9 (#33); Mishnah Sukkah 5:1,4 (#37); Pesikta Rabbati 26 (#92), *Sefer HaHinukh* 384 (#108).

[16] Rambam, *Guide of the Perplexed*, 2:6 (#101).

[17] Perek Shirah (#84).

[18] See the books of Shlomo Hoffman listed in the bibliography.

[19] See Amnon Shiloach and Ruth Tene, *Music Subjects in the Zohar* (Jerusalem: Magnes Press, 1977).

[20] Deuteronomy 31:18–19 (#7).

To sing is to be fully alive. The Talmud describes the prophet Ezekiel coming to a valley full of dry bones. He saw that the bones joined back into the shape of the human skeleton, and that the sinews and muscles reappeared, and skin covered them, and they lay there waiting for his next vision.[21] What happens next? The Talmud picks up the story there, explaining:

> The dead revived by Ezekiel stood on their feet, sang a song, and died.[22]

Ezekiel was witnessing a mass resurrection, but how did he know that the bones had actually returned to life? What was the sign that they had come back to life? It was song! Music, it seems from this story, was a "proof" that life had occurred. Hilariously, the only uncertainty, according to the Talmud, is not whether they sang, but "which song did they sing?!"

Thus, music is fundamental to life. As soon as one breathes, one sings. As King David exclaims in his final and most musical psalm, and elaborated in a midrash:

> *Let everything that breathes (lit: all the breath/soul) praise God, halleluyah!*"[23]
> With every single breath we take, we sing the praises of the Holy One.[24]

Is there a stage of life that music doesn't accompany? The Talmud gives the following account of David, imagining him as singing from before his birth all the way until his death. His songs, it seems, represented his very life:

> [While King David] resided in his mother's womb, he broke into song… Once he emerged into the open air, and he gazed at the stars and the constellations, he broke into song…When he suckled from his mother's breasts and gazed at them, he broke into song…He looked upon his day of death and broke into song…[25]

Moreover, music awakens in us the spirit of life itself. On only its second page, the Talmud relates that the northern wind blew on King David's harp, waking up the great king.[26] Rebbe Nahman of Breslov (d. 1810) elaborates:

---

[21] Ezekiel 37:1-14.
[22] Talmud Bavli Sanhedrin 92b (#62).
[23] Psalms 150:6 (#29).
[24] Yalkut Shimoni, Psalm 150. By contrast, the dead cannot sing praises to God, לא המתים יהללו-קה (Psalms 115:17). Also, the children of Korah were said to have "not died" (Numbers 26:11), and Bavli Sanhedrin 110a (#65) explains that although they had descended to Hell, they were sitting there and singing and thus could not have died.
[25] Talmud Bavli Berakhot 10a (#41).
[26] Talmud Bavli Berakhot 3b (#39).

The northern wind (*ru'ah hatzafon*) is the spirit hidden (*ru'ah hatzafun*) in the heart of each person, and this is the spirit of life.[27]

Music, like the harp in David's story, is one of the amplifiers through which we can hear and express the spirit of life. We may have a spirit of life hidden inside of each of us, but we need the music to draw it out and allow us to find it.

Entering the Song

What is a person? "A piece of meat with eyes."[28]

What is a melody? Merely vibrations in the air.

These are the cold facts of life. And yet, throughout many generations, we, along with our poets and prophets, have tried to suspend our disbeliefs and to dream that a person is more than just flesh, to imagine that a person might grow to love, to care, to appreciate, to wonder, to enjoy! And a melody—it might open our hearts, cause us to rise, communicate with all creatures on earth, even to reach the Divine! These are the musical dreams and hopes which tag along with the stories of a sensitive human heart. How do we allow music to become more than just vibrations, to allow it to move and transform us? How do we enter the musical imagination that is contained in this book?

Song operates in cycles, and its justification is fittingly circular as well. The skeptical philosopher inside of each of us will notice the circularity of many of the concepts in this book—a feedback loop of musical musings. But the circularity is part and parcel of the song. As we'll see, singing gathers us and brings us closer together as an intimate community, and yet closeness and intimacy are themselves prerequisites for making music. Song leads us to silence, but silence leads us back to song. Singing teaches us how to listen, but yet, we must already be listening in order to hear the song. Song is an expression of freedom, but yet the first song was sung in slavery.[29] When do we start singing? It's our choice. Jump in anywhere you please!

Do we have to feel an inspiration first, and then sing—or can we sing, and then feel inspiration emerge from the song? Both! The Talmud taught that divine inspiration could come both before or after song.

---

[27] *Likkutei Moharan* I, 8:9 (#144): A play of words on רוח הצפון / *ru'ah hatzafon* (northern wind) and רוח הצפון / *ru'ah hatzafun* (hidden spirit).

[28] In German, "*Ein Stuck fleisch mit Augen.*" In loving memory of my grandmother, Toni Ettenheim.

[29] See first and second songs of Mekhilta Shirah 1 (#82); see also *Ba'al HaTurim* on Exodus 15:1 (#107).

"To David, a Psalm" (*leDavid mizmor*) teaches that the *Shekhinah* (Divine Presence) rested upon him and then he sang a song; "a Psalm of David" (*mizmor leDavid*) teaches that he [first] sang [that] song, and then the *Shekhinah* rested upon him.[30]

Music inspires and also grows out of inspiration, a cycle of song that generates its own momentum.

A *nigun*, like life itself, moves in endless circles. That's part of the definition of *nigun*—it never really starts and it never really finishes. Even the root of the word *nigun* itself (נ-ג-ן) begins again before it ends, representing this cycle of song.[31]

To enter this musical dream, we must jump in and sing, and the rest of the connections will come over time. For music to move our hearts, we must put our hearts into it. Sing a simple song, with your heart! But this is no easy task; indeed, it may take a lifetime for each of us to learn how to open our mouths and hearts in genuine song and prayer. It is certainly beyond the scope of this book to teach you, really teach you, how to sing. To learn the spiritual craft of song in real life, we must each seek out role models, guides, and mentors, or even just fellow musical travellers, and sit down next to them while they sing and join when we're ready. Music, and the life it contains, is passed through the air from person to person in an ancient chain.

The Chord of Compassion

Music is a thread of mercy (*hut shel hesed*), a connective "chord of compassion,"[32] that takes hold of even the farthest reaches of creation—and the most divergent ways of existing—and pulls them ever closer together. The prophet Isaiah imagined,

> From the ends of the Earth we have heard songs.[33]

None of us can hear all the way to the ends of the physical Earth, but music is a magic carpet that allows us to explore the outer edges of our consciousness, to transcend the limitations of our intellects and knowledge, and to see beyond the stories that we've always told ourselves.

---

[30] Talmud Bavli Pesahim 117a (#45).

[31] Matityahu Glazerson, *Music and Kabbalah* (Jason Aronson: Northvale, N.J., 1996), p. 35.

[32] Talmud Bavli Avodah Zarah 3b (#54), poetic adaptation of Soncino translation. The Talmud suggests that if one studies the song of Torah during the night, a "thread of mercy" will be extended for that person during the day.

[33] Isaiah 24:16 (#17).

Music represents the "all-man's land" between each of our usual entrenched positions, in which the holy connects with the profane, the fixed reaches towards the unfixed, the old becomes new, the angelic meets the human, and the eternal engages with the ephemeral. When we sing, sound merges with silence, sadness with joy, slavery with freedom, poor with rich,[34] night with day,[35] sound with sight,[36] animal with human, war with peace, and perfection with imperfection. Music acts as a mystical interface that connects all of these poles, urging them to talk to each other and to express the life that's contained among all of them.

We need not erase all differences of opinion or experience to arrive together at music. On the contrary, music occurs in the dialogue between the otherwise disparate and detached elements of the world. Song emerges from the reconciliation of different ideas, when we hear each other's experiences and prayers, when we listen for each other's essences, even as we, as individuals or families, may choose widely divergent paths for ourselves. One Lithuanian rabbi even compared the Talmud's tradition of vigorous debate to a musical symphony:

> That is the beauty of our holy and pure Torah. The entire Torah is called a song,[37] and a song is beautiful when all of its voices differ one from another; this is the essence of its polyphonic pleasantness (*ne'imot*). Anyone who swims about in the sea of the Talmud can see the harmony in all of the voices differing from each other [but yet coexisting].[38]

Music, in this sense, represents a form of pluralism. Music is itself born of a dissonant dialogue, a vibrant debate between the tendencies toward resolution and tension. Moments of sympathetic vibrations and harmony, where all of the notes feel at ease, yield to moments of tension, where the notes push against each other and clash in conflict. Music grows from the dialogue between the two harmonic poles of consonance and dissonance.

Rav Kook, too, imagined ever-widening circles of song merging into a greater musical mosaic:

> There is one who sings his soul's song [...]
> There is one who sings the song of the nation [...]

---

[34] Talmud Bavli Ketubot 46b: "Rabbi Yehudah called for two flutists, minimum, to play at every funeral, for even the poorest of people."

[35] Music allows us to fight our battles by day and find inspiration by night. See Talmud Bavli Berakhot 3b (#39).

[36] Exodus 19:15, 20:15 (#5).

[37] Deuteronomy 31:18–19 (#7).

[38] Yehiel Mikhal Epstein, *Arokh HaShulhan*, Hoshen Mishpat, Introduction (#133).

There is one whose soul will expand until it emerges, spreading beyond the boundary of Israel, to sing humanity's song [...]

There is one who will reach still further and higher until he unites with all of existence; with all creatures, with all worlds, and with them all he sings a song. [...]

There is one who ascends in unity along with all these songs, together as one.[39]

Here Rav Kook is describing the different socio-political orientations that characterized his highly sectarian and ideological moment, such as individualism (i.e. "his soul's song"), nationalism (i.e. "the song of his nation"), humanism (i.e. "humanity's song"), and naturalism (i.e. the song of "all existence, all creation"). Yet, he related to them not just as political opinions or personality traits, but as songs, all artistic contributions to the world.[40]

What would it be like if we, too, related to personal and ideological differences as music? How can we learn to hear the particular songs of our own souls and peoples, while also keeping open a sensitive ear to the songs of other peoples? How can we learn to hear the songs being sung of all of creation?

When we sing, if we're lucky, we might float into an ecstatic dreamscape in which our usual habits of thought no longer hold absolute sway over our perceptions. Our vision widens. Our songs cross our conceptual chasms and dismantle our dogmatic divisions, and we learn to hear more of the world, all at once. The Talmud taught that God Godself is able to perceive many worlds at once in much the same way that God listens to the music of the life-angels (*hayyot*).

What does God do at night?...God rides God's lissome cherub, gliding through eighteen thousand worlds...God sits and listens to the song of the *hayyot*.[41]

When we sing, we might come closer to hearing the world the way we've imagined that God hears the world.

With *nigun*, pure music—unfettered by words, freed of intellection division—normal polarities melt away. Perhaps music brings out the love in all of us, and in doing so teaches us to listen to the love that unifies all. That's why Jews incorporate *nigunim* into our spiritual practices. Our wordless melodies transcend all of the divisions that our brains and habits create, surpassing language

---

[39] Abraham Isaac Kook, *Orot HaKodesh* 2:444–445 (#175).

[40] Aryeh Bernstein framed Rav Kook's writing this way to me in 2016, in conversation and in writing.

[41] Talmud Bavli Avodah Zarah 3b (#66).

to connect with the indescribable. Melodies point us towards a dream in which we can all hear the oneness of Creator and creation.[42]

The sages taught that in order to acquire new wisdom one needs to make oneself like an "ownerless wilderness"—to venture purposely into the deserted wild spaces in our souls.[43] Music facilitates our move into these unowned places within ourselves, because sound, too, by its very nature, defies possession.[44] Music's ephemeral expansiveness reminds us of the state of non-ownership from which we can develop as human beings, listen for the songs of all creation, and search for the divine voice.

When we sing a *nigun*, we hope that we might let go of our preordained sets of expectations about how we think the singing is going to proceed and gradually sit in the actual moment of singing. This open mindset allows us to enter into territories that we are less comfortable with; it allows us to engage with the fullness of what we don't know, and to experience a glimpse of another version of the universe. This is the essence of compassion—the realization that what exists beyond our current understanding holds a fullness all its own, one that's just as complete and incomplete as our own selves. Song transports us to these worlds just beyond ourselves, if we let it! When we let go of our expectations and assumptions, we have a chance at hearing the chord of compassion as it unwinds in the world.[45]

In our musical mythology, melodies reach not only across our spiritual spectrums but across the endless expanses of eternity. The entire world, the Zohar teaches us, was created as a song,[46] and it will be through song that the world is ultimately reunited.[47] When we open our mouths and sing, we play our role in the mystical reconciliation of the universe.

Danger: Music!

Despite all of the powerful ways in which music supports our spiritual quests, opens up our minds and brings harmony to the world, throughout Jew-

---

[42] Deuteronomy 6:4, "*Sh'ma…Ehad.*"

[43] Numbers Rabbah 1:1, "One who doesn't make oneself like an open, ownerless desert (*midbar hefker*) cannot acquire the wisdom and the Torah. That's why it says, '*in the Sinai wilderness…*' [i.e. that's why the Torah was giving in the wilderness]."

[44] Rambam, *Mishneh Torah*, Laws of Shofar 1:3 (#99).

[45] Dov Ber Schneuri of Lubavitch, *Tract on Ecstasy* (#142).

[46] Zohar Hadash, Bereishit, p. 298 (#119).

[47] Talmud Bavli Sanhedrin 91a, "All who sing in this world will merit to sing in the world to come."

ish history many of our sages have kept music at arm's length. Why keep a distance from music? Simply put, if music is powerful enough to create the world and to bring about its redemption, then music must also be powerful enough to tear the world apart.

Music can be a powerful tool for opening up the heart; but just as with any powerful tool, we must deploy it with care and sensitivity. If music were a chainsaw, we'd be attuned to the grave warnings in the instructions manual. For all of music's power to affect the world positively, it holds the potential power to tear us apart if we're not careful. Perhaps in this spirit, the Psalmist linked music to a dangerous double-edged sword:

> Lifting songs of God in their throat, and a double-edged sword in their hands.[48]

When we sing, we must keep in mind that the musical sword can be used for the good or the bad; it's a powerful weapon that can create great spiritual unity and lead us to the Divine, or slice that trusting oneness to shreds, leaving us in pieces.

In my years of seriously singing with people, there have been many times when I've been surprised by the outflow of tears, anger, frustration, and difficult emotions that emerge while singing, from myself and from others. People have spontaneously started yelling at me in the middle of a collective song, others have cried for an hour afterwards, spilling out their stories like wine from a broken barrel. Some have fallen in love with people they couldn't court. Music carves us open, wakes up our emotions, and exposes our vulnerabilities. Such emotional vulnerability can certainly form part of a healthy spiritual process; to do so, we must sensitively hold the feelings we've exposed and commit to lifting each other up productively thereafter. But if we're not careful, it can destroy us.

Warnings have abounded of the ways in which music can pull us in what was thought to be the wrong directions. Rashi, for example, mused that the very first musician in the Torah used music for idolatrous purposes.[49] Rashi also suspected that songs—the wrong kind of songs—had led Elisha Ben Abuya, once a great teacher of Torah, to become the archetypal heretic of the Talmud. As Rashi explained, "The songs of the Greeks never left his lips."[50] Others warned

---

[48] Psalms 149:6, "רוֹמְמוֹת אֵל בִּגְרוֹנָם, וְחֶרֶב פִּיפִיּוֹת בְּיָדָם."

[49] Rashi on Genesis 4:20.

[50] Talmud Bavli Hagigah 15b, Rashi's comment there: "אחר...אחר מאי זמר יווני לא פסק מפומיה."

that music leads to licentious intermingling between men and women or causes Jews to break Shabbat. The list of warnings about music goes on and on.

One page in the Talmud stands out when it blames singing, especially singing while intoxicated, for causing many of the calamities that have befallen the Jews throughout history:

> Anyone who drinks to [the playing of] the four kinds of musical instruments brings five different kinds of punishment to this world…
> …bringing exile in the world;
> …bringing famine to the world;
> …causing Torah to be forgotten by its students;
> …bringing lowliness to God's enemies [i.e. God];[51]
> …causing the lowliness of Israel.[52]

On the same page, two other Talmudic sages also condemn music:

> Rav said, "The ear that hears a song should be ripped off." Rava said, "A song in the home is ruin, in the end."

Even today, for various reasons, music is severely restricted in many of the most important moments of Jewish life. According to a common interpretation of Jewish law , playing musical instruments is forbidden on Shabbat and on the holiest holidays of the year.[53] Musical performance of any kind is also avoided for three weeks before the mournful holiday of Tishah B'Av and during the seven week period known as the "Counting of the Omer."[54] But all of these restrictions pale in comparison to the position taken by Rambam (Maimonides), one of the preeminent decisors of *halakhah* (Jewish law), who forbade music altogether—and seemingly forever!—as a symbol of our ongoing mourning after the destruction of the Temple. He wrote:

> It was decreed not to play musical instruments. It is forbidden to participate

---

[51] *Lit.* "The haters of God." This phrase is a euphemism for God.

[52] Talmud Bavli Sotah 48a–b (#59), based on Isaiah 5:11–17.

[53] Music is forbidden on these holy days and Shabbat out of the dual concerns of creating a sacred Shabbat atmosphere and avoiding accidental forbidden work. Rabbi Ethan Tucker has taught extensively about the use of Instruments on Shabbat and Yom Tov, but his essays are not yet published in book form as of this printing. See Ethan Tucker, BeHa'alotekha 5776, "Musical Instruments on Shabbat and Yom Tov," available at www.hadar.org/torah-resource/musical-instruments-shabbat-and-yom-tov.

[54] Music, especially instrumental music, is traditionally forbidden on these days as a sign of mourning. Mourning for the destruction of the Temple on Tishah B'Av and for the thousands of Rabbi Akiva's students who died during the Omer period. Traditions vary as to the exact length of the prohibitions on music during these times of mourning.

in [the playing of] any kinds of musical instruments or in the making of music as well as to listen to them, due to the destruction [of the Temple].[55]

The Rambam's position was not unusual. Other halakhic authorities also prohibited instrumental music and even singing whenever they could.[56]

And yet, throughout the ages, many rabbis have also pushed back against these broad prohibitions, allowing music by limiting the cases that the original restrictions applied to. They would suggest that it was merely singing while drinking wine in a tavern, for example, that was forbidden—not music in general! Or perhaps music was only forbidden to kings and others who are spoiled by endless music! Or perhaps it's alright if it's for the sake of bringing joy to a bride and groom! Or perhaps it's alright if the music is for praising God![57] Or perhaps it's alright as long as the music isn't about secular love, or too lude! And my personal favorite: music is okay at a wedding, "as long a you don't have too much fun!"[58] These types of statements form the basis for an entire genre of Jewish jokes shared often by musicians that all share the punchline, "it might lead to dancing!"

All of these restrictions on music have created a very confusing situation: is music allowed, or not? No one really knows! Moreover, most musicians and music lovers don't seem to care! What we do know is that, allowed or not, Jews do actually sing, all the time. Despite hundreds of years of halakhic warnings and attempts at prohibitions, music could not be kept out of Jewish society.

The Talmud itself acknowledged the difficulties of prohibiting music. When Rav Huna tried to prohibit singing, the markets went haywire:

> When Rav Huna abolished singing, one hundred geese were priced at a *zuz* and one hundred *se'ah* of wheat were priced at a *zuz* [very low prices], but demand dropped off. Rav Hisda came and dismissed him, and geese were in such high demand [and priced] at one for a *zuz*, but they had flown off the shelves.[59]

Even the Rambam, who prohibited music altogether, nevertheless prescribed it in certain cases.[60] A world without music was ultimately unthinkable.

---

[55] Rambam, *Mishneh Torah*, Laws of Fasts 5:14 (#98).

[56] See *Arba'ah Turim*, Orah Hayyim 560.

[57] *Shulhan Arukh*, Orah Hayyim 560:3 (#131). The Shulhan Arukh records a quasi-dialogue between Rabbi Caro and Rabbi Isserles, with Isserles trying to soften the blows against music.

[58] Israel Meir Kagan (Hofetz Hayyim), *Mishnah Berurah* 560:3 (#134).

[59] Talmud Bavli Sotah 48a–b (#59).

[60] Rambam, *Commentary on the Mishnah, Eight Chapters*, Chapter 5.

But even if music has triumphed over its would-be silencers, we must take care not to throw out the important spiritual disciplines and wisdoms that are contained within the warnings about music. To be a musician must mean not only to sing the notes, but to take care of folks when the music affects us and them. When music opens up our love and our tears, we must not abuse or take advantage of the vulnerable spaces therein. Let's instead allow music to bring forth the best, the tenderest instincts in each of us and not open us up to the worst.[61] As the Piezetzner Rebbe (d. 1943) teaches:

> Music…is one of the keys of the soul, waking it and its passions. But it is possible to open our soul, to release some of our spiritual essence and then do nothing at all with it—or possibly damage it! If his joy is vacuous, if his angst leads to nervousness and despair, he will wound that portion of his soul that is exposed. When he falls from such a height, there will be enormous damage to his faith and foundations. The misuse of spiritual power can lead us to deeply improper actions, God help us![62]

I believe that a cautious and sensitive approach to music can allow us to honor the cautions that surround music in the halakhic system and to learn something from its warnings, even as we enthusiastically advance the cause of healthy singing in the world. Can we use music towards the purpose of building, dreaming, collaborating, and unifying, rather than destroying, competing, hurting, and dividing? The stakes are high and choice is in our hands.

Music's Prayer

It was January in Minneapolis, and I was floating in the temporary timelessness of musical prayer, singing and swaying with a beautiful community, when the rabbi opened the northern door and the negative-twenty degree wind rushed in and stunned us. He explained, "This is to remind us that what we do in here, with our prayer and music, must go back out there, must be taken back to the streets."[63] He certainly reminded us that our prayers, no matter how melodic in the sanctuary, would only be fully realized by action in the physical world.

---

[61] As one famous twentieth century Jewish music teacher explained, "Sacred music should help bring forth all that is good and tender in a human being." Abraham W. Binder, "New Trends in Synagogue Music" (1955) quoted in Jonathan L. Friedman, *Quotations On Jewish Sacred Music* (Lanham, MD: Hamilton Books, 2011), p. 44.

[62] Kalonymus Kalman Shapira, *B'nei Mahshavah Tovah*, Number 18 (#179).

[63] Michael Adam Latz, rabbi at Shir Tikvah Congregation, Minneapolis, 2013.

Music is a wordless prayer that opens up our imaginations of the divine Source of all life. Music, the most immaterial and ephemeral and yet most eternal of all the artforms, represents our connection to the Divine, to each other, to everything. We can't see music, we can't grasp it in our hands, but yet we can feel it working through us and the world. As our musical dreams go to work, we might similarly be able to imagine encountering the Divine, whom our liturgy calls "The Holy Blessedness that is Above All Blessing and Songs."[64]

Indeed, the Talmud teaches us that music and prayer are virtually synonymous, declaring,

> Where there is song, there is prayer.[65]

In the long-beloved homiletical-numerical game of *gematria*,[66] the numerical value of the words for prayer, *tefillah*, and song, *shirah*, are identical.[67] From this we can see that music is a form of prayer, and prayer is a form of music. They are like two legs of the spiritual throne, mutually supporting each other.

What is the prayer that music offers? Is it possible that music can open our ears and open our hearts, so that we can better sense the nuance and subtleties of the world around us? If we open our mouths and sing our imperfect songs, can we connect with the divine songs of all creation? Can our prayer chants open the gates of heaven? Can our melodies unlock divine mysteries?

This book has gathered Jewish words and wisdom about music. More than finding the words to describe music, however, the ultimate challenge remains whether those words and those melodies and those dreams can actually affect us and the world around us. Can we allow the sounds of song and the words of Torah to awaken our consciousnesses, and can we use that musical-spiritual energy to help make positive changes in the world?

To be a musician is to be an activist of the spirit. But the music doesn't do this on its own. It requires us to react to the music, to open up, to change along with it. Can we allow the sound of our singing—like the shofar from within each of us—to awaken us, to bring us to positive action?[68] Can we let song help us to do our work in the world with sensitivity and grace?

Ultimately, melodies are just a bunch of notes—whether they're fundamentally meaningless or transcendent depends entirely upon how we choose to lis-

---

[64] As we say in the *Kaddish*, "...דְּקֻדְשָׁא בְּרִיךְ הוּא לְעֵלָּא מִן כָּל בִּרְכָתָא וְשִׁירָתָא תֻּשְׁבְּחָתָא וְנֶחֱמָתָא"

[65] Talmud Bavli Berakhot 6a (#40).

[66] *Gematria* is a form of numerology in which numerical equivalency of letters within a word portends a synchronicity of spiritual concept.

[67] The sum of the values of the Hebrew letters in each word is equal to 515.

[68] *Mishneh Torah*, Laws of Repentance 3:4 (#97).

ten, how we choose to direct our intentions, and whether we let ourselves join the song. Let us find our melodies, and let us find our prayers, and let us bring the world to life!

Adonai, open up my lips, so my mouth can speak your praise.

אֲדֹנָי שְׂפָתַי תִּפְתָּח וּפִי יַגִּיד תְּהִלָּתֶךָ.[69]

---

[69] Psalms 51:17, often recited quietly at the beginning of the *Amidah*.

i
Studies
and
Stories

1

Songs of Prophecy and Torah

Prophecy

וְהָיָה כְּנַגֵּן הַמְנַגֵּן וַתְּהִי עָלָיו יַד־ה'

And when the musician played,
the hand of God was upon him.

—*2 Kings 3:15*

The prophets of ancient Israel surrounded themselves with music. Why did they need music? Music, we might assume, must have opened up the prophets' ears, enabling them to hear the divine voice speaking through them. Music, in this sense, worked like an elite reconnaissance unit sneaking through the prophets' defensive bulwarks and barriers, or like a sweet-talking lover wooing his beloved. Music paved the way for the bestowal of the great gift of divine love, of the prophecies which we have at least partly retained in the words of the Torah and later poetry and writing. Perhaps we, too, can allow music to open us up to our own inspiration, the way that music opened up the pathways of the prophets?

Tradition teaches that the prophets of old required music to help them enter an ecstatic mindset. In one story, the prophet Elisha wanted to start hearing the word of God, so he requested that a musician start to play. As soon as the musician played, Elisha began to prophesy.[1]

In another story, Saul, who had not yet become king, joined a roving band of prophets and musicians who were playing a harp, drum, and flute to help the prophets enter a state of expanded consciousness. These three instruments—harp, drum, and flute—represent the three fundamental elements of music: harmony, rhythm, and melody. Joining the parade of musicians, Saul found that this musical-prophetic experience allowed the spirit of God to rest upon him and allowed him to transform into an *ish aher*, a different person, to find an

---

[1] 2 Kings 3:15 (#15).

17

alternate reality of himself, in which he became capable not only of prophesying but ascending the throne of Israel.[2] Is it possible that music can help us, too, to enter different realms and discover alternate realities in which we might ideally pursue better versions of ourselves?

Referring to these stories of musical prophecy, one fifteenth-century Kabbalist went so far as to suggest that every prophet, aside from Moses, had required music in order to prophesy.

> All his days, [Moses] never required any stimulation from any kind of *nigun* to invoke the spirit of prophecy, for it never withdrew from him at all, always at the ready, from his side, never refraining at all, as, in his supernal power, there is no withdrawal of spirit or the flow of [divine] light, and this was his paradigm. This was not the case with the rest of the prophets, peace be upon them, who needed *nigunim* to awaken the spirit and invoke prophecy upon them...[3]

How does this musical-prophetic process work? Why did prophets require music for prophecy? The Maggid of Mezeritch (d. 1772), the famous student of the Ba'al Shem Tov, explained that music is a sort of model for prophecy. Just as a musical instrument "allows" itself to be played by the musician, so the prophet can allow himself or herself to be played by the "spirit of God."

> Everyone has seen this: when a skilled musician plays, he has ambitions and tries to make his voice sound more beautiful. But this is not the case with the instrument itself, which is silent and has no capacity to have its own ambitions.
>
> This is the meaning of "when the musician plays...:" when a musician, that is, a human being, can become "as if being played" (*kenagen*), that is to say, like an instrument played by a musician, having no ambition of its own, then, "the spirit of the Divine will be upon him."[4]

If prophecy ended thousands of years ago, then what is music's role today in opening up our own prophetic pathways? What is left for us of musical prophecy? Rebbe Nahman of Breslov offers that there might be something left that we can access from the Source of Prophecy. A sacred musician, he explains, is called

---

[2] 1 Samuel 10:5–6 (#9).

[3] *Avodat HaKodesh*, part 4, chapter 23 (#124).

[4] Uziel Meisels, *Tif'eret Uziel* (#152). In his quotation of this verse, Meisels has the more common phrase "spirit of God" (*ru'ah Adonai*), while our editions 2 Kings have the more unusual "hand of God" (*yad Adonai*). Most of our sages quote verses from memory so it is likely that the variation in quotation is a mistake. This mistake also recurs several times in the texts found in this book! However, this is not a significant deviation and probably only a recall error.

a *hazzan*—a Hebrew word with which uses the same root as the word *hazon*, meaning "vision." He continues:

> [The *hazzan*] snatches the song from the place where prophets suckle.[5]

While there are no longer prophets who can hear the word of God directly, the wellspring from which the prophets drew their inspiration not only still exists, but can be accessed through music.

When we sing, we can begin to connect with the larger questions of existence. In one psalm, David declared that his harp allows him to "open up my riddle."[6] Elimelekh of Lizhensk (d. 1787) understands this to mean that songs open up the larger world of mystery:

> "I will open my riddle with a harp" (Psalms 49:5)—This means: …with a harp, as above, or with songs and praises can I open another, grander world that is above this plane of existence, which is called "my riddle," for a riddle is a matter too great to hear/understand with ears alone.

Sometimes, the melodies not only show us the riddles of existence, but help us solve them, too. Music unravels the riddles that words pose for us, because it takes us outside of language altogether, into the place of unlimitedness within each of us. As one late-nineteenth-century writer enthused:

> Only the wordless, the unspeakable, but rich-in-expression, tongue of music is able to answer the riddles of life in such a consoling and satisfactory manner. For only music is able to speak to the inner spirit in its own language, whose words are expressions, and whose arguments are feelings.[7]

In one famous story, the Alter Rebbe, Shneur Zalman of Liadi, sang a *nigun* in the town of Shklov that was reputed to have solved the most difficult questions posed to him by his most learned opponents.[8]

Can music reawaken our primordial questions, too? Can music allow us to expand our consciousness, to ask larger questions, to open ourselves up as we seek to understand the mysteries of life and the riddles of the world? Can music

---

[5] *Likkutei Moharan* I, 3 (#143).

[6] Psalms 49:5, "אפתח בכינור חידתי."

[7] Naphtali Herz Imber, "Music and the Psalms," in *Music: A Monthly Magazine, Devoted to the Art, Science, Technic And Literature of Music* (Chicago: W.S.B. Mathews, 1894). Imber is best known as the author of the words to Israel's national anthem, *HaTikvah* (the melody closely resembles Smetena's Moldau melody).

[8] S. Y. Zevin, *Chassidic Tales on the Torah* (Mesorah Publications: 2012), p. 513.

allow us, too, to connect with the grander mysteries and questions, and to access the spirit of life that's contained within each of us? This is as close to prophecy as we'll ever get!

The Sweetness of Torah

ובנעימה שהיה משה שומע בו
היה משמיע את ישראל

> The melody that Moses heard,
> he repeated to Israel.
>
> —*Mekhilta Yitro 19:19*

Music offers us a way of discovering the sweetness of Torah. It's an invitation to study our ancient wisdom. Were it not for the sweet melodies that I heard on the lips of people who loved to study Torah, I would very likely never have begun to explore the wisdom of the Torah tradition. The melodies pulled me in then made it impossible for me to walk away, for how could a tradition with such beautiful melodies not have other treasures to discover? The Zohar relates that by the side of a mountain at dusk, several scholars were walking as it was getting dark. Suddenly:

> The branches of the trees on the mountain began to hit one another, singing a song...saying, "Holy children of the Divine, scattered among the living of this world, lanterns, pupils of the academy, enter your places to delight with your Lord in Torah!"[9]

Songs are the lanterns that light the dark, enabling us to study the particular spiritual path of Torah, to expand our wisdom and understanding of the ways of the world.

According to one ancient source, music has been intricately connected to Torah ever since Moses first received the Torah on Mount Sinai.

> The Holy Blessed One helped [Moses] by sharing His divine voice—and the melody that Moses heard, he repeated to Israel.[10]

As we can see here, it is taught that Moses himself heard the divine melodies while receiving the words of the Torah, then transmitted them, together, directly to the children of Israel. This is the basis for our tradition of singing

---

[9] Zohar I:7a (#112).
[10] Mekhilta Yitro 19:19 (#81).

the Torah with its *trops* (cantillations), its recurring musical motifs. This music, however, is not simply a nice add-on to the Torah reading. The musical notes themselves are absolutely essential. One collection of medieval German Jewish customs emphasizes that every cantillation of the holy texts is sacred and must be maintained as scrupulously as the letters of the Torah itself:

> [Those who preceded us] established the melodies, such that one would not use the melody of the Torah with Prophets or Writings, or that for the Prophets with Torah or Writings, or that for the Writings with Torah or Prophets. Rather, each melody is established just so, all a law of Moses stemming from Sinai...[11]

The *trops* are the oldest Jewish music that we have, and the fact that several highly divergent *trop* systems exist in Jewish communities around the world doesn't stop each community from claiming that theirs was passed down directly "*MiSinai* (From Sinai)."[12] Indeed, whether the old melodies associated with Torah and prayer came from Sinai or not, singing them allows us to internalize and expand upon the musical-spiritual foundations laid by our ancestors.

In one Talmudic passage, Rabbi Yohanan insists that we must maintain the melodies of the Torah, along with the words:

> Anyone who reads [Torah] without a melody or recites [Mishnah] without a tune, it's about them that Scripture says, "I have also given them laws that are not good."[13]

It would seem from his proof text that he feels that both Torah and *halakhah* suffer when they are studied without music. The Tosafot (a collection of twelfth and thirteenth century Talmud commentators), however, offer a utilitarian justification for music in Torah study. They explain that it was common to recite oral teachings to a tune because the melody "increased their memorability."[14]

Rabbi Moshe Levertov (d. 1941), however, ascribes to singing even deeper importance in relation to Torah study. Music, it seems, activates the pleasantness and sweetness of the Torah.

---

[11] Judah the Hasid, *Sefer Hasidim* 302 (#102).

[12] See, for example, A. Z. Idelsohn, *Jewish Music, its Historical Development* (1929, republished Dover 1992), pp. 44–46, for a "Comparative table or accent motives for the intoning of the Pentateuch."

[13] Talmud Bavli Megillah 32a (#51), quoting Ezekiel 20:25.

[14] Tosafot on that passage (#51), see also Talmud Bavli Megillah 3a (#52).

[This verse from above] indicates someone who does not feel the pleasantness of Torah (*no'am haTorah*) and its sweetness, for they have not activated their spirit at all, awakening it through song.[15]

The *trop* melodies ignite the spirit, he teaches, and thereby open up the sweetness and pleasantness of Torah, which presumably we cannot fully realize without music. He interprets the verse in this way in part based on a play on words between the word *ne'imah*, tune, and *no'am*, pleasantness.

Can we allow the *trops* to lead us, too, towards the sweetness of the Torah? Let's go!

Carrying the Torah, Carrying the Song

"בכתף ישאו"...אין ישאו אלא לשון שירה

"Raised on their shoulders"...
"Raising" means "singing."

—*Talmud Bavli Arakhin 11a*

Once I was teaching wordless *nigunim* at an Orthodox rabbinical seminary in New York City. In the room sat about twenty young men. Half the students were *shuckling* (swaying) back and forth to the music, eyes closed, singing, and bringing forth the proto-ecstasy that's possible with music. The other half of the students sat there with their arms crossed, assuming an "impress me" stance, staring me down, daring me to make my musical exercise relevant to them as scholars. A member of this second group lamented, with obvious disdain, that "for every moment that we're in here singing, we're missing an opportunity to learn a *blatt* of Gemara (a page of Talmud)."

This story illuminates a basic competition that exists between music and words. Which is more important: the notes of the music or the words of the Torah? Is the music there to support and enhance the beauty of the words, or is it possible that it's the opposite, that the music itself is the essential part, in which case the words would simply support the music?

Of course, there doesn't have to be a competition here; both sustain each other. Music and Torah are intricately interwoven, so that throughout the tradition it can be hard to discern which is more important. Some say that music carries the Torah, while others suggest that the music itself rides upon the let-

---

[15] *Ma'amar Nigun*, p. 19 (#164).

ters of the Torah. Taking both together, we can see that music and Torah, like the two sides of an arch, must bolster one another.

Music certainly helps us to understand the verses of Torah. Explaining a verse from Nehemiah, the Talmud reveals that *trops* were actually meant to help us "understand the reading:"

> "They read in the book, God's instruction, with interpretation; and they gave the sense to understand the reading."[16]

> "They read in the book, God's instruction" is the Torah, "with interpretation" is the Targum (vernacular Aramaic translation), "and they gave the sense" is the division of verses (where they begin and end), and "to understand the reading" is the *trop*.[17]

This source indicates that the primary purpose of *trop* is to explicate the text. The *trop*, like punctuation and translation, help us to understand the meanings of the words and sentences, presumably by allowing us to hear the flow of the words and better understand where each phrase starts and stops, and which words are more important, and which words support the others. In this and other texts we looked at above, the text is the king, the music its servant.

But fast forward to the mystical literature. The Zohar reverses the paradigm:

> The letters [of the Torah and vowels] follow their melody, oscillating, like soldiers after their king. The letters are body, the vowels are spirit. Their motions follow the movements (*or*: notes) and stand in place. When a melody of Torah notes moves, the letters and vowels follow. When it pauses, they cease and stand in place.[18]

Who's in charge now? It appears from the Zohar that the melody reigns, leading his army of letters and vowels. While the Talmud texts above suggest that the music largely supports the text, or at best is equal to the text, the Zohar text here introduces a new level of thinking about music in relation to Torah—that the *trops* themselves, which now represent the spirit of the text, are actually leading the letters and vowels. This suggests that the music more directly communicates the essential aspects of the soul, while words mainly function as a bridge to the intellect of humankind.

The sixteenth-century Kabbalist, Moses Cordevero, similarly echoes the kingship of the cantillation. To him, the letters merely shlep for the vowels,

---

[16] Nehemiah 8:8.

[17] Talmud Bavli Megillah 3a (#52).

[18] Zohar I:15b (#113).

who themselves shlep for the *trops*, who represent the soul that rides above the mundane world.

> The letters are the animus (*nefesh*), the vowels are the spirit (*ruʾah*) to the animus, which is the letters, and the accents/cantillation are the soul (*neshamah*) of the spirit of the animus…The vowels ride on the letters, like a rider on a horse, but their subtlety, which is greater than the letters', cannot dwell in the material substance of letters but rather in their echoes, which follows the letter's articulation…The cantillation does not come into contact with a letter but rather rides on top of the vowels, the hidden echo. One must bring great attention to this from oneself, since it cannot be explained in writing, only mouth to mouth.[19]

In this passage from Cordevero, we see a profound respect for music's spiritual capacity, which transcends the intellectual level which is represented by the words. In Kabbalah, the use of *R-K-B* (ר–כ–ב), a root meaning "to ride," implies union, one superior element with another inferior. According to Cordevero, the *trops*, which on the page actually do "ride" upon the letters, vowels, and crowns, and which float out sonically into the realm of the spirit, represent the part of the Torah reading which is closest to the Divine.[20]

While we've just explored texts that prioritize music over text or vice versa, other texts suggest a more mutually supportive relationship between Torah and music in which, through a feat of imaginative collaboration, the Torah can carry the song while the song carries the Torah. Song allows us to carry the Torah, but carrying the Torah also makes singing possible.

The Children of Kehat, son of Levi, for example, were given the task of carrying the Ark containing the Torah.[21] But according to the Talmud, while they may have literally carried the Torah on their shoulders, it was actually their singing that carried the Torah for them.

> "To the children of Kehat, [Moses] gave nothing [no carts, oxen], since the holy work was upon them, raised on their shoulders" (Numbers 7:9) What

---

[19] Moses Cordovero, *Pardes Rimonim*, Gate 29, Chapter 5 (#126).

[20] For more on this, consult: Aryeh Kaplan, *Inner Space: Introduction to Kabbalah, Meditation and Prophecy* (2nd edition) (New York: Moznaim Publishing Corporation, 1991), p. 115, for the Kabbalistic system of "*TaNTO*, תנתא," an acronym for "*Teʾamim, Nekudot, Tagim, Otiyyot;*" Also see Elliot Wolfson, "Biblical Accentuation in a Mystical Key—Kabbalistic Interpretations of the Teʾamim, part II", *Journal of Jewish Music and Liturgy* (1989), esp. pp. 8–11, and DovBer Pinson, *Inner Rhythms: The Kabbalah of Music* (Northvale, N.J: Jason Aronson, Inc., 2000), p. 9 n. 25.

[21] Numbers 3:31.

is the Torah teaching [by the word] "raised?" "Raising" means "singing…"[22]

To carry the Torah is a considerable honor, and indeed, it appears that while singing allowed the children of Kehat to carry the Torah, it was also carrying the Torah that allowed them to sing!

Rebbe Nahman takes the Talmud's already imaginative statement about "singing carrying the Torah" one step further, explaining that

> By means of making music, a person can know if they truly have taken on the yoke of Torah.[23]

Since Torah is itself also called a song,[24] Rebbe Nahman may be suggesting that the nature and spiritual quality of our singing can reflect the extent to which we have internalized the teachings and values of the Torah. This cannot mean that any beautiful or trained voice implies that one has mastered the Torah, but rather that for better or worse, through singing, our spirits are laid bare before us, and we may notice to what extent we are living up to our full potentials as spiritual human beings—i.e. to what extent we have taken on the yoke of the heavens.[25]

But a related story further elucidates the interdependence of song and Torah. Referring to a story in which cows carried the Ark of the Torah, the Zohar explains that the Torah actually allowed the cows themselves to sing:[26]

> When the Ark weighed down on them, and they were weighed out above (*fig.* "found worthy"), they sang a song, and when the Ark was lifted off of them, they mooed like any other cow in the world, not singing a song. Truly, the Ark on their backs made them chant a hymn.[27]

Here, in a musically inclined midrash about singing cows, the Zohar claims that cows moo normally when they are not carrying the Torah, but when the Torah is on their backs, suddenly they can sing! From these texts, it appears that singing supports the Torah, and that the Torah also supports the singing. If it's possible for cows to sing because of the Torah, then it must be possible for us as well. It should only be that Torah helps us to sing our new-ancient song.

---

[22] Talmud Bavli Arakhin 11a (#74). See also a story of Saul Taub of Modhitz (#166).

[23] *Likkutei Moharan* II, 31 (#148).

[24] Deuteronomy 31:18–19 (#7).

[25] Traditionally, the "yoke the heavens" is accepted upon oneself by living with the laws and values of the Torah. We allude to this in the prayers before the *Sh'ma*, which is the liturgy's most prominent quote from Torah (#171): "And all of them received upon themselves the yoke of the kingdom of heaven, one from the other" "וְכֻלָּם מְקַבְּלִים עֲלֵיהֶם עֹל מַלְכוּת שָׁמַיִם זֶה מִזֶּה."

[26] Referring to 1 Samuel 6:12. See also Talmud Bavli Avodah Zarah 24b (#67).

[27] Zohar I:123a–123b (#114).

2

Songs of Ascent

Ladder of Song

האדם צריך לעשות סולמות לעלות על
ידיהם לפעמים השמימה, הנגון הוא אחד
מהסלמות

Sometimes, a person must build ladders
to climb to the heavens. A *nigun* (melody)
is one of these ladders.

—*Piezetzner Rebbe*

The Hebrew word *sulam* means both "ladder" and "musical scale." Melodies form a divine ladder that connects the Earth with the heavens. Perhaps the most famous story of a path to the heavens is the story of Jacob's ladder. It begins:

> And [Jacob] dreamt, and there was a *sulam* standing on the ground, with its head touching the sky, and behold: God's angels were going up and down.[1]

Angels represent the essential human powers within us, and unlike humans, they fulfill one essential function: singing. The Rambam explains,

> And let it be deeply known to you that the essential powers of humankind and of nature and of the soul are called "angels"...that every day the Holy Blessed One creates a choir/class of angels that sing song before Him and then move on.[2]

---

[1] Genesis 28:12.
[2] Rambam, *Guide of the Perplexed* 2:6 (#101).

27

Jacob's ladder must then have been a kind of musical scale, with melodic angels rising and descending along with the prayers of mankind. Jacob ben Asher (d. 1343) also posited that prayerful song is a ladder:

> "*Sulam*" has the numerical equivalence (*gematria*) of "*kol*" (voice), since the sound of the prayers of the righteous is a ladder for angels to ascend.[3]

When we sing, we hope to allow ourselves to experience a state of elevation, a taste of the heavens, a glimpse of the best versions of ourselves.

The musical form of almost every *nigun* mimics a ladder; it tries to get us to rise up and journey with it. Each melody starts low—on the Earth, so to speak—gradually rises in the second section, reaches the heavens in the third, and then descends again when the "B" section repeats at the end, returning us to grounded-ness, representing a full spiritual journey.

If music brings us up, why does the melody ever need to come back down? Why don't we just stay in the heavenly abodes of our musical imagination forever? Well, for better or worse, a ladder leads both up and down. As it says in Genesis, the musical angels go up, and they go down. While singing transcends earthly matters, it also helps us to rediscover the human potential of life on the ground. Singing signals not an escape from life, but an imaginative attempt to remind us of what is yet possible. Music offers us rung after rung to climb to the heavens, where we hope to discover our best selves, so that we can then emulate that holiness in our regular lives.

Rising Songs, Rising Souls

כל בחי' העלאה ממהות למהות...

הוא ע"י השיר

Any ascent from one essence to
another...is by means of song.

—*Shneur Zalman of Liadi*

Music is the soul's native language, the *mamaloshen* of the spirit, the sounds it heard from the angels in its original home in the heavenly abodes. The fifteenth-century Kabbalist, Meir ibn Gabbai, wrote:

> The soul was carved above, from the knot of life, regularly surrounded by the melodies and song of the angels of service, and the song of the cosmos.

---

[3] The letter/numbers of סולם / *sulam* and קול / *kol* both add up to 136. See *Ba'al HaTurim* on Genesis 28:12 (#106).

Now that the soul is in the body, and it hears a melody, it finds ease of spirit, taking pleasure in what it was once regularly surrounded by, cleaving to the bedrock of the melody of the cosmic voice.[4]

When the soul comes down into this world, it learns to speak other languages, but it ultimately takes the highest comfort in music, which reminds it of its first home.

Song lets our souls ascend, with or without words. The *Kedushah* prayer teaches us that angels used to sing "*Kadosh, Kadosh, Kadosh*...Holy, Holy, Holy..."[5] But those words are only Isaiah's translation into Hebrew of something more, meant for our language-loving convenience, because what those angels were really singing was pure music, pure *nigun*, pure beautiful sound.

Musical prayers rise. As the story goes, when the people of Israel sing and pray, their prayers rise upwards toward the Holy One. There, they are collected by the Angel Sandolphyn, the tallest of the angels, who weaves the prayers into crowns, which then float onto the head of the Divine.[6]

One story in the Talmud relates that an enormous crowd assembled for a Passover Seder, and there were so many people that each person only got an olive-sized piece of the paschal lamb, but yet, when they started to sing *Hallel*, their song was so strong that it "burst the roof."[7]

We might note that these prayers only burst through the roof, i.e. ascend, when the music is directed towards the Holy One, the King of the King of Kings. But when the music is directed towards a human king, even one as great as Solomon, the opposite happens. As the people welcomed Solomon as their king, the music descended!

> And all the people went up after him, playing on pipes, and rejoicing with great joy, so that the earth was split by their noise.[8]

According to the fifteenth century mystic Meir ibn Gabbai, the music we produce down here in our world affects the music that's made on high.[9] Our job, he explains, is to fix the flame of the eternal lamp by singing and making music on instruments:

---

[4] *Avodat HaKodesh* part 3, ch. 10 (#123).

[5] Isaiah 6:3, "וְקָרָא זֶה אֶל־זֶה וְאָמַר קָדוֹשׁ קָדוֹשׁ קָדוֹשׁ ה' צְבָאוֹת מְלֹא כָל־הָאָרֶץ כְּבוֹדוֹ."

[6] See Midrash Tehillim 19:7, Pesikta Rabbati 20:4.

[7] Talmud Bavli Pesahim 85b (#44).

[8] 1 Kings 1:40 (#11).

[9] Moshe Idel, "Conceptualizations of Music in Jewish Mysticism," in Lawrence E. Sullivan (ed.), *Enchanting Powers: Music in the World's Religions* (Cambridge, MA: Harvard University Press, 1997), pp. 159–88; citation on pp. 169–172.

[The Hebrew word for "harp" (kinor, כנור) can be broken into] kaf-vav (כ"ו = twenty-six, referring to the numerical value of God's name YHVH) and nun-reish (נ"ר = ner, lamp), a secret that forever burns and sways to unite above. The blue light in the flame yearns and sways upward to fuse with white light, and when it is integrated and united one in another, behold it becomes complete kinor, the union of the Bride with her Beloved from the sweetness of the song.[10]

When we sing praises, ibn Gabbai teaches, we reunite the blue flame with the white, and thus repair the lamp of the human-divine continuum.

Moreover, music accompanied the sacrifices in the Holy Temple and allowed them to not just be burned up but actually transformed into a spiritual state and reach the Divine.[11] Rabbi Shneur Zalman of Liadi (d. 1812, Russia), the first Lubavitcher Rebbe, taught that song is imperative for transcendence. He explained:

Any ascent from one essence to another…is by means of song, which is an aspect of the nullification of what is (bitul hayeish). As it is known, one cannot change from one state of being to another unless one state of being becomes nothing, then it can become something else, with a surplus of blessing.[12]

The Piezetzner Rebbe adds a stirring description of how a melody reaches upwards towards the heavens:

With its voice your soul blazes a trail upward, up to the highest realms, grabbing it with its stirrings, and drawing it with its tongue. Your heart, guts, and interior go out with your spirit's song, and the way of songs is upward, and its ascent and descent, all of its revolutions are carved, each movement of the musician is etched, and the melody is engraved in the timbre of the voice. The melody bears your spirit in its guts, pouring it out before the Divine.[13]

Let's let our songs rise, too, with a surplus of blessing!

---

[10] Meir ibn Gabbai, Avodat HaKodesh, part 4, ch. 24 (#125).

[11] See Sefer HaHinukh #384 (#108).

[12] Torah Or on Genesis 4:20–21 (#140).

[13] Kalonymus Kalman Shapira, B'nei Mahshavah Tovah, Number 18 (#179).

Musical *Mussar*—Balance and Decency

רַנְּנוּ צַדִּיקִים בַּה' לַיְשָׁרִים נָאוָה תְהִלָּה

Righteous ones, rejoice/sing in God! It's
beautiful for the upright to praise!

—*Psalms 33:1*

Rising spiritually through singing may be beautiful—but can music actually lead us to improving our characters, to becoming better human beings in the world on the ground? Can music become a form of *mussar*—a spiritual practice that helps us interact in the world with mutual *menschlikhkeit* (decency)?

According to our tradition, music helps the world to re-balance itself. The Jerusalem Talmud relates the following fantastical story about the *Shirei Ha-Ma'alot*—the fifteen psalms that begin "A Song of Ascents"[14]—and music's miraculous abilities to equalize the inner, primordial chaos—the *tehom*—of the world.[15]

> And so you find that in the moment that David came to dig the foundations of the *Beit HaMikdash* (Temple) he dug down fifteen hundred cubits and didn't find the *tehom*, but in the end, he found a single teapot and wanted to throw it.
>
> It said to him, "You can't [throw me]."
>
> David said, "Why not?"
>
> It said, "I'm here to hold down the *tehom*."
>
> David said, "And since when have you been here?"
>
> It said, "From the moment that the Compassionate One's voice was heard at Sinai proclaiming, 'I am YHVH your God,' the land trembled and sank and I was put here to restrain the *tehom*."
>
> Even so, David didn't listen to it. He threw it away, and the *tehom* started rising and threatened to flood the world…
>
> So David started to sing songs—the [fifteen songs beginning] *Shir Ha-*

---

[14] From Psalms 120 to 134.

[15] The primordial stew of the Earth, or "*tehom*," was capped off and contained at the creation of the world, like a volcano or steam valve, in the very spot where the future Temple would be built.

Ma'alot…and for each song he sang, the *tehom* receded back to its original position.[16]

Oh was King David caught by surprise! He had arrogantly ignored the warnings of a teapot, and he discovered that the *tehom* of the world was much stronger than he was. And so he turned instinctively to song, the only power he knew of that could contain such a force.

The Babylonian Talmud, however, disputes this telling, effectively demanding to know why the songs would have been called "Songs of Ascent" if they actually made the *tehom* descend. Thus, in its alternate telling, when the teapot was removed, the *tehom* began to descend, which would have caused a drought in the land above.[17] Here, too, he quickly composed the fifteen songs of ascent, which also allowed the *tehom* to reposition itself within the balance of the world.

I see in these passages a representation of our own internal chaos and creative spirit. The emotional and psychological lava within our beings is also often only barely held in balance by relatively weak psychological switches—like the teapot in the story. Our opinions and feelings always threaten to bubble out and flood out, overwhelming those around us. By contrast, we can also go to the other extreme and push our feelings and ideas so far down inside us that we risk becoming dried out shells of human beings. We need to cultivate our inner chaos, our inner *tehom*, as the lifeblood of inspiration, but it must also be contained, so that it pulses positively through us without pouring haphazardly into the world. Music holds the power to mitigate the chaos of the Earth, and it similarly can help us to keep ourselves in check, to help us find our humility.

Most people who have made music with other people have discovered that music is like a laboratory for developing decency and humility. Sometimes we need to sing louder, sometimes softer, sometimes not at all. Sometimes we lead, sometimes we follow, sometimes we step out. Music helps us explore our inner life force as it relates to everyone and everything else in the world.

When we're operating honestly in the world and living up to the best ethical suggestions of our traditions, we find that we're singing a divine song. This link between song and ethics is even encoded in the relationship between the Hebrew word for "song" (*shir*) and the word for "upright" (*yashar*). The Jewish tradition often superimposed the two word concepts, as we can see, for example, in the line from Psalms in which singing and righteousness playfully merge in the word "*yesharim*" (upright/singing).

---

[16] Talmud Yerushalmi Sanhedrin 52b (#78). Rabbi Aviva Richman shared this story with me at Mechon Hadar in 2012.

[17] Talmud Bavli Sukkah 53a.

Righteous ones, rejoice (sing, *ranenu*) in God! It is beautiful for the up-right (*yesharim*) to praise.[18]

One Talmudic text describes how even cows, perhaps representing our earthly, mundane sides, straightened themselves and sang songs when carrying the Torah.

"The cows went straight (*vayisharnah*) on the path to Beth Shemesh…"[19] What does "*vayisharnah*" [really] mean? Rabbi Yohanan said, in the name of Rabbi Meir, that they sang a song (*shirah*). And Rav Zutra bar Tuviah said that Rav said, "They straightened (*yishru*) themselves before the Ark and sang a song (*shirah*)."[20]

Here, the author also understands *vayisharnah*" as being related to both "*yashar*" (the straight path) and to "*shirah*" (song). When the cows "straighten up," they realize their job in the world, and they get on the path towards accomplishing their mission. To "straighten up" means to find the backbone to do what's needed in the world, and to become more decent human beings. Song is the great shepherd which corrals us towards becoming our best selves and discovering our inner decency.

In fact, the relationship between *menschlikhkeit* and music is represented in the very name of our people. *YiSRaEl*, which plays on the words *sar* (struggling), *yashar* (upright), and *shir* (song), reminds us that if Jews can become decent human beings as they wrestle with their Divine instincts, then they'll find that they are singing the holy song.[21] The Sefat Emet puts it as follows:

And Israel (*YiSRael*), as it comes to the straight path (*derekh haYaSHaR*), thereby Israel starts singing (*YaSHiR*) a song of God (*SHiR EL*).[22]

Our ancestor Jacob assumed the name *Yisrael* after wrestling with a divine angel. In the first part of his life, Jacob had been a trickster. He conned his brother Esau out of his birthright,[23] deceived his father Isaac for his first blessing,[24] and cheated his father-in-law, Laban, before stealing away with many of

[18] Psalms 33:1 (#23).

[19] 1 Samuel 6:12.

[20] Talmud Bavli Avodah Zarah 24b (#67).

[21] Rabbi Daniel Cotzin-Burg of Baltimore first introduced me to the relationship between the valences of ישראל in 2014.

[22] *Sefat Emet*, Leviticus, Passover, 5658 (#156).

[23] Genesis 25:29–34.

[24] Genesis 27.

the family's flocks.[25] After wrestling with the Angel of God, however, Jacob's life changed—he stopped lying, and he received the name *YisRael* ("wrestled with god"). Even as he acquired a limp, which made him physically less upright, his inner character improved, so his name could also be pointed as *Yashar-El* ("upright before God").[26]

In wrestling with an angel—and in finding his decency—I imagine that Jacob was struggling with and then releasing his personified potential of song. Indeed, the Talmud imagined Jacob's angel just that way, as pure singing potential, waiting for it's moment to sing.

> [The angel] said, "Let me go, the dawn is coming!"[27] [Jacob] said to [the angel], "Are you a thief or a gambler, that you're afraid of the dawn?" [The angel] responded, "I am an angel, and from the day I was created, my time to sing [before God] had not arrived until today."[28]

Just as Jacob's angel left the struggle to sing its holy song, Jacob, too, was permanently transformed by this encounter, and from then on, he too learned to act decently and love the divine song.[29] He passed this musical-spiritual experience down to his descendants in name and melody, the Children of Israel (*B'nei Yisrael*).

---

[25] Genesis 30–31.

[26] Genesis 32:22–32.

[27] Genesis 32:27.

[28] Talmud Bavli Hullin 91b (#69).

[29] According to various midrashim, Jacob loved music and recognized its power. See the story of how Serah serenaded Jacob in Sefer HaYashar (#96). And according to Rebbe Nahman (#150), Jacob sent the "melody of the Land of Israel" down to Egypt.

3

Quieting

Song and Silence

תחלת החכמה שתיקה

In seeking wisdom the
first step is silence.

—*Solomon ibn Gabirol*

I didn't compose any melodies until my first son was born. He refused to sleep. I'd walk him around the room, rocking him back and forth in the timeless tradition. Anyone who has tried to lull sleepless children to sleep knows that if you have ambitions for your evening, that if you even consider working or completing a project, that the baby will know your heart and thus continue to refuse to sleep. But if you are able to quiet your mind and let go of your ambition, and just be there with that child, then the baby goes to sleep.

Interestingly, I found that whenever I succeeded in the meditative feat of becoming internally quiet, and let go of any interest in doing any of my own plans—then suddenly a melody would come into my ear, and I'd start singing it to my son. Ironically, that year, in which I often felt that I couldn't accomplish any work, became the most productive musical year of my life, as every night I'd discover three to four new *nigunim*, as long as I wasn't intending to. I'd emerge from his room eventually and write them all down. I wrote hundreds of melodies that year. But I had to set aside ambition and action, to immerse in a meditative silence, with the help of my baby, to begin to compose.

Perhaps all songs are "born" out of silence.

Silence holds a special place in the Jewish tradition. According to various sources, silence is good for the body, more valuable than words, and even a "cure for everything."[1] Our most famous leaders and prophets remained silent or advo-

---

[1] Pirkei Avot 1:17; Talmud Bavli Megillah 18a.

37

cated silence from time to time as a way of handling trauma,[2] weathering tough times,[3] or as a political strategy.[4] Silence was also an essential spiritual expression[5]—according to some opinions silence was even the highest form of prayer.[6]

But Jews could not remain silent all the time—they had to sing. In that vein, David begged to keep on singing:

> Let my heart sing of you and not keep silent, YHVH my God, I will always praise you![7]

In the ongoing debate between the merits of various types of expression, an aphorism developed among Hasidim:

> Silence is better than words, but singing is better than silence.[8]

Ultimately, however, singing supports silence, and vice versa, even if they initially may seem to be in competition. Songs, with their melodies and harmonies and pulsating rhythms, at once overwhelm us with their beauty, and also teach us to appreciate the character of quiet. One sonic extremity opens up the other.

This is one interpretation of why we say *"Selah"* at the end of certain psalms. *Selah* is the Psalmist's instruction to the singer to pause,[9] to stop for a moment to take in the depth of the words and melodies one has just sung. *Selah* invites us to meditate for a moment and prayerfully reflect. The letters of *Selah*, S-L-H (ס-ל-ה), form an acronym for *"Siman LaM'natzeah Has,* סימן למנצח הס,*"* "a Sign to the Leader/conductor to Hold on/pause."[10]

Song works in partnership with silence to cultivate the spirit. Sometimes song grows out of silence, sometimes silence grows out of song. As we feel the

---

[2] Leviticus 10:3; See also Talmud Bavli Zevahim 115b. Simkha Weintraub sees Aaron's response as potentially an unhealthy repression of his feelings, conversation in Brooklyn, 2012.

[3] Amos 5:13.

[4] Isaiah 30:15.

[5] Talmud Bavli Berakhot 24b: "He who makes his voice heard during prayer is of the small of faith. Rav Huna said, 'This teaching applies only to one who is able to direct his heart when whispering (the words of prayer); but if he is unable to do so, he is permitted (to pray aloud).'"

[6] Talmud Yerushalmi Berakhot 9:1; the opinion cited above is attributed to Rabbi Yehudah of Kfar Neburya.

[7] Psalms 30:13. "לְמַעַן יְזַמֶּרְךָ כָבוֹד וְלֹא יִדֹּם ה' אֱלֹהַי לְעוֹלָם אוֹדֶךָּ." Translation of "כָבוֹד" as "heart" following Robert Alter, *The Book of Psalms* (New York: Norton, 2007).

[8] Hasidic Teaching, quoted in Hanoch Avenary, "The Hasidic Nigun: Ethos and Melos of a Folk Liturgy," *Journal of the International Folk Music Council* 16 (1964), p. 60; also in Jonathan L. Friedman, *Quotations on Jewish Sacred Music*, p 46.

[9] *Brown, Driver, Briggs Biblical Lexicon* on "Selah."

[10] Naphtali Herz Imber, "Music and the Psalms," p. 578.

great expanse between sound and silence and stretch our aesthetic sensibilities, we learn to stretch our spiritual sensibilities as well.

What's left over after song may be even more important than the song itself! According to Rabbi Ze'ev Wolf of Zhitomir, the daily ritual of singing in itself is insufficient to praise God. Rather, the full awesomeness of the Divine is realized in the silence after the songs of *P'sukei D'Zimrah* (verses of song), when one is "left with the residue of song."[11]

So, it would seem that song prepares us for a rich, full silence, the type of silence in which music isn't heard but yet can be felt pulsing through our veins. But it turns out that that very silence also allows us to hear song. Often the seeds of a melody, like the seeds of wisdom itself, are contained within a silent moment. As soon as we get quiet, the silence itself turns around and inspires more music!

Two of our most famous leaders were initially known for being quiet but later became known for their songs. Hannah, whose silent prayer became the Talmud's model for the silent *Amidah*,[12] later opened her mouth "wide" with song,[13] and sang one of the Top Ten songs ever sung in the Tanakh.[14]

Moses, too, who was nearly mute as a result of eating a burning coal,[15] and who hesitated to lead because he could barely talk, became one of the greatest song leaders of our tradition, leading all of the people at once in the famous Song of the Sea.[16] By the end of his life, in a stunning reversal of musical initiative, even the heavens and the angels quieted their singing to listen to the songs of Moses and his people.[17] The truths that Hannah and Moses discovered in quietness allowed them to sing the songs of their souls, and of their people.

To Rebbe Nahman, Moses represented the balance between extreme quiet, which was emblematic of his humility and faith, and extreme song. His songs, rooted in silence, became the ancestor of all spiritual songs in our tradition.

> All songs, whether of this world or the one of the future to come, are only
> by means of Moses, who is the aspect of silence, who merited to sing since

---

[11] *Or HaMe'ir*, Parashat Tetzaveh (#153). He illustrates this idea with wordplay on the seemingly unnecessarily doubled word *shirei*, songs, in the closing prayer of the daily verses of song, which reads, "*HaBoher BeShirei Zimrah*, הבוחר בשירי זמרה."

[12] 1 Samuel 1, Talmud Bavli Berakhot 31a (#42).

[13] 1 Samuel 2:1.

[14] *Ba'al HaTurim* on Exodus 15:1 (#107).

[15] Exodus Rabbah 1:26.

[16] Song of the Sea, Exodus 15:1–2 (#2).

[17] Deuteronomy 32:1; Yalkut Shimoni, Ha'azinu 942; Talmud Bavli Hagigah 12b (#55).

all songs are related to that elevated faith, which includes all songs, all are drawn from it…[18]

A full cup cannot receive, and so we must make room inside for music and its wisdom to enter. Song and silence delicately balance each other. In hours of trying to quiet my baby, I learned to quiet myself first. From that quiet came song, and those songs in turn became lullabies to quiet my baby and my own soul. In a neverending cycle, the very act of singing allows us to hear silence and moves us to silence, and yet silence itself cannot help but lead us back to song.

Calm at the Center of Sound

ובשופר גדול יתקע,
וקול דממה דקה ישמע.

And the Great Shofar is sounded,
and the still small voice is heard.

—*Unetaneh Tokef prayer*

Music cuts away extraneous noise to reveal the divine song hidden in quiet moments. Music carves silence from sound; it organizes the chaotic sounds, and allows us to find the spaces in between. In these spaces, we can hear the sacred nuances of the world.

The greatest musicians, having mastered the notes, work their whole lives to master the silence. My teacher, Cantor Noach Schall, would survey hundreds of pages of music he had penned, which contained a whirlwind of thousands of musical notes, and proclaim, "Here's the best part of all of it!" pointing to the musical rest, where no notes were written.

This concept is nowhere better expressed than in our High Holiday prayers, where we exclaim,

And the Great Shofar is sounded, and the still small voice is heard.[19]

First, we hear the great, loud sounds of the shofar, of our communal singing. But after the loud sounds, we hope that our ears have been opened, so that we can hear the quietest sounds of the universe.

---

[18] *Likkutei Moharan* I 64:5 (#149). For an in depth study of Rebbe Nahman's musical writings, see Chani Haran Smith, *Tuning the Soul: Music as a Spiritual Process in the Teachings of Rabbi Nahman of Bratzlav* (Leiden: Brill, 2010).

[19] *Unetaneh Tokef* prayer. "קול," translated as "voice" above, can also mean "thunder."

Furthermore, Jewish tradition teaches that divine wisdom is found in the quietest moments. What does God's musical voice sound like?[20] According to our mythic stories, the Divine One speaks in varying degrees, from extremely loudly to extremely quietly. While we may be impressed by the loudest sounds, we often come to fully realize the truth of an experience in its quietest moments. Like the greatest of musical artists, the Holy One, too, balances the loudest self-expressions with the most quiet silences. God's awesome loudness paves the way for sensitive quiet.

You might initially suppose that God's voice is overpowering and loud, as it says in Psalm 29, "God's voice breaks the cedars; God shatters the cedars of Lebanon."[21] We know, too, that before the giving of the Torah, the thunderous divine sounds were so loud, so imposing that they sparked a moment of collective synesthesia, in which the shaken Israelites could "see the sounds:"

> As the sound of the shofar grew in strength, Moses spoke and God answered with a voice…And the entire people saw the sounds and the flashes, the sound of the shofar, and the mountain was smoking. The people saw and shuddered, standing far away.[22]

But these overwhelming sounds, the machismo of God's external persona, were only a prelude to the deep silence that pervaded the world when the Torah was given, which one scholar describes as a "silence such as had never been before and will never be again."[23] An ancient midrash relates:

> When God gave the Torah, no bird called, no fowl flew, no cow mooed, the *ofanim* didn't fly, the *serafim* did not say "Holy, holy!" the tide did not turn, humans said not a word, but rather, the whole world fell silent and quieted. A voice emerged, "I am YHVH your God."[24]

Loudness creates awe (*yirah*), and this loudness of God is God's frightening mask. Quietness, however, suggests love (*ahavah*), and here we find that God's loving essence is transmitted quietly.[25] The loud music of youth often gives way to quieter, more nuanced music of maturity. Awe precedes love. Awe may awaken us, but the Torah is given with love, and received in silence.

---

[20] Aviva Richman invited me to consider God's voice as a musical expression of the world, in 2012 at Mechon Hadar.

[21] Psalms 29:5 (#21).

[22] Exodus 19:15, 20:15 (#5). "קול" can be translated as "thunder" or "voice."

[23] Howard Schwartz, *Tree of Souls: The Mythology of Judaism* (Oxford: Oxford, 2007), p. 31.

[24] Exodus Rabbah 29:9 (#79).

[25] See Rashi on Numbers 7:9, "וישמע את הקול-יכול קול נמוך."

The same dynamic pattern is followed in other places, too. Elijah, for example, when searching for God, first experiences all kinds of dramatic sensations, but then, when he listens carefully, he's able to hear the still small voice of the Holy One.

> God passed by, and a great and powerful wind tore through the mountains and shattered boulders before God, but God was not in the wind. And after the wind was an earthquake, but God was not in the earthquake. And after the earthquake was a fire, but God was not in the fire. And after the fire was a *still, small voice.* And when Elijah heard it, he wrapped his face in his cloak and left, standing at the opening of the cave. A voice came to him and said, "Why are you here, Elijah?"[26]

After all of the wind and earthquakes and fire, Elijah knew he was confronting the essence of the Divine when he heard a quiet murmuring, a "still small voice" (a phrase made famous by the King James translation). Could it be that, in a seeming inversion of the normal physics of sound, when we're far away from God, we experience God as a lot of noise and grandeur, but the closer we get, the more we experience the Divine as quiet? Perhaps God's music is like a hurricane with a calm at the center—the closer we come to the Divine, the closer we come to silence, but yet, there's no way to access the silence but through a storm of sound.

Stories from the Temple directly connect this quiet voice paradigm to music. According to the rabbis of our Mishnah, musical instruments produced exponentially amplified sound in the Temple in Jerusalem. All the sounds and songs of the Holy Temple could be heard in Jericho, twenty miles away from the Temple. Thus, from the Temple and outwards, all songs and sounds received a sort of divine amplification, so that it could be heard so far away:

> From Jericho, they could hear the sound of the flutes. From Jericho, they could hear the sound of the cymbals. From Jericho, they could hear the sound of song. From Jericho, they could hear the sound of the shofar. Some say they could even hear the voice of the High Priest when he uttered the Name on Day of Atonement.[27]

And yet, despite all of the amazing music that could be heard emanating from the Temple, the Zohar tells that at the moment that the High Priest entered the innermost chamber, the Holy of Holies, to converse with the Holy One, the music stopped:

---

[26] 1 Kings 19:11–13.
[27] Mishnah Tamid 3:8 (#38).

He enters…[the Holy of Holies] and hears the sound of the cherubs' wings, singing and beating their wings, stretched out above. When he offers the incense, the sound of the wings fades, and they cleave together in silence…The priest, with desire and ecstasy, opens his mouth in devotion, offering his prayers. When he finishes, the cherubs extend their wings as before and sing. Then the priest knows that it has been accepted, and there is jubilation for all.[28]

In contrast to the divine amplification that was heard from outside of the Temple, in which all of the sounds of the Temple resonated more loudly than they might have actually been, the most intimate connections with the Divine in the Holy of Holies appear to have happened in utter silence.[29] Even the angels stopped singing and beating their wings! But, as soon as the prayer was accepted, song resumed.

Music allows us to navigate through the loudness, to find the silence. Music organizes the loud sounds so that we can recognize the power of the quiet, acting as an intermediary between the God's loud, external "persona" and the quiet, holy, inner being where truth is found. Music hangs in the subtle balance between sound and silence. It is music that tunes up our beings, that tunes up the entire world, to allow for an interchange between the soft, inner and the loud, outer manifestations of truth.

Have you ever been in a state of restlessness or chaos, in which your head is so filled with its own machinations that it's hard to appreciate what else is happening in the world around you? I know that's normal for me. But when I sing with people in community, I find myself beginning to expand my focus and notice more, and I become more likely to be able to step outside of myself. As soon as a song has finished, I can suddenly hear, with much greater clarity and awareness, the sounds in the room that I hadn't noticed before, such as the singing of the birds, the humming of a distant air conditioner, the fidgeting of chairs, the sound of a group of people breathing, and other nuances. The quietest ticking of a clock in the room, in fact, might suddenly seem so strong that it's hard to start the next song at any tempo other than sixty beats per minute! Sometimes when we're really lucky we can hear a full pulsating quietness.

Don't take my word for it—make sure to try it yourselves! Gather ten friends, and sing one melody for fifteen minutes, without stopping. At some point, bring the song to a close, and then listen carefully to the quiet. Often, after singing together, we can hear what we didn't even know existed before the

---

[28] Zohar III:67a (#116).

[29] See also, for example, Habakkuk 2:20 (#19): "When God is in His palace, the Sanctuary, the whole world falls silent before Him,"‎"וַה' בְּהֵיכַל קָדְשׁוֹ הַס מִפָּנָיו כָּל־הָאָרֶץ."

song began. It is precisely this deeper awareness, created by intentional singing, which tunes us up to the world around us, and makes us hear the whispers of our inner spiritual beings.

This musical focusing, or tuning up with the quietest noises in the world, allows us to become more sensitive to the nuanced needs of the world, and this, I believe is what it means to hear the still small voice of the Divine. It means to step outside of ourselves so that we can hear voices other than our own, some of which express themselves very quietly. Music facilitates the process of hearing the wisdom and beauty of the quiet, the unnoticed, the unheard. The Piezetzner Rebbe summarizes:

> And you do not need to scream and shout. There is music made with in a whisper or a breath that can still be heard in heaven.[30]

We carry around our quiet truths within our own calm centers, amidst the storms and noisy ruckus of life. We, too, come to understand our truths as we process the echoes of song, as we meditate amidst the dances of life. Yet the question remains for us in every moment: can we hear the quiet voices of the world speaking to us?

---

[30] *B'nei Mahshavah Tovah*, Number 18 (#179).

4

Listening

"Israel, Listen!" Opening our Ears

Music is more than just the notes we play; music is the artistry of the ear. Our most famous Jewish imperative exclaims *"Sh'ma Yisrael"* ("Israel, listen!").[1] It doesn't say *"R'eh Yisrael"* ("Israel, look!"). Why does the Torah, and our subsequent daily repetition of this phrase, frequently ask us to listen, rather than to look, when we are trying to pay attention to the Divine? How does music help us with the process of hearing?

Hearing certainly doesn't have a monopoly on the holy. I have had the chance to daven with a number of people who are deaf, who certainly brought as much energy and beauty to the prayer experience as anyone else. All of our other senses are used all of the time in Jewish life, too. In the course of any Shabbat, for example, we see the light of the candles, taste the wine, feel the water rushing over our hands, and smell the spices, saying a blessing that each of these sensual activities can remind us of the holiness that's possible in life.

And yet, the Torah and Jewish tradition often give a symbolic privilege to hearing, especially in its spiritual sense. This midrash, for example, offers a startling endorsement of of the ear,

> There are 248 major body parts, but *it's through the ear that they all live...* as it says, "listen and you will be alive."[2]

The Talmud, too, places the ears at the top of the hierarchy of the body. For example, consider this passage about compensation payments for bodily injuries:

> Rava said: if he cut off [another's] arm, he must pay him for the value of the arm...if he broke [the other's] leg, he must pay him for the value of the leg... if he put out [another's] eye, he must pay him for the value of his eye...but if he deafened him, he must pay for the value of the whole of his being.[3]

---

[1] Deuteronomy 6:4.
[2] Deuteronomy Rabbah 10:1 (#80), quoting Isaiah 55:3.
[3] Talmud Bavli Bava Kamma 85b (#60).

Rashi explains this practically; without being able to hear, the person wouldn't be able to work anymore, which may have been especially true in his time.[4] But taken together with the midrashic comment above, which considered the ear to be the "life-giving" body part, we can see that hearing, to our Sages, was the most potent mechanism for sensing the spiritual life of the world. It was the ear that could hear the divine voice that could channel spiritual energy to the rest of the bones.

Of all of the senses, hearing was the sense that Jews most frequently turned to as a symbol of how we might resonate with a higher energy.[5] While our vision, taste, and touch tend to focus us on the material world, our ears tend to focus us on the unseen and untouchable, on the immaterial. Hearing allows us to imagine infinity, and therefore it is chosen as the spiritual conveyor in Jewish tradition.[6] One twentieth-century scholar explained:

> Sound stands nearest to the purely spiritual among the phenomena of the world of the senses. Therefore, God has chosen it to be the medium of sensory revelation. Since what is heard is the least dimensional, it is easier to imagine it as something unlimited, and extendible into infinity, than what is visible or tactile. Sense and spirit mutually interact in hearing.[7]

Sound is easiest to imagine as being related to God, because you can't see it, but yet it's there.[8]

Song is designed to help us feel, or at very least imagine, the unity of spiritual purpose in the world. And that's one reason we close our eyes to say the *Sh'ma*, so that we can focus on what unites us rather than on what fractures us. "Don't be led astray by what you see with your eyes," the third paragraph of the *Sh'ma* warns.[9] It is listening that allows us to hear the one-ness of the One who animates the whole world, and to hear the unity of aspects that might look separated to our materialistic eyes.

---

[4] Rashi on Talmud Bavli Bava Kamma 85b (#60), "חירשו—אין ראוי לכלום."

[5] See Rabbeinu Yonah of Gerondi, *Sha'arei Teshuvah* 2:12. See also Pinson, *Inner Rhythms: The Kabbalah of Music*, p. 30, nn. 64–65, on the debates about whether seeing or hearing is the superior sense.

[6] Even the greatest prophets heard only words and riddles, never the full picture of the Divine, that is, other than Moses: Numbers 12:8, "פֶּה אֶל־פֶּה אֲדַבֶּר־בּוֹ וּמַרְאֶה וְלֹא בְחִידֹת."

[7] Adolf Altmann, "The Meaning and the Soul of 'Hear O Israel,'" an essay from 1928, Barbara R. Algin (trans.), in Levi Meier (ed.), *Jewish Values in Jungian Psychology* (Berlin: Jeschurun, 1991), quoted in Friedman, *Quotations*, p. 50.

[8] See, for example, Howard Schwartz, "The Prince and the Slave," in *Miriam's Tambourine: Jewish Folktales from Around the World* (Oxford: Oxford, 1988), p. 305, retold from "*Sippurei Ma'asiyot*." He writes, "And even though music is invisible, still everyone who can hear knows of its existence."

[9] Numbers 15:39.

Music prepares us to "hear spiritually." The *Or HaMe'ir* explained how music helps our spiritual hearing. The melodies of *P'sukei D'Zimrah*, he explained, prune away the hardnesses around our hearts, to prepare for spiritual connection and unification that we hope to feel during the *Sh'ma*:

> Look, first of all, we say *P'sukei D'Zimrah*...Why are they called verses of song (*zimrah*)? Since they pare away (*m'zam'rim*)...the husks [from one's heart and soul]...

> And we continue in this through all the hymns (*z'mirot*): we pare away the husks of the negative qualities we feel within us, and afterwards, we are ready to pray, implying connection, uniting the one's inner thoughts to the loftiness of one's divinity. When the recitation of the *Sh'ma* arrives...then, a complete unity with the Holy Blessed One is achieved.[10]

I've found that often when I listen, I can sense a unity and a unified purpose in a room that's hard to realize with eyes open.

Among the many hundreds of gaudy, ostentatious timepieces that mark the landscape of American synagogue architecture, Jews have also built some impressive synagogues throughout the generations, which are strikingly beautiful to look at. And yet, beautiful or atrocious as they might be, many of these shuls are nearly empty. In a pre-Shabbat tour of one huge Midwestern synagogue, the president of the shul looked out at his fifteen hundred person main sanctuary, explaining that they usually get about fifty people to come. "What have you been spending money on lately?" I asked. "Well, we spent most of our budget last year keeping up our stained glass windows—aren't they beautiful?"

When we focus on what we see—and that's the standard in American material culture in these generations—we lose track of what we are doing, spiritually. Our "grand" architecture has dazzled us for a moment then spoiled us. We have been following the material world that we can lay our eyes on. The traditional Jewish approach is counter-cultural—it encourages us to turn off our electronic devices, close our eyes, sing, and listen to each other's voices in song and prayer. It brings us back to the spiritual purpose, the one-ness that we're trying to create, that we can just as easily create in a very humble room with nothing impressive to look at.

At the end of the Torah, God explains that shortly the Divine face will be hidden from people, but the possibility remains that, from then on, people will

---

[10] *Or HaMe'ir*, Deuteronomy, Rosh Hashanah (#155).

still be able to practice singing the divine song, which according to many sources, is the Torah itself:[11]

> I will surely hide My face on that day because of all the evil done, turning to other gods. Write this song for you now and teach it to the children of Israel. Place it in their mouths, so this song stands as a witness in Israel.[12]

When we're no longer able to see the Divine directly, the Torah says, we must sing the divine song ourselves and listen carefully in the world for divine echoes. Traditionally speaking, Moses was considered the last prophet to have been able to see God's image "face-to-face,"[13] and since then the visual connection with the Divine ceased. The rest of the prophets listened carefully for God's voice. When God stopped talking directly to people with the last of the biblical prophets, the last two thousand years of Jewish mystics and sages hoped to catch the faintest echoes of God's voice echoing in song from Mount Sinai, or to hear a *Bat Kol* (*lit.* daughter of a voice).[14] If we listen carefully, might we hear the vaguest divine echoes, too?

Listening with Our Hearts

אַף עַל פִּי שֶׁזֶּה שָׁמַע וְזֶה שָׁמַע,
זֶה כִּוֵּן לִבּוֹ וְזֶה לֹא כִּוֵּן לִבּוֹ.

Even though this is listening and that is listening, one involves the directing of the heart, and the other doesn't.

—*Mishnah Rosh Hashanah 3:7*

Listening ultimately involves more than just hearing sounds through our ears—it involves allowing sounds to enter our deepest psychological levels, to affect our hearts.

---

[11] Talmud Bavli Sanhedrin 21b suggests that "*Shirah*" refers to the Torah as a whole, as opposed to the *Ha'azinu* song that's following in chapter 32 (as Rashi says in his commentary to the Torah), and the *Arokh HaShulhan* reframes it not just as poetry (*shirah*) but as song specifically (#133). For a summary, see also Jonathan Sacks, Nitzavim-Vayelech (5769), "The Torah as G-d's Song," available at http://rabbisacks.org/covenant-conversation-5769-nitzavim-vayelech-the-torah-as-g-ds-song.

[12] Deuteronomy 31:18–19 (#7).

[13] See, for example, *Yigdal* in the Shabbat Liturgy, line 7. *Yigdal* summarizes the thirteen articles of faith of the Rambam.

[14] Tosefta Sotah 13:3 on "*Bat Kol*": משמתו נביאים אחרונים חגי זכריה ומלאכי פסקה רוח הקדש "מישראל ואעפ"כ היו משמיעין להם על בת קול."

The greatest musician-listener in our tradition was King Solomon. In a dream, Solomon requested that God give him the wisdom to deal with the burden of leading a difficult nation. But the language of Solomon's request is worth exploring. When offered a choice of what to receive from God, Solomon asks for a "listening heart" (*lev shome'a*).

> Give your servant a listening heart to judge your people, to discern between good and evil, else who would be able to judge this weight nation of yours![15]-

A listening heart is able to hear with clarity, and thereby hear the intimate details of the wisdom of the world.

How did Solomon learn to listen? While the Tanakh explains that he was given the art of listening as a divine gift, one teacher of mine has suggested that Solomon also learned how to listen as he grew up in the household of the greatest musician of our tradition. The Davidic household was full of song. After all the singing of his father David, what was left for Solomon? Listening! We learn here that singing (ideally) begets listening.[16]

A listening heart means that one's heart is flexible, able to hear what the world is saying, and able to respond with sensitivity and wisdom. Solomon's listening heart, opened up by the music of his household, was open enough to understand all of the languages of the world, to communicate with the birds and the beasts. By contrast, when Pharaoh's heart was hardened, he could not listen with sensitivity to what the world was telling him, and he descended disastrously to drown in the depths.[17]

A passage from the Mishnah cites two *mitzvot* of the ears—hearing the shofar and hearing the megillah—as it describes the difference between casual hearing and intentional listening.

> If you pass behind a synagogue, or if your house is connected to one, and you hear the sound of the shofar, or the voice of the megillah [being read], if you intend your heart, you've fulfilled [the *mitzvah*], and if not, not. *Even though they are both acts of listening, only in one case did you intend your heart.*[18]

Every *mitzvah* that we do benefits from mindfulness and intentionality, and listening is no exception. We can't just casually listen to the shofar or the me-

---

[15] 1 Kings 3:9–13 (#12).

[16] Dorothy Richman taught this idea in Berkeley, California, in 2013.

[17] Exodus 7:13, "וַיֶּחֱזַק לֵב פַּרְעֹה וְלֹא שָׁמַע אֲלֵהֶם."

[18] Mishnah Rosh Hashanah 3:7 (#34).

gillah—we need to really listen carefully, with our hearts! It's not enough just to hear the sound, the sound must penetrate our beings, we must really notice and process the sounds. When we listen at this level, we imbue our actions with meaning and subtlety, and we transform our inner lives.

After completing the building of the Temple, Solomon, the master-listener, opened his palms to the heavens and begged God to allow his people to live up to their divine missions. Invoking the songs that had just begun to be in the new Temple, he asked God to hear his song, and thereby hear his prayer:

> Hear the song and the prayer, which your servant prays before You today.[19]

As is discussed earlier, song is a form of prayer, and prayer is a form of song—but they both require careful listening. This process is active. Whenever we want God to do something, we must do it ourselves.[20] So, when Solomon asks God to listen, he's reminding himself, and us, that we ourselves must listen to the songs and prayers that we all sing.

When we listen to the depths of our own and each other's music, we find that it's full of longing and praise, full of prayers at its core. Our job is to listen carefully to our songs, to hear the prayers that pour forth from them. We then mimic the Creator, who listens to the prayers pouring forth from Solomon's songs.

There are two sides to the art of music: one is music-making, such as singing or playing notes on one's instrument, and the other is listening, in which one pays special attention to the other sounds in one's environment, and merges one's own music with the other music around. Music can be planned and practiced; listening is spontaneous and unpredictable. Music sends out sonic signals, and listening receives those signals, their echoes, and all of the responses that the world provides. Great musicians are equally adept at producing beautiful sounds on their instruments, but also at listening carefully to the musicians and world around them, learning from what's happening, and curiously synthesizing whatever comes their way, in the moment.

Even the wisest among us still have more to listening to do! Our master listener, Solomon, also expressed that longing to hear with greater clarity, begging:

> Let me hear your voice, for your voice is sweet.[21]

---

[19] 1 Kings 8:28 (#14).

[20] See *Sifrei Devarim*, Parashat Eikev 49, or Talmud Bavli Sotah 14a, or Rambam, *Sefer HaMitzvot*, Positive Commandment #8.

[21] Song of Songs 2:14 (#32)

The more proficient a musician becomes, the less she focuses on the notes she's playing and the more she focuses on listening to the music of the musicians and world around her. This is the spiritual realm of listening, in which the music has led the musician, the ensemble, and the audience towards opening up their ears, opening up their hearts, and paying attention to the life force flowing throughout the whole world.

The Whole World Sings!

מִכְּנַף הָאָרֶץ זְמִרֹת שָׁמַעְנוּ

From the ends of the Earth,
we have heard songs.

—*Isaiah 24:16*

The whole world is singing, but we've barely begun to hear it.

We've heard about songs of the universe from the testimonies of our prophets and poets, as well as from our own fleeting moments of expanded listening, when we clear our minds and listen to the wind and the songs of the birds. For millennia, Jews have dreamed and hoped that we can someday completely immerse ourselves in the songs of all creation.

Perek Shirah, "Chapter of Song," an ancient text, records songs sung by many dozens of different creations in the world.[22] The text describes that every part of the world sings praises, inanimate and animate, macro to micro, from the skies to the Earth, from the mountains to the deserts, from the birds to the fish to the crawling creepers. Their praises have even been conveniently translated into Hebrew for us, and what do you know, their meanings even correspond with the poetry of our own prophets! Here are a few lines:

> The Earth sings…"From the ends of the earth we have heard songs, the beauty of the righteous."[23]

> The Garden of Eden sings, "Wake up, North Wind, and come, South! Blow on my garden, make the spices flow. Let my beloved come to his garden and eat his delicious fruits."…[24]

> The fields sing, "God established the land with wisdom, instituted the

---

[22] See (#84) for the first of Perek Shirah's six chapters.

[23] Isaiah 24:16.

[24] Song of Songs 4:16.

heavens with understanding."…[25]

The rivers sing, "Let the rivers clap their hands, and, as one, the mountains sing for joy!"[26]

The wellsprings sing, "Singers and dancers [say], 'All my wellsprings are in You!'"[27]

Perek Shirah, in its entirety, used to be included in a variety of *siddurim* to remind us of the potency of the natural world. When we offer praise, we imagine ourselves singing alongside all of the other creatures of the world. Our songs are dependent upon their songs. The third chapter of Perek Shirah teaches that even the various vegetations and green growths of the land sing their own unique songs. Rebbe Nahman expands:

> Each and every blade of grass has its own song that it sings…and from the song of the grass is made the shepherd's song.[28]

Our human songs intricately intertwine with the songs of the rest of creation; music is the mystical dream that ties our mutual existences together.

It's not easy to listen to the songs of the world around us, but yet if we don't we're missing the music's primary positive power, which is to awaken our ears to the nuances of the world beyond ourselves. When King David, for example, haughtily forgot to listen to the world's song, he was scolded by a frog:

> It's said of David the King: when he finished his Book of Psalms, he became full of pride, and he said to the Master of the World, "No one exists in the world who can sing praises like me!"…A frog suddenly appeared and said to him, "Don't be arrogant! I sing more praises than you, and each of my songs yields three thousand parables."[29]

David was the composer of the Psalms, the greatest singer that has ever come from the Jewish people. And yet, in this story, a simple frog puts even the great David in his place. Moreover, any time we, as human beings, even as skilled musicians and composers, start to think we have a monopoly on music, we need to take a moment to listen more carefully.

If the universal song is everywhere, then what keeps us from hearing these sounds and songs of all of creation? According to one contemporary teacher,

---

[25] Proverbs 3:19.

[26] Psalms 98:8.

[27] Psalms 87:7 (#24).

[28] *Likkutei Moharan* II, 63 (#147).

[29] *Yalkut Shimoni*, Psalm 150 (#94).

the loud sounds of our obsessive ambitions tend to overpower the sounds of the cycles of the world.[30] This mentality of over-achievement is what our Rabbis derided as the "busy-ness of Rome,"

> If it weren't for the busy sounds of "Rome," the sound of the cycles of the sun might be heard.[31]

On the rare occasions that we are able to listen to the world outside of our own egos, we learn to hear the sounds of the natural world as praises and songs, and we begin to renew the lush, symbiotic existence that anthropocentricity has demolished. Perhaps this is a throwback to rediscovering the place we lost in the mythical Garden of Eden, or it's a path towards our dreams of entering the multifaceted, symbiotic paradise that's yet to come. To be sure, though, listening to the rest of the world does not necessarily mean that we shouldn't also work on our own projects and achievements in the world. The Talmudic source alluded to above comes with a caveat: the line before it actually says exactly the opposite!

> If it weren't for the sound of the cycles of the sun, we might be able to hear the busy sounds of "Rome."[32]

What this paradox suggests to me is that we must try to keep our ambitions (and our songs/sounds!) in balance with an awareness of the songs of the universe.

Such a rare moment of being in tune with the world around us would be nothing short of miraculous—a taste of the world to come! Expanding upon one sage's dictum that reciting Perek Shirah daily would let one experience the world to come,[33] Rav Kook expands that we want to move towards uniting with all of the songs all of the songs of all worlds:

> There is one who will reach still further and higher until he unites with all of existence; with all creatures, with all worlds, and with them all he sings a song. This is the one who, on each and every day promised to him, delves deep into Perek Shirah, a child of the World that is Coming.[34]

---

[30] Pinson, *Inner Rhythms*, p. 158.

[31] Talmud Bavli Yoma 20b.

[32] Thank you to Chaim Kranzler for helping me understand how this paradox can represent the need to balance ambition with awareness.

[33] A quote from Pirkei D'Rabbi Eliezer, which is often quoted at the very beginning of Perek Shirah, see Perek Shirah, prelude.

[34] *Orot HaKodesh* 2:444–445 (#175).

So far in our tradition, after Adam himself,[35] it was only Solomon, King David's son, who learned how to listen to the songs and languages of all of the animals, and who therefore was known as the "complete" king.[36] While Solomon's singing itself wasn't as famous as his father's, his ability to listen, which had been given to him as a gift from God, allowed him to bring all of the kingdoms on Earth together into cooperation, including those of the animals, birds, and fish, who traveled from all over the world bringing songs and stories.[37] Solomon used his father's tools of music and poetry, but made sure to also get outside of himself, to hear the other songs of the universe—and therein lay his true power as a king.

In one midrash, Solomon brought out his father's instruments, and as they were played, all of the animals of the world gathered to await his orders. They came to listen to the music, but Solomon, in his wisdom, used the music as an opportunity to listen to their songs![38]

Though we can barely hear the sensitive and subtle sounds of the world around us, much less the sounds of the spiritual realms, we're slowly learning to listen.

---

[35] Dov Noy, *Folktales of the Jews*, vol. 1 (Lincoln: Nebraska, 2007), p. 485. Noah, too, might have spoken with all of the animals, according to some folktales.

[36] Shlomo means complete, see for example: 1 Kings 5:13 and Kohelet Rabbah 1:1 (and other places in Targum Sheni). See also Ginzburg, *Book of Legends*, p. 123 n. 106.

[37] See Ellen Frankel, *The Classic Tales: 4,000 Years of Jewish Lore* (Northvale, NJ: Jason Aronson, Inc., 1993), in the section on the stories of Solomon; and Howard Schwartz, *Tree of Souls: The Mythology of Judaism*, for more English stories about Solomon speaking the languages of the animals and birds.

[38] *Targum Sheni Appendix I* (The Targum Sheni), ch. 4, (ed. Cassell, 1888), p. 275. This midrash explains how Solomon first heard about the Queen of Sheba.

5

Joining Together through Song

Gathering

וּבִנְעִימָה קְדוֹשָׁה כֻּלָּם כְּאֶחָד עוֹנִים וְאוֹמְרִים
בְּיִרְאָה: "קָדוֹשׁ, קָדוֹשׁ, קָדוֹשׁ"

With sacred song, all answer as one,
speaking with awe: "Holy, holy, holy!"

—*Morning Liturgy*

I used to play the bass drum in a large klezmer marching band, and my brother would play the snare drum. As we marched around the Lower East Side of Manhattan, hipsters would appear on their fire escapes to watch and Puerto Rican sanitation workers would step up from their manholes to dance for a moment as we passed. It was joyous! Everyone danced, everyone loved it, except my beloved fellow Jews, of course, who appeared flummoxed at seeing their music out of the usual context, and thus didn't know what to do with it. But whenever we got to a street corner, we faced a potential problem: my brother would cross the street, but I'd be stuck behind. As one half of the rhythm section moved farther away, it was nearly impossible to connect and sustain the level of amazing musicality we'd generated when we were all standing close together. We eventually learned to wait for the light before traversing the street as a unit.

Music calls us to come together, to unite our energies, and to foster a communal spiritual transformation that's bigger than the sum of our parts. Indeed, music gathers us together, and musicians, if we allow ourselves to do so, can become the gatherers of our people.

The conductor who led the holy Levite orchestra under both Kings David and Solomon, was named "Assaf," an archetypal name which means "Gatherer." Assaf personified the purpose of music, gathering the flock together for collec-

59

tive transformation.[1] He organized the musicians and created such an amazing musical experience that people packed into the Temple not only to bring their offerings but also to hear the music. Assaf operated as the "head" (i.e. the chief), bringing together all the musical limbs into harmony. He was the prototype of a singing-drumming prayer-leader, who not only gathered people together and provided the beat, but allowed people to experience a joint spiritual resonance together, a musical-spiritual exploration.

The Talmud relates a quick exchange about Assaf's cymbals, explaining that the two cymbals that he played—one in each hand—should really be understood as a single drum.[2] Afterall, one must bring the cymbals together to make the sound! Moreover, this vision of two parts being brought together to make music evokes the breadth and power of Assaf's essence as a convener. Not only did he chime his cymbals and conduct the Temple orchestra and choir, but it was his music that helped gather people together at the Temple from all over the land in joint spiritual purpose.

Traditional *davening* includes a *minyan*—ten people who choose to come together to create holy gathering—and yet we find that we are constantly working against an expansion model in which Jews, like American suburbs themselves, tend to move further and further away from each other and from the centers of their cities and shuls. Within synagogues, even those who have chosen to come into the building routinely sit as far away from each other as possible. We have succeeded in creating a "donut effect" in which people spread out to the farthest corners of their shuls, unconsciously showing that they don't fully buy into the communal spiritual process that's at the heart of the Jewish dream. By spreading out, we have lost both the intimacy of joined spiritual venture as well as the bonfire of communal spiritual song.[3]

Gathering together means not only entering into the same enormous room, but also coming close together, physically, and sharing energy, spiritually. To have the courage to come close together means that we might catch a fleeting feeling—in our bones—of the "one-ness" that Jews claim is at the heart of our tradition. The Mishnah suggests that in the ancient Temple, people were gathered very closely together, physically. It says that one of the great miracles that occurred in the Temple was that everybody was packed so closely together, shoulder-to-shoulder in a communal embrace, but yet, when the time came for

---

[1] 1 Chronicles 16:5 (#33).

[2] Talmud Bavli Arakhin 13a (#75).

[3] For more on creating a singing "bonfire," please see the strategies in Joey Weisenberg, *Building Singing Communities* (New York: Hadar Press, 2011), p. 4.

them to bow down, there was miraculously enough room.[4] One teacher of mine once quipped that the real miracle was that even though there was enough room to prostrate, they still stood close together to pray![5]

Changing the letters of A-S-F (ף-ס-א) around, however, we get E-Fe-S (ס-פ-א), meaning "zero." The "ends of the Earth"—and I'd contend, the far corners of the synagogue—are called "AFSei Aretz." Just as this small shift in lettering completely reverses the meaning of the word, so too a small switch in our mentalities can make the difference between bringing the world together and fracturing it further. One of our roles as musicians and singers is to emulate the gathering quality of Assaf, to bring people in from the ends of the Earth to sing together, and to reclaim the one-ness from the zero-ness, the wholeness from the nothingness.

But it's not just for musicians to do this! Everyone could be empowered to sing and to learn about intimacy through that process. As more people realize that they can join the song, more people will realize how far apart we have become.

A paradox of music is that while it brings us together, we also have to come together in order to make music. Where do we start first: by making music, with the aim of bringing people together, or by bringing people together, with the aim of making music? Of course, the answer is, "Yes, go for it!"

The singing and gathering that Assaf led in the Temple mirrored the singing of the angels on high. The *malakhei hashareit*, the angels who served God by singing, used music as a way to join together, to find their common purpose, which was to declare the holiness of the world. First the angels sing, then they are able to come together "as one, *ke'ehad*" and declare, "Holy, Holy, Holy!"[6]

> And all open their mouths, in holiness and purity, *in song and melody,* blessing and praising...lovingly giving each other permission to sanctify their Creator with delight, with crystal language and sacred song, *all answering as one,* speaking with awe: "Holy, holy, holy is God of Hosts, filling the whole world with His Glory."[7]

Angels, who have few opinions and live constantly in the presence of the Holy One, may have an easier time reaching unity than us mortals. For us

---

[4] Pirkei Avot 5:5.

[5] Elie Kaunfer of Mechon Hadar.

[6] Aaron Vittels of Portland, Oregon shared this interpretation. Chaim Kranzler adds that in the *Nusaḥ Sefard*, it adds the word "*ahavah*, love." Only through love and care for the other can we reach "*kulam ke'ehad*" and thereby "*kedushah*."

[7] Daily Morning Liturgy, Blessings Before *Sh'ma* (#171), quote from Isaiah 6:3.

human beings to act "as one,"[8] however, does not mean that we need to all have the same thoughts, or sing exactly the same songs, in exactly the same way. To be "as one" does not necessitate a totalitarian concept of life, in which we all bend our own songs to some superior song. Indeed, we must all bring our own unique spiritual expressions and songs, and sing them together, flexibly, with each other, sharing, learning, adapting, but never leaving behind our own sparks of song.[9]

To be sure, gathering people together is not strictly an act of generosity on the part of the master musician. The musician needs his fellow musicians, and the whole community, as much as they need him. Several hundred years ago, it would be tough to find a cantor without his *meshoyrim*, his choristers, who would harmonize spontaneously with his melodies and *nusah*. One story tells of a well-loved *hazzan* who died and was summoned to sing before the heavenly courts. When he arrived, the cantor insisted he wouldn't be able to sing beautifully without his bass singer there to join him. So the heavenly court waited until the bass singer, too, had died, and then the two sang together again in heaven.[10] Music is meant to be shared, to be sung together.

And yet, even when one is not with other people, music reminds us of our shared senses of humanity acting together in concert. The Rabbi from Levertov describes the musical process as it affects shepherds, the loneliest of subjects on the farthest outskirts of civilization:

> Shepherds tend to sing more than other people, specifically when they have taken themselves, with their flock, to a spot for satisfactory grazing, far away from human civilization. They want to awaken their humanity within themselves, to strengthen and care for their heart, due to their longing for personal fellowship, since this is the essence of a human being...[11]

Can we gather our inner angels and allow music to bring us in from the ends of our earths, to come together in oneness, fellowship, and joint spirit?

---

[8] Think of the final blessing of the *Amidah*: "בָּרְכֵנוּ אָבִינוּ כֻּלָּנוּ כְּאֶחָד, bless us all, as if we were one."

[9] See the *Arokh HaShulhan's* explanation of polyphony as demonstrated by Talmudic inclusion (#133).

[10] Martin Buber, "The Cantor of the Ba'al Shem Tov," in *Tales of the Hasidim* (Tel Aviv: Schoken, 1991), pp. 61–63.

[11] *Ma'amar Nigun*, p. 3 (#161).

The Prayer Leader

כי משתדל לחפש ולבקש למצוא בכולם
נקודות טובות...שעי"ז נעשין נגונים

Striving to search out and seek to find
in everyone points of goodness...from
which you can make *nigunim*.

—*Rebbe Nahman*

The *shaliah tzibur* is the prayer leader of a community, literally the "messenger of the public." The public, however, includes the prayer leader as well as everyone in the community. It's been taught that the word for community, *TZiBuR* (צ-ב-ר) represents the "*TZadikim*" (righteous) and "*Resha'im*" (wicked), as well as the rest of us, who are called "*Beinonim*" (in-betweeners).[12]

It's not a simple task to bring together these various extremes of a community's personality spectrum, and so only certain prayer leaders are considered "fit" for the job. The Talmud lists qualifications for the ideal prayer leader as follows:

> "Rav Yehudah says: [A *shaliah tzibur* should be] one having a large family and has no means of support, and who draws his subsistence from [the produce of] the field, and whose house is empty, whose youth was unblemished, who is meek and is acceptable to the people; who is skilled in chanting, who has a pleasant voice, and possesses a thorough knowledge of the Torah, the Prophets and the Writings, of the midrash, *halakhot*, and *aggadot*, and of all the blessings."[13]

It's easy to become a prayer leader! Just memorize all of the hundreds of prayers and melodies, as well as the entire Tanakh and associated Talmudic traditions, raise a huge family with no money, be humble and handsome, and make sure that people like you and your voice! The Talmud sets a very high bar for becoming a prayer leader, one that none of us can really meet.

Unlikely as it may be that most prayer leaders achieve this list, however, these remain our aspirations, to make sure that we don't become complacent in our positions, to help us to keep pushing along the spiritual artistry of the community. By setting high expectations, our Sages demonstrated how much they wanted singers to transcend their own voices, to understand the universal

---

[12] "*Beinonim*" are a major subject of study in the Lubavitcher Rebbe's book, the *Tanya*.

[13] Talmud Bavli Ta'anit 16a; see the *halakhah* as it appears in *Shulhan Arukh*, Orah Hayyim 53:4–5 (#129).

human wisdom that brings people together, and to use their singing craft to bring that wisdom out in others.

I used to study with an amazing old-school cantor, who saw it as his job to remind me and everyone else how much more we all had to learn.[14] In keeping with his teaching persona and the attitude of his generation of teachers, he never said a good word to me. The best thing he ever said to me was, "That didn't irritate me…at least not too much," and it got worse from there. Nevertheless, every year during the high holiday season, I used to call him up and thank him for all he had taught me. He'd ask, "So how did it go for you this year?" and I'd demur, "Well, it went pretty well—give me a few more years, and I'll probably get it down." "FOR YOU, FORTY YEARS," he'd retort. At first I was a little disturbed that as the years passed, I apparently still always had forty years until I'd know what I was doing. But, like many teachers of his generation, and in keeping with the precepts of the Talmud and halakhic traditions, he had a high bar for what a prayer leader should be capable of. He was the best teacher I ever had.

Even if the bar is set high, however, prayer leaders must still think of the community before themselves. While it's certainly important to sing well, for example, as a prayer leader, it's only one of the qualifications of the job, among many. Joseph Caro's famous code of Jewish law, the *Shulhan Arukh*, explains:

> A communal prayer leader who extends his prayer so others hear his beautiful voice…if it is out of the joy of his heart to praise the Blessed Name with a lovely melody, a blessing should come to him! This is if he prays with seriousness, in fear and awe…

> But if a prayer leader is just trying to have people hear his own voice, and is rejoicing in the mere quality of his voice—this is a travesty.

> Generally, anyone who extends prayer [i.e. to show off] is not doing something good, since it becomes a burden for the community.[15]

According to law-oriented rabbis such as Caro—who, admittedly, might have been jealous of the attention that good singers received at their expense—a good voice is regarded as something that, just as quickly as it boosts the community, could burden the community.

The tent of prayerful song constantly opens and expands. It's not enough just to sing for ourselves—we must also include and teach others our musi-

---

[14] Cantor Noach Schall, of Queens. His extensive published collections of *nusah* and Cantorial motifs should be carefully studied by any advancing *ba'al tefillah*.

[15] *Shulhan Arukh*, Orah Hayyim 53:11 (#130).

cal-spiritual craft, to expand and pass on the tradition. Hygros son of Levi was a great singer with an unusual singing talent,[16] but yet the Mishnah remembered him with shame because he kept his skills and his songs to himself, and didn't share them sufficiently.[17]

Making the community the focus of one's efforts can be tricky in an environment where people are used to sitting passively and watching, which is characteristic of many American synagogues today. In some communities, when I've suggested that my goal was not to perform but to lead everyone else in communal prayer-song, some people have even become outraged, saying, "We pay *you*, so that *we* can sing?"[18]

Concerning oneself with the congregation's prayer more than with one's own singing performance, however, takes off one pressure and adds another. It's actually a tremendous responsibility to lift a whole congregation in prayer, not just yourself! The point of leading prayer isn't to make a perfect-sounding concert, but rather to gather the good energies from each humble participant, and bring those together in a symphony of sometimes-discordant harmony. That said, should it all end up sounding good, too, then all the better!

Rebbe Nahman taught that the ideal prayer leader must constantly seek to judge others favorably as a basis for leading a community in prayer. An ideal prayer leader is one who gathers all of the good points and the good notes from every person in the room and lifts them all up together to form a *nigun*. He explained:

> "Know that you must judge each person with the benefit of the doubt."[19] Even with someone [who seems] entirely wicked, you must search out in them and find a tiny bit of good…
>
> It is by eliciting the points of goodness from the bad that *nigunim* and songs come about…And know that one who can make these melodies, collecting points of goodness that are found within each and every Jew, even the sinners of Israel, it is only this person that can lead a community in prayer.

The prayer leader is called a "messenger of the community," which means that they must be sent by the entire community, that they are able to

---

[16] Talmud Bavli Yoma 38b. As it says there, "When he tuned his voice to a trill, he would stick his thumb into his throat and put his finger between the mustache lines, such that his fellow priests would be suddenly staggered backward."

[17] Mishnah Yoma 3:11 (#36).

[18] This echoes a quip of Macy Nulman's in his book, *Concepts in Jewish Music* (New York: Cantorial Council of America at Yeshiva University, 1985).

[19] Pirkei Avot 1:6.

gather in every point of goodness from each member of those praying, each point included within the prayer leader standing and praying with all of this goodness...

This means judging each person with charity, even the unserious and the wicked, striving to search out and seek to find in everyone points of goodness, from which you can make melodies.[20]

What's startling about Rebbe Nahman's teaching is that it's not just *nigunim* that inspire us to come together. Rather the very act of coming together, and joining the best points of each person one to the next actually creates *nigunim* in the world. The *shaliah tzibur* gathers mystical melodies from the hopeful sparks of humanity. By finding the best in each other, we explore the eternal song.

Imperfect Singing

נטלו את צפויו והיה קולו ערב כמות שהיה

After they removed the [golden] overlay,
it returned the sweetness of its sound.

—Talmud Bavli Arakhin 10b

While singing beautifully and perfectly in tune is good, it's not the only way to sing. The full spiritual spectrum includes both the in tune and the out of tune. To sing, even when out of tune, is a deeply vulnerable and risky process that helps us open up to a full spiritual experience.

The first time I led the high holiday services, I found myself taken aback when the *dukhaning* (priestly blessing) began, in which the Kohanim (priestly class) gather to recite the special, mysterious priestly prayer from under their *talesim* (prayer shawls). As I prompted their prayer by singing the words beginning "Y'varekh'kha" (may God bless you), I was jarred when their response came back, "Y'varekh'kha," in at least twelve different keys at once, completely out of tune, like some kind of primitive sound-painting. Before I could even sing the next word, I was already off to the races, thinking, "Ah, so this is why it was the Levites who sang in the Temple, and not the priests!"

But in the years after that, I began to look forward to that moment of the dukhaning, when we'd get to experience a moment of pure unscripted atonality.

---

[20] *Likkutei Moharan* I, 282 (#146).

Who could plan such a terrifying sound? Not even the best composers. Who knew what sort of dissonant chord they might conjure this year!?

There are two models of music. There's the perfection model, in which musicians practice and refine their performances, attempting to make a certain prearranged piece of music perfect. Of course, even in the perfection model, the music rarely actually achieves "perfection"—it only strives in that direction. Then, there's the imperfection model, in which people begin to make music without even necessarily knowing what piece they're even going to play or sing, and they never have the aspiration or impulse to perfect the music, only to make the music. This music often features moments of being out of tune or time, but this lack of tonal tidiness, when approached with curiosity, can be quite amazing. Indeed, it's less polished, but more adventurous, and sometimes has more nuance and a broader range of expression.

Despite my own personal aspirations towards making music "perfect" from time to time with like-minded professional musicians—and, indeed, even in that configuration it's rarely perfect!—I write here with a slight bias towards the imperfection model, because so many people with beautiful, soulful music and prayers within them have been turned off from singing because they couldn't achieve perfection, which either bothered them or bothered their musical directors who were caught up with perfection themselves. Many hundreds of times, people have approached me and said, "My choir leader told me to stand on the risers but just mouth the words, and since then I've never sung again."

A simple, humble, untrained voice can carry a meaning and beauty that no training can earn. The following Hasidic *mashal* (analogy) describes the phenomenon of a nightingale whose song pleases a king more than a trained orchestra:

> A king had an orchestra, with musicians for each and every kind of instrument, available to play for him at any time. Also, in his palace, there was kept a small bird, a nightingale that trilled and chirped in its cage. The king derived great pleasure from its song, though the bird had no awareness of this at all; it did not know the laws of music theory to sing, [and definitely did not know] more than the masters of music, who are experts in their instruments. But the king's pleasure was to hear its voice, because it is a creature without any consciousness or intelligence, through which it made heard its lovely voice.
>
> So, with a person: does not the Holy Blessed One have bands and bands replete with multitudes of angelic charioteers who, exalt and glorify [God] with speech crystal clear and lovely [tone], with celebration and

song, melodious exultation...Still, the Holy Blessed One receives such pleasure from the human being, an imperfect creature, in an ugly body, so much [worse] than the hosts of [perfect] angels above.[21]

In this story, the humble sound of a song-bird pleases the king more than the most elaborate orchestra, which by extension allows the imperfect sounds of mankind to stir the Holy One as well. The normal singers and daveners in the congregation, who don't seem to have such great voices, can often sing the most stirring prayers, if we can just learn to hear them. Modesty, it seems, makes the music.

Another story, this one from the Talmud, tells of a humble flute that refused to be covered in gold, and of a broken cymbal that lost its character when its cracks were covered:

> Our Rabbis taught: there was a flute in the Temple, which was smooth, subtle, made of reed, and from the days of Moses. The King commanded that it be covered in gold leaf, but it made its sound no longer sweet. After they removed the overlay, it returned the sweetness of its sound, like it was before.

> There was a cymbal in the Temple, made of bronze, whose sound was sweet. It was cracked, and Sages sent for skilled workers from Alexandria, Egypt, who repaired it, but its sound was no longer sweet. They removed the repair, and its sweet sound returned, as it was before.[22]

If even the holy instruments of the temple required their humility, then must not we, too, bring all of our cracks and imperfections to the process of summoning up the spiritual?

The Hasidic world, in particular, with its wordless *nigunim* that were designed to open up song to people of all musical skill levels, cultivated an appreciation for the power of the prayers of ordinary people. Stories abound of normal people whose prayers and simple melodies meant more than those of the most trained performers.

Here's the skeleton of the archetypal music story: once, a long line of experienced cantors assembled to audition to lead the high holidays for the famous Rabbi Levi Yitzhak of Berditchev. One after another they sang long, stirring, virtuosic compositions. At the end of the line stood a simple man, weeping. Through his tears, he explained that he worried that his daughters were be-

---

[21] *Or Yesharim*, M. Kleinman (ed.) (#177).
[22] Talmud Bavli Arakhin 10b (#71).

coming too old for marriage. The great Rabbi quickly responded, "You're hired."

Another story also featured Rabbi Levi Yitzhak of Berditchev's recognition of the power of pure, innocent prayer. In this one, a simple, ignorant boy, who didn't even know the first letter of the Hebrew alphabet, took out his flute in the middle of Yom Kippur *davening*, the holiest day on which traditionally no instruments were allowed. To the horror of the congregants, the boy began to play along with the Unetaneh Tokef prayer. As they picked up the boy to remove him from the room, the Rebbe lifted his hand to stop them, explaining "This boy's pure musical prayer has opened the gates of heaven for all of our prayers!"

In these stories and many others, deep knowledge of mysticism or Torah scholarship, or fantastic musical training, or any of the other trappings of elitist systems fall away when confronted with the simple outpouring of the spirit of humanity.

Even people who cannot sing at all have a lot to offer the song. I was the *ba'al tefillah* for seven years at an old shul in Brooklyn. One of the women there remains one of the few people I've ever met who was truly incapable of singing in tune. Many people claim they can't sing, but the vast majority of them can if they just try a bit—but this woman really could not sing in tune, not anywhere close to the melody that everyone else was singing. And yet, when she walked in, and sang wholeheartedly, completely off key, the entire room would ignite with the feeling of *davening*. She had a deep prayerful energy that filled the room with spirit.

Finally, you need not be young to sing! Many of my greatest role models for singing and dancing have been two or three generations older than me. Their voices had worn out, and they couldn't dance very fast, but their every word and movement held so much meaning. In fact, the old and young used to sing together in the Temple. The Talmud reports that the young singers used to "afflict" the older singers, possibly because they sang so high and beautifully and the older singers couldn't do that anymore.[23] But nevertheless, they all needed each other to make music—some to sing clearly, and some to bring the depth of the human spirit to the process.

Through these experiences and stories, I've come to discover that any voice, in tune or wandering, when empowered, can greatly add to the musical and spiritual energy of the community. That's not to say that musically sensitive folks can't guide the community towards greater tonal cohesion, unity, and har-

---

[23] Talmud Bavli Arakhin 13b (#77).

mony—there's always work to be done! And yet, we must take care never to shut down someone else's musical spirit, at any level because we might not yet appreciate the full power that each person can bring to the community's song, whether in tune or out of tune. Let us ALL sing!

"Amen" and the Courage to Sing

וכל המאריך באמן מאריכין לו ימיו
ושנותיו.

One who extends [the singing of]
"Amen" extends one's life.

—*Talmud Bavli Berakhot 47a*

די גרעסטע אמונה וויפיל א ייד האט, איז
זינגען דער ראש דערפון.

A Jew expresses faith most fully
and most joyfully when singing out
unreservedly (*lit.* sings one's head off).

—*Karliner Rebbe*

Once I was a visiting scholar-musician for a weekend at a very old and very beautiful Orthodox synagogue in New York. This synagogue had an endowment to hire twelve male singers from the Metropolitan Opera to accompany the cantor every Shabbat. These singers would gather in the choir loft, three or four levels above the assembled community, so that their beautiful four part choral "Amens" would drift down to the community like the sound of the angels coming from on high. It was beautiful, and yet I felt something irritating me about the situation.

At dinner, in my slightly naive and *chutzpadik* way, I asked the choir director, "It was beautiful hearing the Amens coming from the rafters, but wouldn't it be even better if the choir came down, surrounded the cantor, and then let us all surround you, so that we could really all connect and feel like we're part of the Amen, too?" "Absolutely not," he said, "that would not work at all." But nevertheless he invited me to join the choir to sing the next morning.

When I arrived in the choir loft for *Shaharit* (morning prayers), I found twelve unshaven Russian men reclining on their chairs, with their shirts hanging out and their hair messed up, reading the daily news. The only thing that was missing was vodka and cigars, though I wouldn't put that past them either. As soon as the choir leader's baton went up, they promptly stood up, belted out, "AAAMMMMENNN," and then sat down and returned to their newspapers.

What does it mean to sing "Amen"?

The word "Amen" is supposed to be the paradigmatic expression of a cultivation of faith, of creative co-wonderment. When we sing "Amen," we declare, "Yes, we feel (or are trying to feel!) the awesomeness of the world, together, in this moment!"

Amen itself is just a two syllable word, but when we stretch it out in song, it becomes *emunah*, faith. *Emunah* is what it would be like if we were all engaged in an extended state of "Amen."[24] Towards that end, the Gemara suggests that we elongate out our Amens.

> One who extends [the singing of] "Amen" extends one's life.[25]

When we sing Amen, and even stretch it out as the Gemara suggests, we cultivate a sense of *emunah*.

Emunah carries multiple valences. Yes, *emunah* connotes "steadfastness" and "faith," as reflected in the story from the Torah in which Moses held his hands in the air with steadfastness, with *emunah*, until his army prevailed.[26] *Emunah*, however, also suggests caretaking. To have *emunah* means to cultivate a sense of awe and wonder, to stay with something and take care of it until it reveals its beauty. Mordechai, for example, was called the "OMeN, אומן" (caretaker) of Esther.[27] Finally, *emunah* suggests creativity and craftsmanship, as artists are called "OMaNim, אומנים."[28] Put together, then, *emunah* means a creative cultivation of faith, or the faith to cultivate creativity, and so on. *Emunah* is the artistry of belief.

Every time that we sit down to sing together, it requires tremendous courage, steadfastness, patience and *chutzpah* to allow the music to grow. In other words, to sing at all, it takes *emunah*. We aspire to sing until something special and beautiful happens, until music becomes more than just its motifs. But creating beauty is not easy in the face of the many kinds of psychological resistance—from ourselves and from others—that we're likely to encounter every time we start singing. When we persevere with the song, however, we allow it

---

[24] See *Tur*, Orah Hayyim 124, connecting Amen to *emunah*.

[25] Talmud Bavli Berakhot 47a.

[26] Exodus 17:12, וַיְהִי יָדָיו אֱמוּנָה.

[27] Esther 2:7.

[28] Talmud Bavli Sukkah 51b (#47).

to take hold and move people's hearts, and we might find ourselves exploring a collective feeling of *emunah*.

Indeed, it takes perseverance to sing with people, especially to reach to the point where people's hearts are moved by song. I used to travel around the outer boroughs of New York City, singing old Yiddish songs with various small groups of Holocaust survivors, groups that barely exist anymore. The old Yiddish-speaking women were always so happy to hear a young man singing their childhood songs, and I'd have to gracefully avoid a torrent of lipstick kisses. In the back of the room, however, would be a bank of *shtark* (tough) looking *altercockers* (old-farts) wearing fedoras. They'd sit with their arms crossed, shaking their heads with mild disgust, and the message I received was, "You *yunger-cocker* (young-fart) who never experienced anything in his whole life." If I looked at them, it would be hard to go on with my singing—because they were too intimidating, and it seemed impossible to faze them. I persevered and continued to sing anyway, and when I finished playing, and everyone was leaving, the men would sometimes come up to me and, with a total change of affect, gush, "Yosselle (Joey), your songs just touched our hearts." I would sigh, "Well, don't you think you could have given me that impression just a little bit earlier?"

Indeed, to put it mildly, people don't always help us to create collective song. Once, a man in Maryland stood close in front of me, making continuous cutting motions at his throat, urging me to "finish it already" from the very beginning of the *davening*. A woman in New York vigorously interrupted to declare that she was a *visenshaft* (research oriented) Jew and that she found all of the singing useless. One time in Dallas, the morning after what I thought was a beautiful evening of singing, an eighty five year-old man informed me that the Vilna Gaon (the famous Lithuanian *misnagdik* sage and leading opponent of the Hasidic movement) had appeared to him in a dream the previous night to tell him that singing *nigunim* was "a big waste of time." But this very man then sat for the next three hours, transfixed, singing with me, nevertheless. Even *misnagdim* have been moved by music!

These fulminations are frustrating but at least a little bit funny. What's more discouraging, however, is not the active condemnation of singing—for these stories at least acknowledge that song is happening—but rather the complete non-recognition that any attempt at song or prayer is even happening. This attitude gives rise to the social hour that begins at *davening* time in some shuls, and the rabbi who wanders around the room counting heads, and the president who is "doing his presidential duty" of ostentatiously perusing the perimeter and slapping all the men's-club cronies on the back in the middle of the supposedly silent *Amidah*...and the list only starts there.

Small wonder then, that Pierre Pinchik, one of the greatest—and most dramatic—cantors of the twentieth century, used to wait until *Sh'ma Yisrael*, and then cynically lift his fringe wrapped finger and point directly at a talking member of the congregation, firing his finger like a gun, until the talker looked up and quieted down.[29] This was a famous diva cantor pulling rank, but did it help anyone enter the atmosphere of prayer?

The Talmud, however, proposed another approach to helping people join the grandeur of the prayer, and that was to start with encouraging people to fully pronounce just one word, "Amen." What if everyone could sing just that one word, with complete intention? The Talmud boasts of a cantor, from several millennia before Pinchik, who used a flag to prompt the largest "Amen" ever recorded in our tradition:

> Anyone who did not see Dyoploston in Alexandria, Egypt, has not seen the glory of Israel. They said: it was like a great basilica, a colonnade within a colonnade. Sometimes there were 1,200,000 people, double the amount that left Egypt! There were seventy-one golden thrones, matching the seventy-one in the great Sanhedrin, each one made from no less than twenty-one *kikars* of gold. A wooden dais was in the middle of it all, and the congregation's *hazzan* would stand on it with flags in his hand. When he reached [the time for the community] to answer "Amen," he would raise the flag aloft, and all the people would answer "Amen!"[30]

Indeed, with such a large crowd, when it came time for the people to say "Amen," the cantor had a problem—how would they say "Amen" if they couldn't hear his prayers in that hugest of auditoriums? He couldn't leave the assembled people behind—he needed to elicit an honest and timely "Amen" from an enormous crowd and found he could do so only by waving an "Amen" flag when it was their turn. The Talmud trusted that they knew which prayers they were responding to.[31] The story continues:

> However, they did not sit all mixed together. Rather, the goldsmiths sat by themselves, the silversmiths by themselves, the blacksmiths by themselves, the metal-weavers by themselves, and the wool-weavers by

---

[29] Story from Cantor Noach Schall.

[30] Talmud Bavli Sukkah 51b (#47). In Talmudic sources *hazzan*, does not necessarily mean the "cantor/singer" but more like "shul officer," but we've left in the multiple valences for the musical purposes of this book.

[31] See Talmud Bavli Berakhot 47a, which says you can't have an "orphaned Amen," i.e. saying Amen without knowing what you're responding to. See Rashi on "יתומה."

themselves. When a poor person entered, they would recognize their colleagues and turn there, and it was from them that their family's and their own charitable sustenance would come.[32]

This crowd, as it's described in the story, didn't just say "Amen" as a pro-forma statement of faith—rather it embodied the very core concept of *EMuNah* (belief/artistry) itself. Their collective "Amen" was uttered by a group of self-organizing artists and craftsmen called *"OMaNin,"* who sat organized by their specialties. Not only that, but each of these artist groups were aware of their responsibilities for taking care of their poor, for being the caretakers of society, *"AMaNim."* The Talmud's story, then, represents an ideal version of *emunah*, in which people come together en masse to care for each other, to develop their artistries and crafts with which to build the world, and to sing the songs of the Divine with collective "Amens."

Song is inextricably connected to the process of developing and expressing *emunah*. It is singing, with strength and togetherness, which both cultivates and then expresses our *emunah*. When we sing, we offer a creative "Amen" of song, our response to all the world's gifts. As the Karliner Rebbe states:

> A Jew expresses *emunah* most fully and most joyfully when singing out unreservedly (*lit.* "singing one's head off").[33]

The cultivation of *emunah* is the cultivation of our ability to see beyond ourselves. It is through singing that we realize our *emunah*, and through our *emunah* that we are able to hear the songs of the universe, as the Slonimer Rebbe describes:

> "A pure and unadulterated *emunah* provides a Jew with a unique perspective on all of creation. Who can see the Creator, of the blessed Name, from within it, from within the innermost heavens, from within the earth and all that is on it. Who can sense the power of the Cause in the effect, how You infuse all with life. In the light of this *emunah*, she can hear the song of creation that emanates from each created thing."[34]

---

[32] Perhaps it was these Amen-uttering craftsmen who were hired to fix the holy musical instruments in the great Temple of Solomon, "ושלחו חכמים והביאו אומנין מאלכסנדריא של מצרים, ותקנוהו" (Talmud Bavli Arakhin 10b (#71)). Ultimately, their fixes didn't work.

[33] As quoted in *B'nei Mahshavah Tovah*, 18 (#179).

[34] Shalom Noah Berezovsky, *Netivot Shalom*, Opening Poem (#178); see also Tanhuma B'Shallah, ch. 10: "As a reward for *emunah* that the Divine Presence rested on them and they sang a song, as it was said, 'They believed in God[...] and then Moses sang.'"

A full *emunah*, however, which carries connotations of artistry and of care-taking, allows us to mimic the omni-directional listening of the Creator, to hear the sounds and music calling out from the entire world around us, to float in the river of the world's songs. Can we allow our Amens to remind us to nurse the world, to bring out its beauty, to build and craft the world while also faithfully remembering the limits of our own creation? Can we do these things even in the face of sabotage and opposition? Can we allow our Amens to remind us of the songs that are sung by all of creation?

6

Holy Instruments

וזה שמנגן ביד על הכלי, הוא מקבץ ומלקט ביד
את הרוח טובה

One who, with his hand, plays a musical
instrument, with that hand he gathers in
and collects a spirit of goodness.

—*Rebbe Naḥman*

Musical instruments are vessels of holiness that are capable of bringing the Divine Presence into the world. Not only do we play beautiful, inspiring music through instruments, but music teaches us how to make our very selves into instruments of the transcendent tune.

The world's first musician, a harp player named Yuval, was born at the beginning of Genesis.[1] By introducing Yuval so early, and describing him as the brother of the world's first shepherd, the Torah establishes music and musical instruments at the core of the civilized human experience. According to Rashi, the earliest instruments were used for worship purposes, and by the time of the Temple, musical instruments had become indispensible in the cultivation of the sacred.[2]

Not only could holy music be made from the Temple's instruments, but in fact the Temple's instruments were themselves made from the very same material as the pillars of the Temple itself—a special wood which had never been seen before and would never be seen again.[3] From this shared material, we can

---

[1] Genesis 4:20–21 (#1).

[2] Rashi on Genesis 4:20–21; albeit to "worship the stars," of which Rashi disapproved.

[3] 1 Kings 10:12 (#13); see also 2 Chronicles 9:11, for a similar reference to the special *almug* wood.

imagine that music supported the Temple's holy activities in the same way that pillars held up its physical structure.[4]

Indeed, the job of musical instruments isn't just to make beautiful sounds, but to awaken the spiritual energies within each of us. A thirteenth-century Castilian mystic imagined:

> [The High Priest's] power is awakened with the beauty of song and the purity of prayer…So do the [Levite] musicians, according to their position and ability, direct their fingers to the hollows and strings of their instruments, awakening a song and a melody, directing their hearts to the Omnipresent. Thus, blessing is aroused, and the *Shekhinah* rests on them, each person according to their work and reach.[5]

Let's step back for a second. In the Tanakh, hundreds of verses describe dozens of different musical instruments.[6] Nine instruments appear in the final psalm alone.[7] Of all of these, the drum, the flute, the harp, and the shofar are the four main types of instruments that appear over and over again. Of these, the drum, flute, and harp symbolize the rhythms, melodies, and harmonies that form the basis of all music, leaving the shofar to represent the primal scream that animates all the others.

The instruments don't only make music; they also play literary roles in the stories of the Tanakh and Talmud. Take the drum, for example. Often played by women, such as the prophetess Miriam,[8] the drum signifies a celebration of life,[9] or operates as a tragic foil, emphasizing the celebration that might have been, as in the sad story of Jephthah and his daughter, whose fate is sealed at the moment she comes out of her house, drumming.[10] The drum, of course, was also

---

[4] The materials that comprised musical instruments, especially ones designed for sacred employ, mattered greatly. The Talmud, too, considered instruments to be holy vessels, and therefore also wondered, for example, whether a flute could be made out of the bone of an animal that had been used for idolatrous purposes. See Talmud Bavli Avodah Zarah 47a (#68).

[5] "Treatise on the Left Emanation" (#120); for a discussion of the text, see Moshe Idel, "Conceptualizations of Music in Jewish Mysticism," in Lawrence Sullivan (ed.), *Enchanting Powers: Music in the World's Religions* (Cambridge: Harvard, 1997), p. 163.

[6] For a large compendium of Tanakh music sources, as well as a list of instruments in the Tanakh, see Shlomo Hoffman's books in the bibliography.

[7] Psalm 150 (#29).

[8] Exodus 15:20 (#3).

[9] See the dancing women in 1 Samuel 18:6.

[10] Judges 11:34. See also Laban's lament in Genesis 31:27. See also how drums played a role in the story of Dinah's rape, according to Pirkei D'Rabbi Eliezer 38 (#86).

responsible for unifying the rhythm of the Temple's holy proceedings, which is why there could be infinite harps and trumpets, but only one drum.[11]

On the other side of the literary spectrum stood the flute, which usually appeared as the instrument of mourning and weeping.[12] Because of this specialty of the flute, it was required that there be at least two "weeping" flute players at any funeral.[13]

While the drum and the flute played supporting roles in the literary story of music, it was the *kinor* (ancient harp) and the shofar that really seized the imaginations of our sages; to these instruments was given the task of pronouncing mythical motifs and mystical modalities. The harp was the instrument of inspiration and meditation, the instrument that played by itself at night, the instrument that symbolized the Jewish people when they come together in ideal harmony with the world. The shofar, on the other hand, was the instrument that woke us up and made us cry, that demands that we change and improve, and that urges us to look ahead and create the peaceful times that our tradition dares to dream are possible.

The harp and the shofar work together, however, to create a harmonic link between the bookends of the broadest expanses of eternity. According to one story, the most famous harp and shofars were created simultaneously, at the very same early moment in Jewish mythical memory, out of the sinews and horns of the *Akeidah*'s ram, which tradition teaches was created before the very first Shabbat:[14]

> The ram…was created at twilight [on the sixth day of creation]…its sinews became the ten strings on the harp David played…Its horns: the left one was blown at Mount Sinai…and the right one, bigger than the left, will one day be blown in the future to come, as it was said, "And on that day, a Great Shofar will be blown, and God will be ruler over the whole world."[15]

Not only was Abraham's ram created on the sixth day of creation with other miraculous vessels of Jewish lore, but the music that came from its horns and sinews would go on to last until the coming of the Messiah. The harp and shofar, prepared at the beginning of holy time, fittingly prepare us for our musical-spiritual journeys that stretch until the end of time.

---

[11] Talmud Bavli Arakhin 13a (#75).

[12] See Jeremiah 48:36, Job 30:31.

[13] Talmud Bavli Ketubot 46b.

[14] This midrash gives a fuller meaning and purpose to the mysterious ram that was sacrificed in the place of Isaac by Abraham at the *Akeidah* in Genesis 22:13–14. According to Pirkei Avot 5:6, this ram was created at the last moment before the very first Shabbat on the sixth day of creation.

[15] Isaiah 27:13; Pirkei D'Rabbi Eliezer 21 (#85).

The story of musical instruments in Jewish history, however, isn't always so positive or straightforward. After the destruction of the great Temple in Jerusalem, the Levites jumped into the fire with their holiest instruments,[16] while the rest of the harps were hung up in the willow trees along the banks of the Babylon,[17] or carefully hidden by priests until Messianic times.[18] After that, all instruments—and possibly all musics—were officially prohibited in Jewish life, as a sign of mourning for the Temple.[19] We lost our lyres. A number of folktales even recount epic journeys to find the holy harps we left behind—including a story of one man who looked up and down on every tree along the rivers of Babylon, hoping to find David's harp, in vain.[20]

But even though Jews have made their marks as performing musicians and composers in nearly every musical culture in which they have ever lived, the role of instruments in the spiritual Jewish tradition itself is still either forbidden, ambiguous, or underdeveloped. Could we still still be waiting to rediscover our old harps? Let us hope we can find them soon!

Let's look now at the two most famous instruments—the harp and the shofar—in more detail.

The Harp

והסוד על כנסת ישראל שהיא המשוררת
והיא כנור דוד

> The secret is that the Community of Israel was the music-maker; She is the harp of David.

> —*Meir Ibn Gabbai*

On the one hand, the harp is the instrument of an individual's meditation and inspiration.[21] As we saw earlier, at the midnight hour, the northern wind of inspiration strummed sweet harmonies on David's harp, so that it seemed to play by

[16] Pesikta Rabbati 26 (#92).

[17] Psalms 137:1–6.

[18] Massekhet Kelim, ed. Jellinek, pp. 88–91, Mishnah 9 (#93). See also Ginzberg, *Legends* (2 volume version), p. 1091.

[19] Rambam, *Mishneh Torah*, Laws of Fasts 5:14 (#98); See also Ezekiel 26:13 (#18).

[20] Howard Schwartz, *Miriam's Tambourine: Jewish Folktales from Around the World*, pp. 163–167.

[21] Psalms 92:1–4 (#25).

itself, allowing the king to meditate upon the wisdom of the Torah.[22] In this way the harp can also inspire spiritual wisdom in any other listener,[23] for it opens up the mysteries and riddles of life.[24] Hearing the harp could even heal those whose minds had become caught in the trap of narrowness. In this way, the harp soothed the sadness of our ancestor Jacob and later calmed the crazy King Saul.[25]

The harp, with its calm, harmonious tones and pleasant timbre, encourages a sense of softness and openness. One medieval rabbi compared the hollow, open places inside us, which might resonate with the Divine Spirit, to the reverberant physical spaces in which music truly resonates.

> It is known that in a hollowed out or pierced space, a sound is heard much more strongly because of the spiritual atmosphere that has entered there, like a harp or other such instruments, which generate sound without any speech, like drafty hallways on high floors, or caverns, or mountains, or bathhouses, or ramshackle houses...Know that the human body is all holes and hollows, and from this one can understand how the *Shekhinah* dwells in the hollowed and hole-y body that can generate sound.[26]

Through the process of making music, we try to expand the openness within us, to welcome divine resonance. If we can find this state of openness within ourselves, then God might play us, too, the way a musician plays a harp.[27]

While the harp brings out the melodic meditation and inspiration in an individual, its most outstanding feature is its capacity for harmony. Like the piano of today, the harp in its time was the prototypical instrument of harmony. While the flute, trumpet, and shofar can only play one note at a time, the harp allows many strings to vibrate together with a beautiful resonance. But the harp didn't just make musical harmony—it came to symbolize the dream of harmony between people, as well. Meir Ibn Gabbai, the sixteenth-century mystic, explained that David's harp is itself the sound of Israel singing together:

> "A harp was suspended above David's bed, and when midnight struck, a northern wind would blow and [the harp] would start to play." Its secret is

---

[22] Talmud Bavli Berakhot 3b (#39), *Likkutei Moharan* I, 8:9 (#144).

[23] Quoting the psalmist's imperative to "Praise God with a harp" (Psalms 33:2), the Radak explains that the harp "awakens and assists the spirit of wisdom (*hanefesh hahokhmah*)" (#105).

[24] Psalms. 49:5, "I will open my riddle with a harp;" see Elimelekh of Lizhensk's commentary (#135).

[25] 1 Samuel 16:23 (#10).

[26] Abraham Abulafia, *Mafte'ah HaRayon* (#121). Also found in: Moshe Idel, "Music and Prophetic Kabbalah," in Israel Adler & Bathja Bayer (eds.), *Yuval: Studies of the Jewish Music Research Center Vol. IV* (Jerusalem: Magnes Press, 1982), p. 153 n. 13.

[27] See Uziel Meisels, *Tif'eret Uziel* (#152).

that it is the community of Israel that sings, and She is the harp of David.[28]

A community is made up of many different people who vibrate at different frequencies. United, these differences resonate together to make a mystical song. When we gather to sing, make music, or just be together, we, too, can become the inspirational harp hung above King David's bed! It won't happen without conscious effort, though. We must constantly ask ourselves: can we intentionally gather together to transcend our disparities and allow the Divine Spirit to strum on our collective strings?[29]

This mythical, transhistorical harp, which symbolizes the gathering and harmony between people, grows and develops over time, along with the spiritual technology of the people. In fact, the very strings themselves bear meaning! In the five strings of David's harp, Rebbe Nahman saw the five books of the Torah.[30] In the Talmud, the messianic era will be heralded by the seven-stringed harp gaining an additional string[31]—or, in other versions, a tenth string, corresponding to the tenth and final new song that's sung at the end of time.[32]

My dream is that as more people come together to consider and create the divine harmony of the world, the harp of Israel grows to include more and more strings, until we all arrive in the world to come, in which everyone is singing.

The Shofar

תְּקַע בְּשׁוֹפָר גָּדוֹל לְחֵרוּתֵנוּ

Sound the Great Shofar for our freedom!

—*Weekday Amidah Prayer*

If the harp acts as a resonant receiver of divine inspiration and a symbol of the potential unity of people, the shofar acts as a change agent, a piercing cry that awakens us from our meditations or from our slumber, and calls us to action. Like the trumpets (*hatzotzrot*) that called the Israelites to move in the desert, the shofar heralds, it announces, it summons, it communicates with God,

---

[28] *Avodat HaKodesh,* part 4, ch. 24 (#125).

[29] The *Kenesset Yisrael* (Gathering of Israel) is also a Kabbalistic pseudonym for the *Shekhinah.*

[30] *Likkutei Moharan* I, 8:9 (#144).

[31] The number eight (i.e. one more than the run-of-the-mill seven-day week) is often associated with the supernatural.

[32] Psalms 33:2–3 (#23): "הודו לה' בכנור בנבל עשור זמרו לו שירו לו שיר חדש." On the ten-stringed harp, see Numbers 10:1–10 (#6).

and it urges us (and God) to act in the world justly. It is, as my friend Cantor Jack Kessler put it, a "primeval sound carrying messages from out of time."[33]

The shofar calls us to awaken and act, exclaiming:

> Wake up, you sleepers from your slumber! Get up from your nap, nappers! Sift through your actions and return with repentance (*teshuvah*)! Remember your Creator![34]

The shofar is not what one wants to hear while sleeping. It wakes us up with its physical power. But it also wakes us up spiritually, reminding us to analyze our actions, turn back to the path of justice, and to remember our duties.

The shofar is designed as a sonic signal for us to break out of our patterns, to rework our habits, to consider the world from a fresh perspective, and to do *teshuvah*. Thus, one rabbi in the Talmud teaches that we should use a curved shofar, especially on Rosh Hashanah, as a symbol of this mental "twisting" that is needed in the shofar season, and especially on the Day of the Shofar's Call (*Yom Teru'ah*), as Rosh Hashanah is also known.[35]

The shofar also reminds us of the crying, pain and suffering in the world:

> The length of a *teru'ah* is the length of three sobs (*yevavot*).[36]

The most poignant crying is that of a mother losing a child. In one midrash, the shofar is associated with the crying of our matriarch Sarah in the painful moments that she heard erroneously, through Samael's (Satan's) trickery, that her son had been killed by her zealous husband:

> When Abraham returned from Mount Moriah, Samael was furious [to see] that he had not been successful in preventing Abraham our ancestor's sacrifice [of Isaac]. What did [Samael] do? He went and said to Sarah, "Haven't you heard what happened in the world?" She replied, "No." He said, "Abraham took his son Isaac, slaughtered him, and sacrificed him on an altar as a burnt offering! The boy cried and wailed that he could not be saved." Immediately, she began to weep and howl. She wept three times, corresponding to the three shouts (*teki'ot*), and the three howls to the three wails (*teru'ot*). Then her soul took its leave, and she died.[37]

---

[33] Conversation in Philadelphia, November 2015.

[34] *Mishneh Torah*, Laws of Repentance 3:4 (#97).

[35] Talmud Bavli Rosh Hashanah 26b (#48).

[36] Mishnah Rosh Hashanah 4:9 (#35).

[37] Pirkei D'Rabbi Eliezer 32. In the earlier part of this midrash, Samael had wanted to make Abraham abandon the plans to sacrifice Isaac, and thus not "pass the test" that God was giving him. Abraham, by almost going through with the sacrifice until the last moment, passed the test, frustrating Samael, who resorted to the other destructive lie that ended up killing Sarah.

We reread painful episodes relating to Ishmael, Isaac, and their mothers on Rosh Hashanah, right before hearing the shofar, to remind ourselves of the tears of the world.

With the shofar, however, we don't just recall the suffering of our own families and peoples; we recall the suffering and humanity of all families and peoples, even those of our worst enemies. Here, we're taught that the sound of the shofar reminds us of the tears shed by the mother of Sisera, the war captain of the Canaanites who terrorized the Israelites:[38]

> It was written, "It will be a *teru'ah* day for you" (Numbers 29:1). They translate this, "It will be a day of wailing for you." It was written regarding Sisera's mother, "Sisera's mother peered from the window and wailed [after her son didn't return home]" (Judges 5:28). One scholar suggested that she groaned [long sighs], and another that she howled [short piercing cries].[39]

By conjuring up the memories of these terrible stories, the *shevarim* (broken notes) breaks our hearts open and allows us to cry ourselves.

While the shofar reminds us of crying, it also reminds us of the other end of the emotional spectrum: it has accompanied the greatest celebrations and events in Jewish history! One midrash exclaimed:

> The shofar was created only for good, since the Torah was given [at Sinai] with [the accompaniment of] the shofar…And with the shofar did the walls of Jericho fall…And in the future, at the time of the revelation of the Messiah, will the Holy Blessed One blow the shofar…And with a shofar will the Holy Blessed One gather in the exiles of Israel to their place… Thus is it said: "Raise your voice like a shofar" (Isaiah 58:1).[40]

In this sense, the shofar represents the widest set of emotions present in the humanity, from dispirited sadness to unparalleled joy.

On Rosh Hashanah we begin the shofar service on with the words, "*min hameitzar karati*—from the narrow place I called out."[41] The shofar's shape itself imitates the path from constriction to freedom. As the breath moves through the winding path of the shofar from the narrow end to the wider end, it symbolizes the path from narrow-mindedness to expanded consciousness, from slavery

---

[38] Judges 4–5.

[39] Talmud Bavli Rosh Hashanah 33b; Rabbi Annie Lewis showed me these texts about crying and the shofar, in a text compilation for a class for the Germantown Jewish Centre in 2015.

[40] Tanna D'Vei Eliyahu Zuta 22 (#90).

[41] Psalms 118:5.

to freedom.[42] Perhaps it is for this reason that the Talmud says the shofar should not be turned around and blown the other way.[43]

Even when we're not sounding the shofar itself, we remind ourselves of the freedom that the shofar signifies when in the course of traditional prayer practice we exclaim the following thrice daily:

Sound the Great Shofar for our freedom![44]

It seems then that the shofar doesn't only remind us of the good and bad things that happen to us, from the outside. Rather, it reminds us that we need to get into the action ourselves. When we blow the shofar, we are understood to be causing God to move from the throne of justice to the throne of mercy.[45] In demanding mercy from God, though, we, too, fancy ourselves as partners of God, who must also move from our chairs of harsh judgement to demand compassion in the world.[46]

The shofar, unlike the harp, does not develop with new technologies. Whereas the harp is built and refined by people, growing and developing with time, the shofar comes from the natural world and remains the same forever. Its sound was there at the beginning of time and will be there at the end of time, and it will be the same all the way through, a beacon of natural consistency in an ever-changing world of new technology. The raw voice of the shofar at once reminds us of the natural world, untouched and unenhanced by human technologies and domination, and also of the transnatural world, of the primeval voice of truth from outside of time and technology. So that we can hear the shofar's wild voice unvarnished, the Talmud goes to great lengths to maintain the integrity of the shofar's sound:

If [the shofar] was coated with gold [in the place where you put your mouth], it is not kosher. But if not in that place, then it is kosher. If its insides were coated with gold, then it is not kosher. [If] the outside [was coated], if it changes its sound at all, then it's not kosher, but if not, then it's fine. If it was pierced and then plugged, if it hinders the sound, then it is not kosher, but if not, then it's fine...If a shofar is installed inside of another shofar: if the inner one's sound can be heard, then it exempts [one's obligation], but if only the outer one can be heard, then it does

---

[42] Rabbi Arthur Waskow in conversation, October 22, 2014.

[43] Talmud Bavli Rosh Hashanah 27b (#49): "הפכו ותקע בו לא יצא."

[44] One of the blessings of the *Amidah*.

[45] Pesikta D'Rav Kahana 23:3 (#91).

[46] See Sifrei Devarim Parashat Eikev 49, or Talmud Bavli Sotah 14a, or Rambam *Sefer HaMitzvot* Positive Commandment #8.

not exempt…If pieces of shofars were glued together, it is not kosher…If any amount was added to it, whether of its own material or not, it is not kosher. If it was pierced and then plugged, it is not kosher, whether of its own material or not. Rabbi Natan said, "If its own material was used, then it is kosher, but not if different material was used." If its sound is thin or thick or raspy, it is kosher; all of the shofar's [own] sounds are kosher.[47]

From this set of rules, we learn that the sound of the shofar, not to mention the shofar itself, must above all be honest. All of the shofar's own sounds are kosher, but it must sound like itself. That honesty does not have to be pretty. In fact, the shofar's voice is considered kosher if it is wavering or raspy—as long as it sounds like itself.[48] In this spirit, the shofar reminds us to listen to other voices of truth in the world, even those that are not easy to hear, as long as they are honest and true.

---

[47] Talmud Bavli Rosh Hashanah 27b (#49).

[48] Ari Kaiman shared this idea with me at Yeshivat Chovevei Torah in 2014.

7

Songs of Struggle

Battle Songs

רוֹמְמוֹת אֵל בִּגְרוֹנָם וְחֶרֶב פִּיפִיּוֹת בְּיָדָם:

Lifting songs of God in their throats, and
a double-edged sword in their hands.

—*Psalms* 149:6[1]

Music is a fighting force, and it accompanies us and helps us through all
of our struggles just as it has accompanied armies as they marched into battle.
Towards that end, many of the words that we use for music double as words that
we use for fighting and struggling. For example, the root *Z-M-R* (ז-מ-ר), which
has the meaning of "song," also connotes "pruning," "cutting," and "fighting." In
one famous line, Moses declared:

God is my strength and song/cutting force.[2]

Playing on the double meaning of *zimrah*, the divine song and a strong fighting force become indistinguishable.

The root *Sh-Y-R* (ש-י-ר) evokes "song," but also "wrestling," "struggling," and
"ruling." As we discussed above, the very name of our people "Israel" evokes
both singing (*ShiR El*) and struggling (*YiSRael*), as reflected in the story of Jacob's wrestling with the soon-to-be-singing Angel.

Finally, the root *N-G-N* (נ-ג-נ) means "melody," and also evokes "shield,"
and "defence" (*MaGeN*).

---

[1] See also Talmud Bavli Berakhot 5a: "One who recites the *Sh'ma* on one's deathbed, it is as if
one grasps a double-edged sword in one's hand."

[2] Exodus 15:2 (#4).

Music manifested directly in our now-mythical melees. Joshua, the first great warrior-leader of the Jewish people, broke down the walls of Jericho with the music of shofars and shouts.

> When the people heard the sound of the shofars, that the people shouted with a great shout, and the wall fell down flat, so that the people went up into the city, every man straight before him, and they took the city.[3]

To win a different battle, Joshua even took over the Sun's Song in order to prolong the day.[4]

But there was no paradigm of warrior-musician more famous that King David. King David sang at night, and fought by day. In the Talmud, we encounter this story of David, music, and war:

> A harp was hung above the bed of David, and once midnight arrived, a northern wind would blow on it, making its own melody. David awoke at once and delved into Torah until dawn broke.
>
> After the break of dawn, the sages of Israel entered, saying to him, "Our lord, the king, your people Israel need sustenance." He said to them, "They should go and sustain each other." They said to him, "A handful cannot satisfy a lion, and a pit cannot be filled with [its own] clumps of dirt." He said to them, "Go out and take plunder [i.e. go to war]."[5]

Did you find this ending as disappointing as I did? The liberal, pacifist side of me would have preferred that King David's night of singing and Torah study would have led to a more peaceful approach to life during the day—certainly not to war! And yet I must consider that David was rising to the battle-heavy destiny that was set out for him as his role in life and in mythical Jewish history. David would have preferred to stay in his room and continue to sing and study Torah, but ultimately he was persuaded to come into the world and use his wisdom to meet the challenges that are the daily occupation of any ruler.

A Yiddish folktale shows the "fighting" power of music in its spiritual and psychological sense. In this story, in which a boy searches for the path back to the archetypal Garden of Eden, one character explains that an instrument is the only tool that can disperse deadly serpents, which traditionally represent the collective temptations of the world:

---

[3] Joshua 6:20 (#8).
[4] Midrash Tanhuma, Aharei Mot 9 (#89).
[5] Talmud Bavli Berakhot 3b (#39).

With a sad voice the boy asked Sarah if there was any way to get past the serpents.

Sarah smiled and said, "Yes, but only with the help of Miriam's Tambourine...Know that the sound of this tambourine has great power; it causes those with pure souls to be filled with joy, and evil creatures to cringe and flee as fast as they can. Now please hurry, for if I go as long as a day without hearing the music of my tambourine, my eternal life will come to an end."[6]

Can music work the same way in our lives as well? Can we, too, choose to use music to fight in our internal battlefields? Can song strengthen us in our personal struggles to master our own inner demons, to choose positive actions, and to reopen our own spiritual Edens? Can music awaken the royalty in each of us from our slumbers and inspire us to fulfill our destined roles in the world, even if those roles require significant struggles—even battles? Let it be so!

Swords into Songs: Making Peace

מעשה ידי טובעין בים ואתם אומרים שירה?

The work of My hands are drowning in
the sea, and you want to sing?!

—*Talmud Bavli Megillah 10b*

We must fight from time to time, and music helps sustain us and inspire us in our battles, as we've explored above. But even as song leads us into battle, it also lays the groundwork for peace. Music reminds us that even as we must sometimes fight, we can still urge ourselves to consider the essential humanity of even our worst enemies.

Jewish tradition provides a few models in which songs and music remind us of the humanity of our enemies. When our enemies die, there should be no rejoicing in their downfall.[7] The Talmud tells that when the angels wanted to sing a song of praise as the Children of Israel came out of the sea, and the Egyptians drowned, but God scolded them, saying:

---

[6] Schwartz, *Miriam's Tambourine*, p. 4; Schwartz attributes this story to an oral story recorded in the Yiddish "*Ma'aseh MeHeHayyat*" Vilna 1908 AT 465C, which I still haven't seen in the original.

[7] Mekhilta of Rabbi Yishma'el, B'Shallah, Massekhta D'Shirah 1 (#82).

The work of My hands are drowning in the sea, and you want to sing?!⁸

This is complicated. It can't be simply that we must not sing in praise of the downfall of our enemies; after all, God did not rebuke Israel for singing the song of the sea, but only the angels. And yet, the Gemara suggests that there must be some consideration of the humanity of even our worst enemies. In a further recasting of the above story, Shmelke of Nikolsburg goes so far as to explain that the angels in fact wished to sing to ease the pain of the dying Egyptians:

> The [true reason the] ministering angels wanted to sing was so the Egyptians would hear their sweet voices, and their souls could leave [in peace].⁹

Here's another example of limiting a song after a struggle: when the dangerous Moabite enemy was killed by an act of God, Jehoshaphat was tempted to sing the familiar formulation of "*Hodu ladonai ki tov*—Give thanks to God because God is good."¹⁰ Out of consideration for the enemy, however, he refrained from saying "God is good," and just sang, "*Hodu ladonai*—Give thanks to God."

These warnings against the gloating of war urge us to sow the seeds of peace even while we're fighting our battles. Towards that end, the prophet Isaiah begged us to consider a time in which our spears will stop being used for killing and instead will revert back to their use in cutting in the fields. Tellingly, the word for pruning hooks, "*maZMeiRot*," includes the musical root "*ZeMeR*," linking the longing to go back to working the land to a strong desire to sing in peace.¹¹

> They will beat their swords into plowshares and their spears into pruning hooks. Nation will not take up sword against nation, nor will they train for war anymore.¹²

Toward this end, we seek to follow the model of Solomon, the composer of the Song of Songs, the son of the great warrior-singer David, who ushered in a great period of peace, in which he didn't have to fight any wars, and in which he could listen carefully to every creature on Earth.

Furthermore, we'd like our music to offer us the wisdom to pursue the war or peace that's necessary in any moment. A folktale illustrates how music pre-

---

⁸ Talmud Bavli Megillah 10b (#53).

⁹ Shmelke of Nikolsburg, as quoted in *Shemen HaTov* (#136).

¹⁰ 2 Chronicles 20:21.

¹¹ See Song of Songs 2:12, "עֵת הַזָּמִיר הִגִּיעַ," variously translated as "the time of pruning has arrived" or the "time for singing has arrived."

¹² Isaiah 2:4.

pares us for taking on the missions in our lives, whether they be warlike or peaceful. A king is promised that his son will learn the life wisdom that can come only from music:

> Let the lad stay with me for a week or for two, and I shall guide him in royal ways and instruct him and within him shall place the *spirit of sound*. And after that, *wisdom* will enter his heart and knowledge and wisdom shall be part of him, and he shall be wise and brave and ready for *peace or for war*.[13]

When the struggles of the daytime world come knocking on our doors, heralding our own impending struggles and "realities," can we, too, summon the courage to go out into the world to fight our battles and sing our songs with as much wisdom and peacefulness as we can muster?

At best, however, music comes along at just the right moment and lets us set aside our differences.

I used to play a weekly klezmer gig at a popular bar in Williamsburg, Brooklyn. The building was shaped like a long triangle; on one side sat the deeply Hasidic community of the Satmar Jews, while the other side was heavily Puerto Rican. Our klezmer band played right in the doorway, at the point that seemed to separate those two worlds.

One evening, we looked out over our shoulders as we were playing, to see that a fight had broken out between some of the Hasidim and some of the Puerto Ricans. To add to the trouble, six carloads of *shomrim*—burly Hasidic vigilantes—had just shown up to protect their own, and some extra Puerto Ricans had gathered on the other side as well. A rumble was in the making.

Without careful consideration, my bandmates and I looked at each other, winked, and pushed open the triangle point door and walked out into the middle of the fight while we continued to play lively dance music. Totally taken by the surprise of music, both sides looked up and momentarily forgot that they were supposed to be fighting. It only took that moment! The *shomrim* joined the dancing and we received many invitations that evening to come for Shabbat and to play at future weddings.

May it be that we should no longer have to use our songs as double-edged swords but rather as tools of gathering together for mutual sustenance, support and joy. Let our swords be turned back into songs!

---

[13] Emanuel Bin Gorion (ed.), *Mimekor Yisrael: Classic Jewish Folk Tales* (Bloomington: Indiana University Press, 1976), I.M. Lask (trans.), p. 1370, "The Power of Song."

8

Brokenness and Wholeness

Tears. Joy.

הַזֹּרְעִים בְּדִמְעָה בְּרִנָּה יִקְצֹרוּ

Those who sow in tears will reap in song.

—*Psalms 126:5*

Singing encourages us to experience the full range of the human emotional and spiritual spectrum, from brokenheartedness to elation. Music makes us cry, then shows us joy; it breaks open our hearts and then rebuilds our happiness.

Crying and singing are the twin processes by which we cultivate an open state of being. When tears and songs flow out of us, they encourage vulnerability, signaling that we're open for personal growth, that we may yet develop into new and more sensitive versions of ourselves. The Tikkunei Zohar teaches about two palaces, or heavenly abodes, that can be entered through either of these twin processes of crying and singing:

> There is a palace of tears to which no one can gain entrance except through crying, and there is a palace of song (*nigun*) that can be entered only through song.[1]

Crying is what happens when one's internal feelings bubble up and flow out of one's heart as tears. Singing is the same—it's also a process of deep feelings that flow out from the heart, be they of sadness or joy or deep yearning, expressed as song. In this way, song and tears are not only the keys that open the heart, and in turn open the heavenly palaces of our dreams, but they may also be opened in this actual world.

The unlocking of the heart is this outpouring of our deepest feelings and yearnings. At its best, our traditional prayers and sacred poetry can unlock our

---

[1] Tikkunei Zohar, Tikkun 11 (#118).

hearts in this way. When we can't access our essential feelings through the fixed written prayers, however, we must unlock our hearts through crying, as the Talmud explains:

> Even if the gates of prayer are closed, the gates of tears are never closed, as it was said, "Hear my prayer and listen to my call for help. Do not be silent at my tears."[2]

To express our deepest prayers, we must try to cry when we sing. As Isaiah Horowitz, often called the Holy Sh'LaH, wrote,

> One must awaken oneself and see that one's prayers are tearful...Even if sometimes one cannot truly bring oneself to tears, one's voice during prayer, in vocalizing the words, should still be humble and broken, as though one were crying.[3]

If we can't cry real tears, we should at least act the part and try to cry! Perhaps this "act" of crying while singing can help us to cultivate a brokenness, to summon up the real tears and the real prayers that are waiting within us underneath the disguised layers of our stoic façades and muscular masks.

It was towards the purpose of cultivating tears that the great Eastern European cantors and prayer leaders sang with *kvetches* (cries) and *krechts* (sighs). In their singing, we could hear the sound of yearning, pleading, and of begging, and those sounds could bring people to tears, and thus to prayer. Modern synagogues could stand to learn from our tradition by creating space for us to cry together, as often our tears are the only prayers we can truly offer.

It is, in fact, melody that exposes our inner feelings andallows us to cry. The Piezetzner Rebbe explains:

> A melody, ultimately, is only a kind of exposure of the spirit and its feelings. They are revealed in speech, as when one speaks with a friend of their thoughts and feelings of pain or joy, but this is even more true with the [timbre of] the voice...when one's sorrows are overwhelming, God forbid, and one can no longer find the words to speak, then one will break down into crying and weeping, using only his voice, no words.[4]

Crying, however, is not the end of the story. Tears, when paired with song, could allow us to find joy, to find moments where we can appreciate the fullness of life. Through brokenness we find wholeness—as we shatter our exter-

---

[2] Psalms 39:13 in Talmud Bavli Berakhot 32b.

[3] Isaiah Horowitz, *Sh'nei Luhot HaBrit*, Massekhet Tamid, Perek Ner Mitzvah (#127).

[4] Shapira, *B'nei Mahshavah Tovah*, Number 18 (#179).

nal hardnesses, we might then uncover the flexible wholeness within. Towards this end the shofar's song, with its broken notes, called *shevarim*, is designed to break us open. Once broken, we're ready to rebuild, and collect ourselves into the *tekiyah gedolah*: the long, sustained, whole note that we're trying to become, the note that also symbolizes the completeness that we dream the world could permanently achieve before the end of time. Of course, even the greatest shofar blower's final note comes to an end eventually, and then we have to restart the cycle of breaking and rebuilding.

Every Shabbat after meals, we sing, "Those who sow in tears, will reap in *rinah*."[5] *Rinah* means both joy and song. With this line, we imagine that if we can allow ourselves to cry, to fully go into the realm of tears, that we will ultimately open up the pathways back to joy, and thus back to song. In other words, if we can hit the bottom of the emotional spectrum, we can activate the pathways for rising to the top as well. This journey represents the process of imagining, as if in a dream, the return of joy.

One great prayer leader taught me that the verse might be also parsed as, "Those who sow in tears with song...will reap," meaning that those who can manage to sing while they are crying, and to cry while they are singing, will ultimately reap.[6] In other words, those who can find song from within their tears will facilitate the re-gathering of our exiled tears, like a flash flood that suddenly emerges from an isolated stream in the desert.[7]

Of course, music is joy just as much as it is sadness. Our stories could not imagine a joyous time that is not also full of music. When the Jews came out of Egypt, they celebrated with song.[8] When David returned the ark to Jerusalem, there was music and dancing.[9] When Solomon was anointed king, there was a great musical celebration.[10] The Mishnah, too, cannot imagine joy without lots and lots of music. Consider the Mishnah's extensive description of the joyous, musical party that accompanied the Water-Drawing Festival (*Simhat Beit HaSho'evah*) in the Temple:

> Anyone who has not seen the rejoicing at the Water-Drawing Festival has never seen joy in their lives...Pious people and the accomplished would

---

[5] Psalms 126:5 (#26). Many sing this Psalm, commonly referred to as *Shir HaMa'alot*, before reciting the Grace after Meals on holidays and other festive occasions. Shabbat is a time for dreaming and singing of the path towards a refined world.

[6] Elli Kranzler, who said he heard it from Rabbi Shlomo Carlebach.

[7] See the rest of Psalm 126.

[8] Exodus 15:1–2 (#2).

[9] 2 Samuel 6:5,15–16.

[10] 1 Kings 1:40 (#11).

dance before [the assembled] with lit torches in their hands, singing songs and praises, with the Levites on their harps, lyres, cymbals, and horns, all kinds of sounds without limit. [They stood] on the fifteen steps from the general section to the women's section, like the fifteen Songs of Ascent in Psalms, on which the Levites would stand with their musical instruments and sing songs. Two priests stood at the upper gate, leading from the general section to the women's section, with two horns in their hands. The rooster crowed, and would play a *tekiyah*, a *teru'ah*, and another *tekiyah*. They reached the tenth step: *tekiyah*, *teru'ah*, *tekiyah*. They reached the [women's] section: *tekiyah*, *teru'ah*, *tekiyah*.[11]

Musicians in the Temple were responsible for creating the joy that could allow for spiritual transformation. Music constitutes the ever-challenging process of creating joy—and that is the main work that musicians have to do today, as well! The Talmud explains:

What is this joyful and good-hearted service? It says: it is song.[12]

Music extracts joy from the vast panoramas of our melancholy. We can't find joy if we don't first admit that we're sad, so music tries to expose our vulnerability first and then show us what we can do with that vulnerability. Indeed, this is what a musician's job is: find the good notes from within the bad notes, to find the joy from within the sadness. According to Rebbe Nahman, as the musician plays his instrument, he gathers in the spirit of goodness from amidst the spirit of sadness of the world. This very ingathering of joy ultimately allows a new *nigun* to form in the world:

One who plays a musical instrument by hand, gathers in, with that hand, and collects a spirit of goodness, a spirit of prophecy, from the midst of a sadness of spirit. One must understand music to gather in, collect, and locate the parts of spirit, one by one, to compose a *nigun*—and the same goes for the joy—that is, to compose a spirit of goodness, a spirit of prophecy, the opposite of a sadness of spirit.[13]

When we reach into our sadness and extract joy, we imitate the divine process, for according to one Psalm,

You transformed my mourning to merriment. You untied my sackcloth and wrapped me in joy. So my glory can sing to You and no longer be si-

---

[11] Mishnah Sukkah 5:1–4 (#37).

[12] Talmud Bavli Arakhin 11b (#74).

[13] 1 Samuel 16:16; *Likkutei Moharan* I, 54:6 (#145).

lent, YHVH, my God, I will praise You forever.[14]

The divine process, however, does not subsume our own agency in the process of recovering the joyful song of life. If the Holy One has the agency to convert sadness into happiness, we must also, and we do that by singing. Abraham Joshua Heschel explained that the person who goes through the process of weeping and reflection can convert his own "sorrow into song:

> He who stands on a normal rung weeps;
> he who stands higher is silent;
> but he who stands on the topmost rung
> converts his sorrow into song.[15]

Let us, too, face our sorrows and find our songs!

Healing

וְלָקַח דָּוִד אֶת־הַכִּנּוֹר וְנִגֵּן בְּיָדוֹ וְרָוַח לְשָׁאוּל
וְטוֹב לוֹ וְסָרָה מֵעָלָיו רוּחַ הָרָעָה:

> David would take the harp and play
> it with his hand; and Saul would be
> refreshed/re-expanded and be well, and
> the evil spirit would depart from him.

—*1 Samuel 16:23*

Music heals the spirit and balances our bodies. While music does not directly cure physical diseases, it can certainly assist in the spiritual and psychological realms of healing. When we are unwell, music dispels our depressions; it connects us with our internal life forces; it reminds us of our essential humanity; it raises our spirits; it balances our internal chaos; it joins us with others; it celebrates life; and it reminds us of what paths we might yet have left to walk in the world.

Let's look at how David's harp, for example, soothed King Saul. King Saul did not initially want to be king, but once he became king, he became pathologically attached to the position, such that the thought of losing the throne drove him to a severe depression. Only one person—the young musician David—could help him.

---

[14] Psalms 30:12–13 (#22).

[15] Abraham Joshua Heschel, *A Passion for Truth* (New York: Farrar, Straus and Giroux, 1973), p. 283.

When Saul listened to the sound of the harp, the constricting spirit would leave him and his mind would be refreshed or even expanded. Of course, Saul demanded only the best harpist in the land, who, ironically, was the young David.[16] The Talmud would not be surprised that music helped soothe Saul's spirits, as it claims,

> Three things restore a person's mind: [good] sounds, [good] sights, and [good] smells.[17]

The first thing that brings back a person's judgment is "good sounds." Rashi comments that the Talmud must mean music, indicating that beautiful music played on instruments or the notes of a *zemer* help restore a person's internal harmony and clarity.[18]

Even Rambam, who generally forbade instruments and music altogether,[19] recognized that music could help a person escape from depression:

> If melancholy is awakened within one, one can dispel it by listening to singing and different melodies, or by strolling through gardens or beautiful buildings, or by sitting with lovely images, or other activities which expand the soul/spirit, and the anxiety and melancholy will dissolve.[20]

Indeed—as Rambam was also a prominent doctor and healer for Jews and non-Jews alike—it appears that he prescribed music as a treatment for severe depression and anxiety. The fields of music therapy and sound healing today continue these modes of treatment.

The therapeutic process of musical healing reflects the process of spiritual healing in general. One story of healing in the Talmud relates that the famous healer Rabbi Yohanan healed suffering people by first connecting with them and then by lifting them up. When Rabbi Yohanan himself became sick, he, too, required someone else to come to his side, for, as the anonymous narrator explained, "A prisoner can't let himself out of prison."[21]

Music itself specializes in the process of connecting and "lifting", and music is one of the keys that lets us out of our unhealthy prisons. But like the case of

---

[16] See Abarbanel on 1 Samuel 16 for a full discussion of David's unique combination of skills as a wise warrior who "knew song" (#109).

[17] Talmud Bavli Berakhot 57b (#43).

[18] Rashi on Talmud Bavli Berakhot 57b, on "קול." Rashi also says that the pleasant voice/song of a woman might also help.

[19] *Mishneh Torah*, Laws of Fasts 5:14 (#98).

[20] Rambam, *Commentary on the Mishnah, Eight Chapters* (Introduction to *Pirkei Avot*), Chapter 5, "On a Person's Direction of Spiritual Potencies towards a Singular Objective" (#100).

[21] Talmud Bavli Berakhot 5b.

the wounded healer above, it often takes someone else to make the music with you, to create the sense of companionship and connection, that really allows one to open the doors of our sick dungeons and climb out. We rely upon each other for our singing strength, as the Koretzer Rebbe taught:

> Sometimes, when a person sings, he cannot raise his voice. But when someone comes to help and sings strongly, this in turn gives the first person the ability to raise his own voice [to match]. This is of the secret significance of uniting, soul to soul.[22]

A second person unlocks the dreams, the songs, and the understandings of his fellow. Healing works the same way. This is why we are enjoined to visit the sick, which is a *mitzvah* with no measure.[23]

In one musical midrash, Serah, daughter of Asher, serenades her depressed grandfather Jacob back to emotional health. For twenty-two years since losing his son Joseph, Jacob had lived a depressed life, and hadn't been able to see beyond his sadness and anger.[24] Fearing that their father Jacob would drop dead from shock upon hearing the good news of Joseph's survival, his sons sent along Serah, the daughter of Asher, the best harpist of her day, to soothe their father through a song.

> [Jacob's sons] returned from Egypt, and went to Canaan in joy and gladness to Jacob, their father. They came to the border of the land, saying to each other, "What should we do with this matter, before our father? If we come to him suddenly, and recount what happened, he will be so shocked that he won't be able to bear hearing [more] from us."

> So, they kept traveling until close to their homes and found Serah, daughter of Asher, who was coming out to greet them. This young woman was exceptionally wise, and she knew how to play a harp. They called to her, and she came and kissed them. They took her with them, gave her a harp, and said, "Please go to our father, sit before him, play this harp, and speak these words to him…"

> They directed her to go to their home, take her harp, and hurry back to them, to come and sit before Jacob. The harp was lovely as she played and said, with soothing speech, "Beloved Joseph is alive, ruling over the whole of Egypt. He did not die!"

---

[22] Pinhas of Koretz, *Midrash Pinhas*, vol. 1 (Lvov, 1872), §90 (#137).

[23] See, e.g., Talmud Bavli Nedarim 39b.

[24] About Jacob's anger and depression, see Shimon Ben Tzemah Duran, *Magen Avot*, Part 2 ch. 2, 15b.

She continued to play, saying these things. Jacob [was able to] hear her words; they were a sweetness for him. He heard her words again, then a third time, and joy entered his heart due to the gratifying nature of her words. The spirit of God came upon him, and he knew all her words were true. Jacob blessed Serah with these words [of his own], "My daughter, death will never rule over you, eternally, for you have revitalized my spirit."[25]

Reclaiming his divine spirit through her song, Jacob blessed his grand-daughter musician with eternal life. Serah did live forever, according to tradition,[26] as did her harp; in one modern midrash, Serah's harp is the very same harp that King David would play generations later.[27]

Of course, we don't have to rely on the stories or wisdom of ancient rabbis for our information about musical healing. Indeed, many of us who have played music for sick people (or been serenaded while sick ourselves) have discovered this. I knew a man who had been a fighter for justice. I saw him in his hospital bed, skinny and debilitated, near the end of a terminal bout with cancer, with his wife and daughters surrounding him. When his daughters started singing, he stood up, hoisted his body and medical tubes up off the bed, and began to dance, looking upwards with his beautiful, determined smile. He died several days later. While the music didn't heal his body, it reminded him of his essence, it lifted him up, and it allowed him to dance, then die with dignity.

I also know a dear man whose dementia prevents him from speaking and, increasingly, from communicating in any way with his loved ones. He looks lost, sad, and detached from the world that we imagine ourselves to be in. Yet when I begin to sing *Shalom Aleikhem*, the song he used to sing on Friday nights, his eyes light up, his hand starts beating rhythms, and he opens his mouth, singing the words and the melody. For a fleeting moment, he reclaims the spirit within him, even if it's only the echoes of a life once lived. The man who cannot talk can yet sing.

Music is an awesome tool that raises us up and revitalizes us. It allows us to reclaim our hopes and connections and rediscover the divine life within us. The power of a *nigun* to raise us up, according to Rebbe Nahman, is unlimited—it, too, like the goodness inherent in visiting the sick, "cannot be measured."

> It's good for a person to accustom himself to reviving himself with a *nigun*, because *nigun* is a powerful and mighty tool, and it has the great strength

---

[25] *Sefer haYashar*, Parshat VaYigash (#96).

[26] Serah was in the list of Israelites who went down to Egypt (Genesis 46:17) and also in the list of Israelites who made it out of Egypt, into the wilderness (Numbers 26:60). Our rabbis tried to explain her exceptionally long life with this musical midrash.

[27] Jill Hammer, *Sisters at Sinai* (Philadelphia: Jewish Publication Society, 2004), p. 184.

to awaken a person and point his heart towards the Blessed Name. And even one who doesn't know how to play music [or sing out loud], can sing to himself and through that revive himself. For the "lift" of a *nigun* cannot be measured.[28]

Music also awakens our inner humanity, reminding us of the spark of love and beauty that's hidden inside of us. When we're unwell, or when our bodies don't work properly or resemble who we really think are, we need music to help us reclaim ourselves from within our suffering conditions. Perhaps music can do this because it summons up old feelings of life that were once associated with a particular piece of music, like a song from one's healthy youth, or because music itself brings up deep emotion, which perhaps more than anything confirms that we're alive. As the Rabbi from Levertov explained:

> The *nigun* awakens the trace of a memory of love and attachment...even when it is hidden in a person, such that they can no longer feel it in themselves, for it has disappeared from them. Even so, it is hidden and still remains to be brought to mind by means of the *nigun*.[29]

A taxi-cab driver once told me a story about music reconnecting a person with the world.[30] He said that a man had gotten into his car but refused to say a word, or even look at him—he looked angry and depressed, and essentially non-communicative. The driver turned on some reggae music very softly in the front seat. A few minutes later, the man leaned forward and asked, "Could you turn that up a little bit?" A few minutes later, "A little higher?" and then, "A little more?" Pretty soon a smile came to the man's face, and he started talking and sharing stories with the driver. Music, the driver later told me, had freed this man and brought him back to life.

The vibrations of musical notes have an amazing healing effect upon our bodies and minds that we're only just beginning to consider scientifically, but our ancient stories and spiritual traditions had noticed—if not fully explained— that healing power of music hundreds of years earlier.[31] One thirteenth-century teacher, for example, observed that music reminds our internal organs how to interact with each other, how to renew their mutual "joy:"

> See, when a lyre and harp combine their sound, combining their voices,

---

[28] Nahman of Breslov, *Sihot HaRan* 273 (#151).

[29] *Ma'amar Nigun*, 17 (#163).

[30] Named Kwame, in Philadelphia, 2016.

[31] For some popular studies on the science of music as it affects the brain and body, see Daniel J. Levitin, *This is Your Brain on Music* (Dutton: New York, 2006) and Oliver Sacks, *Musicophilia: Tales of Music and the Brain* (New York: Vintage Books, Random, 2007).

the ears hear the fluctuation and interchange in the pangs of love, the strings struck by the right hand or left, vibrating, bring a sweet taste to the ears. From the ears, the sound passes to the heart, and from the heart to the guts and joy is renewed between them, through the pleasure of a melody's fluctuation.[32]

Music may balance our bodies and allow us to remember our inner essence—and yet, in one story, music itself becomes the very reason to remain living!

> Once, the Holy Jew (Rabbi Ya'akov Yitzhak Rabinowitz, of Pshischa) saw, with his holy spirit of prophecy, that the holy Maggid of Koznitz was deathly ill, so he immediately ordered two of his men, one named Rabbi Samuel Yedlinsker, and the other named Rabbi Samuel Sekshiner, to travel to the house of the holy Maggid while he still lived. There they will take in a Shabbat with the holy Maggid, for they are immensely skilled singers and can, with their songs, restore and return [the Maggid] to this world. Due to [the Holy Jew's] command, they were protected and [smoothly] traveled to Koznitz and came before the holy Maggid, who still lived. He asked them from where they had come, and they answered that the Holy Jew had sent them there. Rabbi Samuel Yedlinsker said that he was able to sing, and the holy Maggid honored him with [leading] *Kabbalat Shabbat*, and Rabbi Samuel Sekshiner would enhance his leading as a harmonizer (*meshoreir*). When the holy Maggid heard the melodies (*nigunim*) of *Kabbalat Shabbat*, his health began to improve, more and more with each one. He felt within himself that the *nigunim* were the specific medicine for his illness. Said the holy Maggid, "The Holy Jew saw, in his radiant lens [of prophecy], that I had already walked throughout all realms, but I had not yet been to the world of song. So he sent me these men who could return me to this world, through their *nigunim*."[33]

Music is a key that opens the prisons of our sicknesses. Even if our physical diseases don't dissipate, music allows us to see the life that we yet have within us, to appreciate what's there, to find the joy within the sadness, and to break out of the gloom and anger that surround our sicknesses. And since all of us can locate ourselves somewhere on the continuum between wellness and illness, music can serve to let us all out of our self-imposed prisons, to reclaim our joint humanity.

---

[32] Abraham Abulafia, *Gan Na'ul* (#122).
[33] Louis Newman, *Hasidic Anthology*, p. 65, story 9, quoted from J.K.K. Rokotz, *Niflaoth HaYehudi*, (Warsaw, 1908), p. 59.

9

Praise and Gratitude

Freedom and Miracles

כל מי שנעשה לו נס ואומר שירה בידוע שמו־
חלין לו על כל עונותיו ונעשה בריה חדשה...

> It is well known that everyone for whom
> a miracle has been performed and who
> subsequently sings a song will be forgiven
> all their sins and will become a new
> creature.
>
> —*Yalkut Shimoni*

Singing is the ultimate expression of freedom, an essential rejoicing at the end of a cycle of suffering. Music is a recognition of the miracles of life.

The most famous freedom song of our tradition is the Song of the Sea. It begins, "And thus Moses sang, with all of the Children of Israel, this song to God."[1] This song recounts the stunning moment when Moses and the Israelites escaped the slavery of Egypt by walking through the Sea of Reeds on dry land. It was sung by Moses, Miriam, the dancing women, and the entire Jewish people,[2] and has become the most important song of freedom in our tradition, reminding us of the birth of our nation. Even the fetuses in their mother's bellies sang along.[3]

But the Song of the Sea was only one of many songs of freedom sung by our ancestors. Almost all of the war heroes and righteous leaders of the Tanakh

---

[1] Exodus 15:1–2 (#4).

[2] Some say that because the poem has a chiastic structure, with "*Mi Khamokha*" being the very middle, and Miriam and Moses equally far away from the middle, that they were co-composing, or antiphonally responding to each other. Conversation with Cantor Jacky Chernett, London 2016. The Talmud discusses other ways in which Moses traded verses with the people (see #57).

[3] Talmud Bavli Sotah 30b–31a (#58).

immediately sang songs and praises upon averting tragedy, or upon bringing their people from suffering to freedom, as can be seen in the Ten Songs of the Tanakh.[4]

"This song"—But is it really just one song? Are there not ten songs?

The first was sung in Egypt, as it was said, "You will have a song like a night a feast is made holy" (Isaiah 30:29).

The second was on the [Reed] Sea, as it was said, "Then Moses sang" (Exodus 15:1).

The third was at the well [in the desert], as it was said, "Then Israel sang" (Exodus 21:17).

The fourth was sung by Moses [near the end of his life], as it was said, "Moses concluded writing all the words of this song" (Deuteronomy 31:24).

The fifth was sung by Joshua, as it was said, "Then Joshua spoke before God on the day God delivered…" (Joshua 10:12).

The sixth was sung by Deborah and Barak, as it was said, "Then sang Deborah and Barak ben Avinoam…" (Judges 5:1).

The seventh was sung by David, as it was said, "David spoke to God the words of this song…" (2 Samuel 22:1).

The eighth was sung by Solomon, as it was said, "A Psalm, a song for the dedication of David's house" (Psalms 30:1)…

The ninth was sung by Jehoshaphat, as it was said, "Jehoshaphat counseled with the people and stationed those to sing for God and praise the beauty of the Holy One, as they exited before the army, saying 'Praise God, Whose love is eternal'" (2 Chronicles 20:21)…

The tenth will be in the coming future, as it was said, "Sing to God a new song, and praise to the ends of the earth" (Isaiah 42:10).[5]

Perhaps we can even say that after a miracle, you must sing. The Haggadah, for example, obligates us to sing after recounting the story of the miraculous Exodus from Egypt:

Therefore we are obligated to thank, praise, laud, glorify, exalt, lavish,

---

[4] For other lists of the "Top Ten Songs of the Tanakh," see also Tanhuma B'Shallah 10, Midrash Zuta Shir Hashirim 1:1, *Ba'al HaTurim* on Exodus 15:1 (#107).

[5] Mekhilta D'Shirah 1 (#83).

bless, raise high, and celebrate the One who made all these miracles for our ancestors and for us: who brought us out from slavery to freedom, from sorrow to joy, from mourning to this good day, from darkness to great light, and from servitude to redemption. And let us sing before [God] a new song, *halleluyah*![6]

According to a midrash, the transformation that might follow a miracle is predicated upon taking the time to sing a song to the Divine One:

Not everyone who wants to sing a song can sing a song, but anyone who has experienced a miracle and subsequently sings a song, all their sins will be forgiven and they become a new creature.[7]

If we don't sing after each miracle that we experience, we may miss tremendous opportunities for personal and global transformation. Since each day and each moment is a miracle, perhaps there are always reasons to sing, even without awaiting a special miracle.

Consider this story of one who forgot to sing. A great miracle happened for the righteous Jewish king, Hezekiah. The Assyrian army of Sennacherib had razed dozens of smaller cities and was perched outside of Jerusalem, ready to invade, when the whole army was destroyed overnight through divine intervention. Hezekiah, who was known for his great righteousness and piety, unfortunately neglected to sing a song of praise to the Holy One after this miracle. According to the Talmud, had he only sung a Song of Praise, Hezekiah would have become the Messiah![8]

The Holy Blessed One wanted to make Hezekiah the Messiah...The Attribute of Judgment came before the Holy Blessed One and said, "Master of the universe! If David, king of Israel, who sang so many songs and praises before You, You did not make Messiah, Hezekiah, for whom You performed all these miracles but sang before You not one song, You'll make him Messiah?!"[9]

Later in the story, the Earth tries to rescue Hezekiah's chance at becoming the Messiah by singing for him, but it didn't work. He needed to sing on his own behalf! We all must sing the songs of our own miracles.

---

[6] Passover Haggadah.

[7] *Yalkut Shimoni*, B'Shallah 254 (#95).

[8] Hezekiah did sing the first time (Isaiah 38:10), but not the second time after Sennacherib's army was destroyed.

[9] Talmud Bavli Sanhedrin 94a (#63).

And yet singing is not limited to the already-free, to the post-miracle existence. Indeed, we sing songs while yet enslaved to remind ourselves of our humanity, to recognize our path towards freedom. We sing to create freedom, to generate the miracles. As shown above in the Ten Songs, the first song that was sung by Jews was sung while still in Egypt, and only the second upon its emancipation. In the depths of slavery, the Israelites cry out, they make noise; they sing the blues. That sound goes up to God and activates God.[10]

Min hameitzar, the verse from Psalms that we sing on festivals and before sounding the shofar, reminds us that if we sing while we're still caught in a state of narrowness, of constricted consciousness, then we may find our freedom and experience a divine expansiveness:

> From the narrow place (*meitzar*) I called out to God;
> I was answered with divine expansiveness (*merhav-Yah*).[11]

Given that no one is entirely free or entirely enslaved, and that we're all on a continuum between servitude and self-determination, there's no reason to wait to sing—freedom is expressed through song, but yet our songs themselves may very well lead to freedom. At the moment that we open our mouths, are we not already free?

What's more, the end of the struggles of this world will be brought about by singing. As the Zohar declares:

> Israel will arise from exile with a song.[12]

Through the process of composing divine songs, we will build the worlds we dream of, we will transcend our trapped situations and we will yet emerge from our exiles, where we will then sing again!

Overflowing Praise

אָשִׁירָה לַה' כִּי גָמַל עָלָי:

I sing to God, for He has taken care of me.

—*Psalms 13:6*

---

[10] Exodus 2:23–24; conversation with Aryeh Bernstein, 2016.
[11] Psalms 118:5.
[12] Tikkunei Zohar, 3a (#117).

We've all received gifts from heaven. All of us who have breath filling our lungs and blood pulsating through our veins and thoughts streaming through our minds—we've received gifts that we haven't earned, the gifts of life. Song is what happens the moment we realize the un-repayable debt we owe to the Divine Source of Life. What else could we offer back to the Divine?

King David asked what one theologian suggests is the defining question of Judaism:

How can I repay God for all the care he has shown me?[13]

But David offered an answer elsewhere in the Psalms:

I sing to God for He has taken care of me.[14]

At the very moment when our breath leaves our mouths, they sing songs. Song is what happens at the moment of freedom. Singing is how we express our appreciation of the gifts of life.

And yet, even if we sing praises with every breath we take, we still could never praise enough. Included in the poetry of the Shabbat morning prayers is:

Even if our mouths were as full of song as the sea,
our tongues with joy as the many waves,
our lips with praise as the expanse of the sky,
our eyes shining like the sun and the moon,
our hands spread out like eagles' wings,
our legs as swift as gazelles,
we still could not satisfy the praises due to You, YHVH our God, God
of our ancestors."[15]

Even with our best efforts at singing and praising, the Divine is still, as we say in the Kaddish, "*le'ela min kol birkhata veshirata tusbehata…*, above all of our blessings and songs and praises."[16]

That said, even if our songs will never be sufficient, we still need to sing! Indeed, according to the Jewish tradition, singing is, in fact, obligatory. Commenting on the verse from Proverbs, "Honor God with your wealth,"[17] a midrash in Pesikta Rabbati explains:

If you have a sweet voice, and you are sitting in the synagogue, get up

---

[13] Psalms 116:12.

[14] Psalms 13:6 (#20). This insight is from Shai Held, in a class at Mechon Hadar, 2014.

[15] Shabbat Morning Liturgy (#169).

[16] לְעֵלָּא מִן כָּל בִּרְכָתָא וְשִׁירָתָא תֻּשְׁבְּחָתָא וְנֶחֱמָתָא, דַּאֲמִירָן בְּעָלְמָא.

[17] Proverbs 3:9 (#30).

and praise the Lord with your voice!...Hiyya, the son of Rabbi Eliezer haKapar's sister had a lovely voice, and he would say to him, "Hiyya, my son, stand and glorify God with that which you have been gifted."[18]

And on the same verse, Rashi explains:

"With your wealth"—[This means] from all you are graced with, even a sweet voice...[19]

As we'll see, praise does not appear to be optional—we must give honor to the Divine, with whatever means we have. Joseph Caro, the great master of Jewish law, took Rashi's idea even further. Not only should we honor the Divine with the "wealth" of a sweet voice, but in fact, it's a commandment. If we *can* sing, we *must* sing![20]

Moreover, there's a spiritual value to singing that cannot be achieved through talking. The Piezetzner Rebbe explains that we must sing our praises of the Holy One, not merely speak of them:

One who speaks of the praises and glory of the Divine is like one who recounts that there is a great light [like the sun] that shines in a certain place far away. *But one who sings a song of praise and glory for the Divine is like one who brings a candle close from far away.* This [singing] arouses in him an extra visioning power of the children of the prophets (*b'nei ne-vi'im*)[21] that is within him, and through his song and spirit it is somewhat revealed.[22]

Here the Piezetzner reminds us that singing expresses far more than mere words, especially when it comes to praising the Divine. To sing, he explains, allows us to actually feel the divine warmth and see the godly light, whereas words only give us a vague impression of something that continues to feel far away.

But how do we actually begin to offer praise and gratitude? How do we actually summon up our songs? Rav Kook explores how it happens in the most ecstatic experiences, in which one is overcome by the recognition of God's energy within, and that energy suddenly overflows from one's mouth as song:

How does one [come to] make melodies and sing songs of praise? The

---

[18] Pesikta Rabbati 25:3 (#88).

[19] Rashi on Proverbs 3:9 (#30).

[20] *Beit Yosef* on *Tur*, Orah Hayyim 53 (#128).

[21] There is a principle that Jews "If they aren't prophets, they are the descendents of prophets" (see, for example, Talmud Bavli Pesahim 66a). This is meant to say that the instincts and practices of Jewish communities should be trusted as a form of prophecy.

[22] Shapira, *Hovat HaTalmidim*, "Torah Prayer and Singing to God" (#159).

spirit of your soul comes, and the overwhelmingness of the Divine fills the heart. And your heart feels how it is too limited to contain all of its sensations, and holy pleasure suffuses all of its limbs. Your mind expands and illumines, discerning the truth of the immensity of its vision, yet also its diminution, due to its being copied from a supernal original. It is lifted and ascends and is sanctified, and a compulsion felt inside grows and becomes stronger within, filled with power, like lightning, glow-full but then darkened, as a thought of lowliness passes through your mind running counter to this magnificent state. But another flash of lightning appears, and all is light and love and mercy. The goodness of God's greatness, the envisioning of divine beauty, in immensity and awe, with strength and splendor, is appointed and infuses all chambers of your heart. It keeps thinking, and the feeling grows. Consciousness becomes one, lifelines radiating continuously, giving no rest. Suddenly, supernal pleasure knocks, the voice of my beloved; He is here! [Your consciousness] is called, it awakes, and your mouth opens with song.[23]

Perhaps this is the ideal state of spiritual practice, of being carried away by the flow of the divine river. Many of us, though, who are never fortunate enough to experience a truly ecstatic mystical moment like Rav Kook was describing, have to work hard to offer praises, to approach life with a sense of gratitude and smallness, and even to sing songs. We simply ask, over and over again, that our mouths, too, might be opened, like the mystic's.[24]

Music is the process of listening carefully to the world around us and offering our own songs back to the universe. In this way music is fundamentally interwoven into the Jewish spiritual process. When we sing, we not only create a cozy cultural blanket that warms us, but we weave praises into the fabric of the universe, or put another way, "I will sing sweet melodies and weave beautiful songs."[25]

---

[23] Abraham Isaac Kook, *Shemoneh Kevatzim* 5:84 (#176).

[24] Psalms 51:17, and beginning of *Amidah*, "אֲדֹנָי שְׂפָתַי תִּפְתָּח וּפִי יַגִּיד תְּהִלָּתֶךָ."

[25] *Shir HaKavod*, or *Anim Z'mirot* (#103).

10

Renewing the Songs of Life

The Metamorphosis of a Melody

שירו לו שיר חדש: חדשו לו שיר תמיד

"Sing a new song to the Divine:"
Refresh the melody to the Divine, always.

—*Radak on Psalms 33:3*

My grandfather, of blessed memory, used to take me and my siblings down to the industrial port area of Milwaukee, where his friend ran a scrap metal business. We would watch with delight as broken cars were dropped from fifty feet to shatter their glass, leaving the metal frame, which would be melted down and resold as recycled metal.

Music performs a "salvage operation"[1] on the spirits of humankind, as it lifts us up and reminds us of our joint humanity. But melodies, too, must be recycled and renewed; as we are rescued by melodies, we must feed the energy back into the melodies.

In one Yiddish story, after a melody is initially composed for a wedding, it then disappears and reappears in various guises throughout the years, including in much slower form at a funeral, and then it, too, almost dies altogether—but, amazingly, it returns again from the dead:

> And a *nigun* lives, and a *nigun* dies; and one forgets a *nigun*, like one forgets someone who has been buried!
>
> Young and fresh it once was, that *nigun*! With fresh life it had burst forth...but with time it became weak, it had lived through its prime, and its energy left it...It was a thing of the past, it was nullified...Its last breath went into the air, and somewhere quiet it went...and it was no more!

---

[1] Cantor Jack Kessler of Philadelphia, has described his work in the world as a "salvage operation."

But even a *nigun* can be resurrected…

Suddenly an old *nigun* is recollected, it bubbles up and springs out of one's mouth…not intentionally, a new feeling infuses it, a new soul, and it is almost a new *nigun* that comes to life…

That is indeed a metamorphosis of a *nigun*.[2]

So we have it that a *nigun* has a life of its own, which may ebb and flow in its inspiration over many years, or die altogether.

Some have mused, however, about how to keep a melody fresh over time. The Ba'al Shem Tov told a story about a musician whose king figures out how to keep the musician's music ever vibrant:

Once, there was a king, who had a servant who knew how to make the most beautiful music in the world. The king especially loved one of his melodies, so he commanded that it be played before him in the palace, every day, multiple times a day. So it was done.

As the days passed, the *nigun* became stale in the musician's eyes; the desire and excitement he once felt was gone. What did the king do to reawaken the excitement and loving desire for the musician? He had it announced every day, each time, that he wanted to hear this *nigun* that was so dear in his eyes, [and each time] a new person would be brought from the market, who had never heard the *nigun* before. And so it was that when a new person came to listen, he elicited enthusiasm for the *nigun* anew in the musician.

The king did this many times. After a while, the king sought advice on what to do with the musician, since it was getting hard to find a new person each time to listen to him. The advice he received was to [blindfold][3] the musician, so he could [not] see the form of a person, and every time the king wanted to hear his favorite *nigun* again, he would tell the musician that a new person had come from nearby, who had never heard this *nigun* before, and fresh pleasure would be born in the musician once more.[4]

In this story, a musician is fooled into believing that there's a fresh audience for his melody, and in imagining fresh ears hearing his music, he's newly inspired

---

[2] I.L. Peretz, "Metamorphoses of a *Nigun*," 1922, pp. 4–5, Vilna (#174). Peretz frequently included music and musicians in his stories. This story focuses on one melody. This is a short excerpt from a twenty-five page long story.

[3] Blindfolding is my own euphemism for the more grisly act that the story originally insisted upon—removing his eyes altogether.

[4] *Or HaMe'ir*, Deuteronomy, Ecclesiastes (#154).

to play the same melody daily, with constantly renewed vigor, for years on end. By reorienting our imagination, can we, like the musician, find a way to rejuvenate our own melodies? Can we "fool" ourselves into musical vitality as well?

The psalmist once wrote, "Sing a new song to God."[5] What does it mean to "sing a new song?" At face value, the line implies that we ought to literally compose new melodies all the time. Some Hasidic courts, for example, would insist upon singing a brand new *nigun* for every Shabbat. Imagine the creative imperative of composing new songs all the time! Singing a brand new melody, however, is not the only way to understand "sing a new song." David Kimhi (d. 1235) proposed that to "'sing a new song to the Divine' [means to] refresh the melody to the divine, always."[6] In the Radak's view, it seems that we do not have to literally sing a brand new melody all the time, but rather we must continuously reinvent our old notes as new, to constantly reclaim the divine melody that is played through us.

Still, there are some questions I have about melodies that are still not easy: can one hear a melody afresh if the singer or composer was, for example, abusive? Or if the music was a featured soundtrack to genocide? How far can we go in hearing melodies as innocent notes, just waiting for renewed life? What impact does the artist's life have on how we experience the music?

To compose a new melody is a creative imperative, and to reinvent an old melody—that's a spiritual imperative. The Maharil (d. ca. 1427), who was known for advocating for the continuation of local traditions and customs throughout the Jewish world, urged Jews of his time not to change the melodies of their communities.[7]

The Hofetz Hayyim, interpreting the Maharil's words, suggests that changing melodies would "confuse the communal consciousness."[8] He's likely referring to the fixed prayer melodies, the *nusah hatefillah*, which mark the revolving time-cycles of the year.[9] But by insisting that we retain our traditional melodies,

---

[5] Psalms 33:3 (#23).

[6] Radak on Psalms 33:3 (#104).

[7] Rema, quoting Maharil, in *Shulhan Orah*, Orah Hayyim, 619.

[8] *Mishnah Berurah* on Orah Hayyim 619 (#132).

[9] "*Afilu benigunim*, even with melodies" (#132) might refer to *nusah hatefillah*, but might also refer more broadly to famous melodies in any given community. Cantor Sherwood Goffin has written some very helpful articles about the *halakhah* around melodies that seem to have come straight from Mount Sinai ("*MiSinai*" melodies) and how those rules might apply to today (see for example, Sherwood Goffin, "On the Proper Use of Niggunim for the *Tefillot* of the *Yamim Noraim*" YU *Torah Online*, 2012, www.yutorah.org/lectures/lecture.cfm/759536/cantor-sherwood-goffin/on-the-proper-use-of-niggunim-for-the-tefillot-of-the-yamim-noraim).

I think he's suggesting that we need to do the hard work of retrofitting the old sounds, of summoning the spiritual sparks that transcend the melody itself.

Friends with a Melody

My mother used to tell me that if at any point in life I had even a single true friend I'd be lucky, for a true friend is rare. The same is true, I've come to think, for music. If at any point, there's even one melody in your life that moves your soul and opens yours heart, you are lucky.

Like with any friend, however, it takes a long time to really get to know a melody. When we first hear a melody, we shake its hand and say, "Nice to meet you, Melody," and we try to remain on polite terms with it until it becomes our friend. It can take years before a melody is truly a friend; you might meet a melody a dozen times before it begins to speak to you honestly in the language of truth and companionship. And you must certainly sing a melody many dozens of times before it enters your *kishkes* (insides), before it becomes a part of you, and before you become a "vessel of song" (i.e. a "*Kli Zemer*"/"Klezmer") for that melody. And you must sing a melody for years before it merges with your being, so that the melody becomes you and you become the melody.

But eventually, just like any deep friendship or love partnership, we must constantly reexamine a melody, and imagine, with curiosity, what we might draw from it. Can we turn it over, stretch it out, speed it up, slow it down, harmonize with it, sing it higher and lower, louder and softer, and keep asking ourselves, "What might this melodic friend be today?" We might imagine the seemingly endless potential of a single melody the way our Rabbis imagined the "thousand" distinct notes that could be played by the *magreifah*, a mystical ten-holed instrument that was played the Temple.[10] An instrument, and a melody, has nearly endless potential!

We all search for brand new melodies, but we can also make our old melodies sing anew. When we hear a new melody, a melody we haven't heard before, it can freshen us up, and remind us about the spiritual potential of music. But then again, the older melodies were once young in our minds, as well!

We must write new melodies, but the process of writing new melodies ought to allow us to rediscover the beauty of our older melodies. Ultimately, as one of my teachers put it, "all melodies are just a bunch of notes."[11] A *nigun* only lives if

---

[10] Talmud Bavli Arakhin 10b–11a (#72).

[11] Cantor Noach Schall, private lessons, 2007.

we live with it. So, it's what we do with them, and how we sing them, that matters. As I.L. Peretz muses:

> A letter, it's how you read it. A *nigun*, it's how you sing it!…
>
> First there is the body of a *nigun*, but it still needs a soul! And the soul of a *nigun* is, of course, a person's feelings: his love, his rage, his grace, his vengefulness, his heart's longing, his regret, his pain—all, all that a person feels, can he put into a *nigun* and the *nigun*—can come to life![12]

To bring a *nigun* to life, to make friends with it, requires the time to spend with it, the patience to let it become what it can be, the trust that the beauty will emerge, and the *chutzpah* to try. Rather than bar-hopping and speed-dating through dozens of melodies, always hoping that the next melody will be better than the one we're singing now, we can seize the opportunity to sing one melody for an hour or longer, exploring every nook and cranny of the melody, pouring our souls into it, and encouraging it to become our friend. The process of repeating a melody over and over again creates tremendous depth of experience—but I warn you, creating depth is profoundly counter-cultural. Be careful!

River of Fire: The Musical *Mikveh*

כל יומא ויומא נבראין מלאכי השרת מנהר
דינור ואמרי שירה ובטלי

> Day after day the ministering angels are
> created anew from the river Dinur, and
> they sing praises and are then destroyed.
>
> —*Talmud Bavli Hagigah 14a*

As we learn to reinvent a *nigun*, we learn to reinvent ourselves, our own melodies of life. We sing melodies and we become melodies. Music is so intricately interwoven into our lives that when we speak of our "songs," we could be referring to the melodies that we sing, or to the songs our lives become. At the end of the day, can we refresh our songs, and refresh ourselves, to prepare for the next round of singing and life? When we bring a *nigun* to life, the *nigun* will bring us to life.

The angels, too, must keep their songs fresh, every day. But how do the angels keep their songs alive? It's told that at the end of every day that they sing,

---

[12] I.L. Peretz, "Metamorphosis of a *Nigun*," excerpt pp. 4–5 (#174).

they jump into the River of Fire, where they are incinerated, and then completely reformed and renewed for their job of singing praises to their Creator the
following day:

> Day after day the ministering angels are created anew from the river Din-
> ur, and they sing praises and are then destroyed...The angels are refreshed
> every day and sing to the Holy Blessed One and then the return to the
> River of Fire from which they came, and soon God comes back and re-
> news them and returns them to what they were originally.[13]

But what are angels, and how do their songs relate to our songs? Angels, as
we explored above, represent the very powers that make us human, and their
main job is to sing. By gathering our inner angels together in song, the Holy One
allows us to hear the awesome echoes of existence itself. But yet, like all music,
these ethereal echoes prove to be ephemeral; the music ends in a moment, and
we need to start all over again.

The River of Fire was a *mikveh* for the angels, a place of purification and
renewal—and song itself is a *mikveh* for us. Angels personify the singing essence
of the world, and their continuous renewal represents the process of how we also
renew our own divine songs. We humans might not incinerate ourselves at the
end of each day, but we still try to refresh our life-songs every day, continuously.
As the traditional daily *davening* reminds us:

> They [the angels] offer songs to the blessed God, to the Ruler, God Who
> Lives and Is. They sing songs and make praises heard...[The Divine] is
> that which renews the work of creation with goodness, every day and in
> every moment—always.[14]

May it be that we sing every day as though it were our first time singing!

לָאֵל בָּרוּךְ נְעִימוֹת יִתֵּנוּ. לְמֶלֶךְ אֵל חַי וְקַיָּם זְמִרוֹת יֹאמֵרוּ
וְתִשְׁבָּחוֹת יַשְׁמִיעוּ...הַמְחַדֵּשׁ בְּטוּבוֹ בְּכָל יוֹם תָּמִיד
מַעֲשֵׂה בְרֵאשִׁית.

---

[13] Talmud Bavli Hagigah 14a (#56).
[14] Daily Morning Liturgy, *Yotzer Or* (#170).

ii

*Open
Library*

TORAH

1. Yuval: Father of all Musicians

בראשית ד, כ-כא / *Genesis 4:20–21*

וַתֵּלֶד עָדָה אֶת-יָבָל הוּא הָיָה אֲבִי יֹשֵׁב אֹהֶל וּמִקְנֶה: וְשֵׁם אָחִיו יוּבָל הוּא הָיָה אֲבִי כָּל-תֹּפֵשׂ כִּנּוֹר וְעוּגָב:

And [Ada] bore Yaval; he was the ancestor of all who dwell in tents and raise cattle. And the name of his brother was Yuval; he was the ancestor of all those who played the lyre and the harp.

2. The Song Of the Sea, The Most Famous Song of Freedom

שמות טו, א-ב / *Exodus 15:1–2*

אָז יָשִׁיר-מֹשֶׁה וּבְנֵי יִשְׂרָאֵל אֶת-הַשִּׁירָה הַזֹּאת לַה' וַיֹּאמְרוּ לֵאמֹר אָשִׁירָה לַה' כִּי-גָאֹה גָּאָה סוּס וְרֹכְבוֹ רָמָה בַיָּם: עָזִּי וְזִמְרָת קָהּ וַיְהִי-לִי לִישׁוּעָה זֶה אֵלִי וְאַנְוֵהוּ אֱלֹהֵי אָבִי וַאֲרֹמְמֶנְהוּ...

Then Moses and the Children of Israel sang this song to YHVH, saying, "I will sing to YHVH; God has the power, drowning horse and chariot in the sea. God is my might, Yah is my song (*zimrat-ya*) and will be my salvation. This is my God, I will glorify Him; my ancestral God, I will exalt Him.

3. Miriam: Dancing, Leading

שמות טו, כ-כא / Exodus 15:20–21

וַתִּקַּח מִרְיָם הַנְּבִיאָה אֲחוֹת אַהֲרֹן אֶת־הַתֹּף בְּיָדָהּ וַתֵּצֶאןָ כָל־הַנָּשִׁים אַחֲרֶיהָ בְּתֻפִּים וּבִמְחֹלֹת: וַתַּעַן לָהֶם מִרְיָם שִׁירוּ לַה' כִּי־גָאֹה גָּאָה סוּס וְרֹכְבוֹ רָמָה בַיָּם:

Miriam the prophet, the sister of Aaron, took up the timbrel in her hand, and all the women went out after her, dancing, with drums. To them, Miriam sang out, "Sing to YHVH, God is victorious! Horse and rider, He has thrown into the sea!"

4. Song is a Strong Force

שמות טו, ב / Exodus 15:2

עָזִּי וְזִמְרָת קָהּ וַיְהִי־לִי לִישׁוּעָה

Yah is my might and my strength/ song, [Yah] has become my redemption…

5. Shofar and Synesthesia

שמות יט,טו; כ, טו / Exodus 19:15, 20:15

וַיְהִי קוֹל הַשֹּׁפָר הוֹלֵךְ וְחָזֵק מְאֹד מֹשֶׁה יְדַבֵּר וְהָאֱלֹהִים יַעֲנֶנּוּ בְקוֹל...

As the sound of the shofar grew in strength, Moses spoke and God answered with a voice…

וְכָל־הָעָם רֹאִים אֶת־הַקּוֹלֹת וְאֶת־הַלַּפִּידִם וְאֵת קוֹל הַשֹּׁפָר וְאֶת־הָהָר עָשֵׁן וַיַּרְא הָעָם וַיָּנֻעוּ וַיַּעַמְדוּ מֵרָחֹק:

And the entire people saw the sounds and the flashes, the sound of the shofar, and the mountain was smoking. The people saw and shuddered, standing far away.

6. Trumpets Summon Israel to Move

במדבר י, א־ב / *Numbers 10:1–2*

וַיְדַבֵּר ה' אֶל־מֹשֶׁה לֵּאמֹר: עֲשֵׂה לְךָ
שְׁתֵּי חֲצוֹצְרֹת כֶּסֶף מִקְשָׁה תַּעֲשֶׂה
אֹתָם וְהָיוּ לְךָ לְמִקְרָא הָעֵדָה וּלְמַסַּע
אֶת־הַמַּחֲנוֹת:

YHVH spoke to Moses, saying, "Make for yourself two trumpets of silver; have them hammered. They will be for you to call the community and for the camps to set out.

7. My Face Will be Hidden, Put this Song in their Mouths

דברים לא, יח־יט / *Deuteronomy 31:18–19*

וְאָנֹכִי הַסְתֵּר אַסְתִּיר פָּנַי בַּיּוֹם הַהוּא
עַל כָּל־הָרָעָה אֲשֶׁר עָשָׂה כִּי פָנָה
אֶל־אֱלֹהִים אֲחֵרִים: וְעַתָּה כִּתְבוּ
לָכֶם אֶת־הַשִּׁירָה הַזֹּאת וְלַמְּדָהּ
אֶת־בְּנֵי־יִשְׂרָאֵל שִׂימָהּ בְּפִיהֶם לְמַעַן
תִּהְיֶה־לִּי הַשִּׁירָה הַזֹּאת לְעֵד בִּבְנֵי
יִשְׂרָאֵל:

I will surely hide My face on that day because of all the evil done, turning to other gods. Write this song for you, now, and teach it to the children of Israel. Place it in their mouths, so this song stands as a witness in Israel.

PROPHETS

8. Joshua Breaks Down Walls with Music

יהושע ו, כ / *Joshua 6:20*

...וַיְהִי כִשְׁמֹעַ הָעָם אֶת קוֹל הַשּׁוֹפָר
וַיָּרִיעוּ הָעָם תְּרוּעָה גְדוֹלָה וַתִּפֹּל
הַחוֹמָה תַּחְתֶּיהָ וַיַּעַל הָעָם הָעִירָה
אִישׁ נֶגְדּוֹ וַיִּלְכְּדוּ אֶת הָעִיר.

[W]hen the people heard the sound of the shofars, the people shouted with a great shout, and the wall fell down flat, and the people ascended and entered the city, each person straight ahead, and they took the city.

9. Prophets Travelled with Musicians

שמואל א י, ה-ו / *1 Samuel 10:5–6*

וִיהִי כְבֹאֲךָ שָׁם הָעִיר וּפָגַעְתָּ חֶבֶל
נְבִיאִים יֹרְדִים מֵהַבָּמָה וְלִפְנֵיהֶם נֵבֶל
וְתֹף וְחָלִיל וְכִנּוֹר וְהֵמָּה מִתְנַבְּאִים:
וְצָלְחָה עָלֶיךָ רוּחַ ה' וְהִתְנַבִּיתָ עִמָּם
וְנֶהְפַּכְתָּ לְאִישׁ אַחֵר:

When you reach the city, you will encounter a band of prophets descending from the high place, before them a harp, a drum, a flute; and they will prophesy. The spirit of God will rush over you, and you will prophesy with them, transforming into a different person.

10. David's Harp Soothes Saul

שמואל א טז, כג / *1 Samuel 16:23*

וְהָיָה בִּהְיוֹת רוּחַ־אֱלֹהִים אֶל־שָׁאוּל וְלָקַח דָּוִד אֶת־הַכִּנּוֹר וְנִגֵּן בְּיָדוֹ וְרָוַח לְשָׁאוּל וְטוֹב לוֹ וְסָרָה מֵעָלָיו רוּחַ הָרָעָה:

It came about whenever the [depressive] spirit from God came to Saul, David would take the harp and play it with his hand; Saul would be refreshed/re-expanded and be well, and the evil spirit would depart from him.

11. Earth Splits

מלכים א א, מ / *1 Kings 1:40*

וַיַּעֲלוּ כָל־הָעָם אַחֲרָיו וְהָעָם מְחַלְלִים בַּחֲלִלִים וּשְׂמֵחִים שִׂמְחָה גְדוֹלָה וַתִּבָּקַע הָאָרֶץ בְּקוֹלָם:

And all the people went up after him, playing on pipes, and rejoicing with great joy, so that the earth was split by their noise.

12. The Listening Heart

מלכים א ג:ט–יג / *1 Kings 3:9–13*

וְנָתַתָּ לְעַבְדְּךָ לֵב שֹׁמֵעַ לִשְׁפֹּט אֶת־עַמְּךָ לְהָבִין בֵּין־טוֹב לְרָע כִּי מִי יוּכַל לִשְׁפֹּט אֶת־עַמְּךָ הַכָּבֵד הַזֶּה:

Give your servant a listening heart to judge your people, to discern between good and evil, able to judge this weighty nation of yours!

(continued)

וַיִּיטַב הַדָּבָר בְּעֵינֵי אֲדֹנָי כִּי שָׁאַל
שְׁלֹמֹה אֶת־הַדָּבָר הַזֶּה: וַיֹּאמֶר אֱלֹהִים
אֵלָיו יַעַן אֲשֶׁר שָׁאַלְתָּ אֶת־הַדָּבָר הַזֶּה
וְלֹא־שָׁאַלְתָּ לְּךָ יָמִים רַבִּים וְלֹא־שָׁאַלְתָּ
לְּךָ עֹשֶׁר וְלֹא שָׁאַלְתָּ נֶפֶשׁ אֹיְבֶיךָ
וְשָׁאַלְתָּ לְּךָ הָבִין לִשְׁמֹעַ מִשְׁפָּט: הִנֵּה
עָשִׂיתִי כִּדְבָרֶיךָ הִנֵּה נָתַתִּי לְךָ לֵב
חָכָם וְנָבוֹן אֲשֶׁר כָּמוֹךָ לֹא־הָיָה לְפָנֶיךָ
וְאַחֲרֶיךָ לֹא־יָקוּם כָּמוֹךָ: וְגַם אֲשֶׁר
לֹא־שָׁאַלְתָּ נָתַתִּי לָךְ גַּם־עֹשֶׁר גַּם־כָּבוֹד
אֲשֶׁר לֹא־הָיָה כָמוֹךָ אִישׁ בַּמְּלָכִים
כָּל־יָמֶיךָ:

This request was good in the Lord's eyes, that Solomon had asked this. God said to him, "Since you have asked for [a listening heart], not asking a long life for yourself, or wealth, or the life of your enemies, but rather to understand and discern judgment, so I will do as you have said, giving you a wise and understanding heart whose like has never been and after which will never arise. Even that for which you have not asked I will provide: wealth and honor no king before your days has ever had."

13. Instruments of Holy Wood

מלכים א י, יב / *1 Kings 10:12*

וַיַּעַשׂ הַמֶּלֶךְ אֶת־עֲצֵי הָאַלְמֻגִּים מִסְעָד
לְבֵית־ה' וּלְבֵית הַמֶּלֶךְ וְכִנֹּרוֹת וּנְבָלִים
לַשָּׁרִים לֹא־בָא כֵן עֲצֵי אַלְמֻגִּים וְלֹא
נִרְאָה עַד הַיּוֹם הַזֶּה:

The king transformed the *almug* trees into pillars/supports for the Temple and the palace, and made harps and lyres for the musicians. *Almug* trees like these had never before entered Israel, which have not been seen since, even today.

14. Hear the Song, Hear the Prayer

מלכים א ח, כח / *1 Kings 8:28*

לִשְׁמֹעַ אֶל־הָרִנָּה וְאֶל־הַתְּפִלָּה אֲשֶׁר
עַבְדְּךָ מִתְפַּלֵּל לְפָנֶיךָ הַיּוֹם:

Hear the song and the prayer that your servant prays before You today.

15. Music Opens Elisha's Prophecy

מלכים ב ג, טו / *2 Kings 3:15*

וְעַתָּה קְחוּ־לִי מְנַגֵּן וְהָיָה כְּנַגֵּן הַמְנַגֵּן
וַתְּהִי עָלָיו יַד־ה':

"Now bring me a musician!" And when the musician played, the hand of God came upon him.

16. Drunken Songs Not Enough

ישעיה ה, יא־יב / *Isaiah 5:11–12*

הוֹי מַשְׁכִּימֵי בַבֹּקֶר שֵׁכָר יִרְדֹּפוּ מְאַחֲרֵי
בַנֶּשֶׁף יַיִן יַדְלִיקֵם: וְהָיָה כִנּוֹר וָנֶבֶל תֹּף
וְחָלִיל וָיַיִן מִשְׁתֵּיהֶם וְאֵת פֹּעַל ה' לֹא
יַבִּיטוּ וּמַעֲשֵׂה יָדָיו לֹא רָאוּ:

Oy to those who arise early in the morning to chase drink and get lit with wine till late at night. At their feasts, there are harps and lyres, drums and flutes, and wine, but they do cannot recognize the work of God, they don't see the act of His hands.

17. Music from the Ends of the Earth

ישעיה כד, טז / *Isaiah 24:16*

מִכְּנַף הָאָרֶץ זְמִרֹת שָׁמַעְנוּ

From the ends of the Earth we have heard songs.

18. Songs and Music No More

יחזקאל כו, יג / *Ezekiel 26:13*

וְהִשְׁבַּתִּי הֲמוֹן שִׁירָיִךְ וְקוֹל כִּנּוֹרַיִךְ לֹא יִשָּׁמַע עוֹד:

I will make the noise of your songs cease, and the sound of your harps will no longer be heard.

19. Sacred Silence

חבקוק ב, כ / *Habakkuk 2:20*

וַה' בְּהֵיכַל קָדְשׁוֹ הַס מִפָּנָיו כָּל־הָאָרֶץ:

When God is in His palace, the Sanctuary, the whole world falls silent before Him.

Writings

20. How Can I Repay God? With Song.

תהלים יג, ו / *Psalms 13:6*

אָשִׁירָה לַה' כִּי גָמַל עָלָי׃

I sing to God for He has taken care of me.

21. God's Loud Voice

תהלים כט, ד-ט / *Psalms 29:4–9*

קוֹל-ה' בַּכֹּחַ קוֹל ה' בֶּהָדָר׃

God's voice is in the strength. God's voice is in the glory.

קוֹל ה' שֹׁבֵר אֲרָזִים וַיְשַׁבֵּר ה'
אֶת-אַרְזֵי הַלְּבָנוֹן׃ וַיַּרְקִידֵם כְּמוֹ-עֵגֶל
לְבָנוֹן וְשִׂרְיֹן כְּמוֹ בֶן-רְאֵמִים׃

God's voice breaks the cedars; God shatters the cedars of Lebanon, and makes them dance like calves, Lebanon and Siryon like little oxen.

קוֹל-ה' חֹצֵב לַהֲבוֹת אֵשׁ׃

God's voice carves flames.

קוֹל ה' יָחִיל מִדְבָּר יָחִיל ה' מִדְבַּר
קָדֵשׁ׃

God's voice makes the wasteland quake; God rocks the desert of Kadesh.

קוֹל ה' יְחוֹלֵל אַיָּלוֹת וַיֶּחֱשֹׂף יְעָרוֹת
וּבְהֵיכָלוֹ כֻּלּוֹ אֹמֵר כָּבוֹד׃

God's voice makes hinds give birth and strips the forest bare. In God's temple, all say "Glory!"

22. Downcasted-ness to Dancing

תהלים ל, יב-יג / *Psalms 30:12–13*

הָפַכְתָּ מִסְפְּדִי לְמָחוֹל לִי פִּתַּחְתָּ שַׂקִּי
וַתְּאַזְּרֵנִי שִׂמְחָה: לְמַעַן יְזַמֶּרְךָ כָבוֹד
וְלֹא יִדֹּם ה' אֱלֹהַי לְעוֹלָם אוֹדֶךָ:

You changed my mourning to dance. You opened my sackcloth and wrapped me in joy. So my glory can sing to You and no longer be silent, YHVH, my God, I will praise You forever.

23. Upright Song

תהלים לג, א-ד / *Psalms 33:1–4*

רַנְּנוּ צַדִּיקִים בַּה' לַיְשָׁרִים נָאוָה תְהִלָּה:

Righteous ones, rejoice in God! It is beautiful for the upright to praise.

הוֹדוּ לַה' בְּכִנּוֹר בְּנֵבֶל עָשׂוֹר זַמְּרוּ־
לוֹ: שִׁירוּ לוֹ שִׁיר חָדָשׁ הֵיטִיבוּ נַגֵּן
בִּתְרוּעָה:

Praise God with the harp, make a song with that ten-stringed instrument. Sing to God a new song; play it loud and play it well.

כִּי־יָשָׁר דְּבַר־ה' וְכָל־מַעֲשֵׂהוּ בֶּאֱמוּנָה:

For the word of God is right; all of God's deeds are done in trust.

24. Divine Wellspring of Creativity

תהלים פז, ז / *Psalms 87:7*

וְשָׁרִים כְּחֹלְלִים כָּל־מַעְיָנַי בָּךְ:

For the singers, and for the dancers [or: flautists], all my wellsprings are in you [Zion].

25. Meditative Shabbat Harp

תהלים צב, א–ד / *Psalms 92:1–4*

מִזְמוֹר שִׁיר לְיוֹם הַשַּׁבָּת: טוֹב לְהֹדוֹת
לַה' וּלְזַמֵּר לְשִׁמְךָ עֶלְיוֹן: לְהַגִּיד בַּבֹּקֶר
חַסְדֶּךָ וֶאֱמוּנָתְךָ בַּלֵּילוֹת: עֲלֵי־עָשׂוֹר
וַעֲלֵי־נָבֶל עֲלֵי הִגָּיוֹן בְּכִנּוֹר:

A psalm: a song for the Sabbath Day. It is good to thank God, to make music for Your supernal name, to tell of your kindness in the morning and of your care-taking at night, on the ten-stringed instrument, on the lyre, with meditations on the harp.

26. Those Who Sow in Tears, Will Reap in Song/Joy...

תהלים קכו, א–ו / *Psalms 126:1–6*

שִׁיר הַמַּעֲלוֹת

A song of ascents.

בְּשׁוּב ה' אֶת־שִׁיבַת צִיּוֹן הָיִינוּ
כְּחֹלְמִים: אָז יִמָּלֵא שְׂחוֹק פִּינוּ
וּלְשׁוֹנֵנוּ רִנָּה אָז יֹאמְרוּ בַגּוֹיִם הִגְדִּיל
ה' לַעֲשׂוֹת עִם־אֵלֶּה: הִגְדִּיל ה' לַעֲשׂוֹת
עִמָּנוּ הָיִינוּ שְׂמֵחִים:

When God brought home those who returned to Zion, it was like a dream. Then, our mouths were full with laughter, and our tongues with song. Then, they said, amidst the nations, "God has acted greatly with them." God has acted greatly with us, and we were happy.

שׁוּבָה ה' אֶת־שְׁבִיתֵנוּ כַּאֲפִיקִים בַּנֶּגֶב:
הַזֹּרְעִים בְּדִמְעָה בְּרִנָּה יִקְצֹרוּ: הָלוֹךְ
יֵלֵךְ וּבָכֹה נֹשֵׂא מֶשֶׁךְ־הַזָּרַע בֹּא־יָבוֹא
בְרִנָּה נֹשֵׂא אֲלֻמֹּתָיו:

Reverse our captivity, God, like the wadi in the Negev. Those who sow in tears will reap in joyous song. Though you walk, weeping, carrying seed to scatter, you will return joyfully singing, carrying what you have reaped.

27. Hanging Up Their Harps

תהלים קלז, א–ו / *Psalms 137:1–6*

עַל־נַהֲרוֹת בָּבֶל שָׁם יָשַׁבְנוּ גַּם־בָּכִינוּ בְּזָכְרֵנוּ אֶת־צִיּוֹן: עַל־עֲרָבִים בְּתוֹכָהּ תָּלִינוּ כִּנֹּרוֹתֵינוּ: כִּי שָׁם שְׁאֵלוּנוּ שׁוֹבֵינוּ דִּבְרֵי־שִׁיר וְתוֹלָלֵינוּ שִׂמְחָה שִׁירוּ לָנוּ מִשִּׁיר צִיּוֹן:

By Babylon's rivers, there we sat and wept, and remembered Zion. On the willows, there we hung up our harps. For there our captors required of us songs, and our tormentors, joy, saying, "Sing us one of those songs of Zion!"

אֵיךְ נָשִׁיר אֶת־שִׁיר ה' עַל אַדְמַת נֵכָר: אִם־אֶשְׁכָּחֵךְ יְרוּשָׁלַיִם תִּשְׁכַּח יְמִינִי: תִּדְבַּק־לְשׁוֹנִי לְחִכִּי אִם־לֹא אֶזְכְּרֵכִי אִם־לֹא אַעֲלֶה אֶת־יְרוּשָׁלַיִם עַל רֹאשׁ שִׂמְחָתִי:

How can we sing God's song in a foreign land? If I forget you, O Jerusalem, let my right hand forget its skill! Fix my tongue to the top of my mouth if I don't remember, if I don't raise up Jerusalem at the beginning of my happiness.

28. Songs are a Double-Edged Sword

תהלים קמט, ו / *Psalms 149:6*

רוֹמְמוֹת אֵל בִּגְרוֹנָם וְחֶרֶב פִּיפִיּוֹת בְּיָדָם:

Lifting songs of God in their throats, and a double edged sword in their hands.

29. Praise the Lord with Nine Instruments and Every Breath!

תהלים קנ / *Psalms 150*

הַלְלוּקָהּ

Halleluyah!

הַלְלוּ־אֵל בְּקָדְשׁוֹ הַלְלוּהוּ בִּרְקִיעַ עֻזּוֹ:

Praise God in His Temple, praise Him in His mighty skies.

(continued)

הַלְלוּהוּ בִגְבוּרֹתָיו | Praise Him with His powers,
הַלְלוּהוּ כְּרֹב גֻּדְלוֹ: | praise Him per how great He is.

הַלְלוּהוּ בְּתֵקַע שׁוֹפָר | Praise Him with the blowing of the
הַלְלוּהוּ בְּנֵבֶל וְכִנּוֹר: | shofar, praise Him with the lyre and the harp.

הַלְלוּהוּ בְתֹף וּמָחוֹל | Praise Him with drum and dance,
הַלְלוּהוּ בְּמִנִּים וְעוּגָב: | praise Him with winds and strings.

הַלְלוּהוּ בְצִלְצְלֵי־שָׁמַע | Praise Him with the chiming
הַלְלוּהוּ בְּצִלְצְלֵי תְרוּעָה: | of *Sh'ma*, praise Him with the trumpet's trills.

כֹּל הַנְּשָׁמָה תְּהַלֵּל קָהּ הַלְלוּקָהּ: | Let everything that breathes praise God, *halleluyah*!

30. Good Voice, Must Sing

משלי ג, ט / *Proverbs 3:9*

כַּבֵּד אֶת־ה' מֵהוֹנֶךָ... | Honor God with your wealth…

רַשִׁ"י, שם: מהונך - מכל מה שחננך אפי' מקול ערב (אל תקרי מהונך אלא מגרונך): | **Rashi's commentary on this verse:** "With your wealth"—[This means] from all you are graced with, even a sweet voice. (Don't read "with your wealth [*honekha*]" but rather "with your throat [*g'ronekha*].")

31. Song of the Morning Stars

איוב לח, ז / *Job 38:7*

בְּרָן־יַחַד כּוֹכְבֵי בֹקֶר וַיָּרִיעוּ כָּל־בְּנֵי אֱלֹהִים: | When the stars of morning sang together, the children of God trilling together.

32. Let Me Hear Your Voice!

שיר השירים ב, יד / *Song of Songs 2:14*

יוֹנָתִי בְּחַגְוֵי הַסֶּלַע בְּסֵתֶר הַמַּדְרֵגָה
הַרְאִינִי אֶת־מַרְאַיִךְ הַשְׁמִיעִינִי
אֶת־קוֹלֵךְ כִּי־קוֹלֵךְ עָרֵב וּמַרְאֵיךְ נָאוֶה:

My dove in the clefts of the rock, in a hidden place in the cliff, let me see your face, let me hear your voice, for your voice is sweet, and your appearance is lovely.

33. Assaf, The Gatherer of Song[1]

דברי הימים א טז, ה-ט / *1 Chronicles 16:5–9*

אָסָף הָרֹאשׁ וּמִשְׁנֵהוּ זְכַרְיָה יְעִיאֵל
וּשְׁמִירָמוֹת וִיחִיאֵל וּמַתִּתְיָה וֶאֱלִיאָב
וּבְנָיָהוּ וְעֹבֵד אֱדֹם וִיעִיאֵל בִּכְלֵי נְבָלִים
וּבְכִנֹּרוֹת וְאָסָף בַּמְצִלְתַּיִם מַשְׁמִיעַ:
וּבְנָיָהוּ וְיַחֲזִיאֵל הַכֹּהֲנִים בַּחֲצֹצְרוֹת
תָּמִיד לִפְנֵי אֲרוֹן בְּרִית־הָאֱלֹהִים: בַּיּוֹם
הַהוּא אָז נָתַן דָּוִיד בָּרֹאשׁ לְהֹדוֹת לַה'
בְּיַד־אָסָף וְאֶחָיו:

Assaf the chief (*lit.* "head"), his second-in-command Zekharyah, Ye'iel; Shemiramot, Yehiel, Mattityah, Eliav, Benayahu; Obed-edom, and Ye'iel with harps and stringed instruments, Assaf sounding the cymbals, and the priests Benayahu and Yahaziel with the trumpets, always before the Ark of the God's Covenant. Then, on that day, David first offered gratitude to God through the hands of Assaf and his brothers:

הוֹדוּ לַה' קִרְאוּ בִשְׁמוֹ הוֹדִיעוּ בָעַמִּים
עֲלִילֹתָיו: שִׁירוּ לוֹ זַמְּרוּ־לוֹ שִׂיחוּ
בְּכָל־נִפְלְאֹתָיו:

"Thank God, call out His Name! Make the nations know what He does! Sing to Him, play for Him, speak of all His wonders!"

---

[1] Assaf, the great Conductor, was appointed by David to lead the procession of the Ark as it made its way into Jerusalem.

MISHNAH

34. Hearing with the Heart

משנה ראש השנה ג, ז / *Mishnah Rosh Hashanah 3:7*

...וְכֵן מִי שֶׁהָיָה עוֹבֵר אֲחוֹרֵי בֵית
הַכְּנֶסֶת, אוֹ שֶׁהָיָה בֵיתוֹ סָמוּךְ לְבֵית
הַכְּנֶסֶת, וְשָׁמַע קוֹל שׁוֹפָר אוֹ קוֹל
מְגִלָּה, אִם כִּוֵּן לִבּוֹ, יָצָא. וְאִם לָאו, לֹא
יָצָא. אַף עַל פִּי שֶׁזֶּה שָׁמַע וְזֶה שָׁמַע,
זֶה כִּוֵּן לִבּוֹ וְזֶה לֹא כִוֵּן לִבּוֹ:

If you pass behind a synagogue, or if
your house is connected to one, and
you hear the sound of the shofar, or the
voice of the megillah being read, if you
intend your heart, you've fulfilled [the
mitzvah], and if not, not. Even though
they are both acts of listening, only in
one case did you intend your heart.

35. The Crying of the Shofar

משנה ראש השנה ד, ט / *Mishnah Rosh Hashanah 4:9*

שִׁעוּר תְּרוּעָה כְּשָׁלשׁ יְבָבוֹת.

The length of a *teru'ah* is the length
of three sobs.

36. Teach Musical Craft to Others

משנה יומא ג:יא / *Mishnah Yoma 3:11*

וְאֵלּוּ לִגְנַאי, שֶׁל בֵּית אַבְטִינָס לֹא רָצוּ
לְלַמֵּד עַל מַעֲשֵׂה הַקְּטֹרֶת. שֶׁל בֵּית
גַּרְמוּ, לֹא רָצוּ לְלַמֵּד עַל מַעֲשֵׂה לֶחֶם
הַפָּנִים. הַגְרָס בֶּן לֵוִי הָיָה יוֹדֵעַ פֶּרֶק
בַּשִּׁיר וְלֹא רָצָה לְלַמֵּד. בֶּן קַמְצָר לֹא
רָצָה לְלַמֵּד עַל מַעֲשֵׂה הַכְּתָב....

These were mentioned for shame:
those in the house of Garmu, who did
not want to teach how to make the
Bread of Presence; Those in the house
of Avtinas, who did not want to teach
how to make the incense; Hygros,
son of Levi, who knew verses of song
but did not want to teach them; The
descendents of Kamtzar, who did not
want to teach the scribal arts...

37. The Greatest Music Party Ever, at the Temple...

משנה סוכה ה:א, ד / *Mishnah Sukkah 5:1, 4*

כָּל מִי שֶׁלֹּא רָאָה שִׂמְחַת בֵּית
הַשּׁוֹאֵבָה, לֹא רָאָה שִׂמְחָה מִיָּמָיו: [...]
חֲסִידִים וְאַנְשֵׁי מַעֲשֶׂה הָיוּ מְרַקְּדִים
לִפְנֵיהֶם בַּאֲבוּקוֹת שֶׁל אוֹר שֶׁבִּידֵיהֶן,
וְאוֹמְרִים לִפְנֵיהֶן דִּבְרֵי שִׁירוֹת
וְתִשְׁבָּחוֹת. וְהַלְוִיִּם בְּכִנּוֹרוֹת וּבִנְבָלִים
וּבִמְצִלְתַּיִם וּבַחֲצוֹצְרוֹת וּבִכְלֵי שִׁיר
בְּלֹא מִסְפָּר, עַל חֲמֵשׁ עֶשְׂרֵה מַעֲלוֹת
הַיּוֹרְדוֹת מֵעֶזְרַת יִשְׂרָאֵל לְעֶזְרַת נָשִׁים,
כְּנֶגֶד חֲמִשָּׁה עָשָׂר שִׁיר הַמַּעֲלוֹת
שֶׁבַּתְּהִלִּים, שֶׁעֲלֵיהֶן לְוִיִּם עוֹמְדִין
בִּכְלֵי שִׁיר וְאוֹמְרִים שִׁירָה.

Anyone who has not seen the rejoicing at the Water Drawing Festival (*Simhat Beit HaSho'eivah*) has never seen joy in their lives... Pious people and the accomplished would dance before [the assembled] with lit torches in their hands, singing songs and praises, with the Levites on their harps, lyres, cymbals, and horns, all kinds of sounds without limit. On the fifteen steps from the general section to the women's section, like the fifteen Songs of Ascent in Psalms, the Levites would stand with their musical instruments and sing songs.

וְעָמְדוּ שְׁנֵי כֹהֲנִים בְּשַׁעַר הָעֶלְיוֹן
שֶׁיּוֹרֵד מֵעֶזְרַת יִשְׂרָאֵל לְעֶזְרַת נָשִׁים,
וּשְׁתֵּי חֲצוֹצְרוֹת בִּידֵיהֶן. קָרָא הַגֶּבֶר,
תָּקְעוּ וְהֵרִיעוּ וְתָקְעוּ. הִגִּיעוּ לְמַעֲלָה
עֲשִׂירִית, תָּקְעוּ וְהֵרִיעוּ וְתָקְעוּ. הִגִּיעוּ
לָעֲזָרָה, תָּקְעוּ וְהֵרִיעוּ וְתָקְעוּ...

Two priests stood at the upper gate, leading from the general section to the women's section, with two horns in their hands. The rooster crowed, and would play a *teki'ah*, a *teru'ah*, and another *teki'ah*. They reached the tenth step: *teki'ah*, *teru'ah*, *teki'ah*. They reached the [women's] section: *teki'ah*, *teru'ah*, *teki'ah*...

38. Divine Amplification from Temple

משנה תמיד ג, ח / *Mishnah Tamid 3:8*

מִירִיחוֹ הָיוּ שׁוֹמְעִין קוֹל שַׁעַר הַגָּדוֹל
שֶׁנִּפְתַּח. מִירִיחוֹ הָיוּ שׁוֹמְעִין קוֹל
הַמַּגְרֵפָה. מִירִיחוֹ הָיוּ שׁוֹמְעִין קוֹל
הָעֵץ שֶׁעָשָׂה בֶּן קָטִין מוּכְנִי לַכִּיּוֹר.
מִירִיחוֹ הָיוּ שׁוֹמְעִין קוֹל גְּבִינִי כָּרוֹז.
מִירִיחוֹ הָיוּ שׁוֹמְעִין קוֹל הֶחָלִיל.
מִירִיחוֹ הָיוּ שׁוֹמְעִין קוֹל הַצֶּלְצָל.
מִירִיחוֹ (הָיוּ) שׁוֹמְעִין קוֹל הַשִּׁיר.
מִירִיחוֹ הָיוּ שׁוֹמְעִים קוֹל הַשּׁוֹפָר. וְיֵשׁ
אוֹמְרִים, אַף קוֹל שֶׁל כֹּהֵן גָּדוֹל בְּשָׁעָה
שֶׁהוּא מַזְכִּיר אֶת הַשֵּׁם בְּיוֹם הַכִּפּוּרִים

The sound of the great gate opening
[in the Temple] could be heard all
the way in Jericho. From Jericho,
they could hear the sound of the
magreifah. From Jericho, they could
hear the sound of the wood prepared
by Katin's son for the washbasin.
From Jericho, they could hear the
sound of Gevini the announcer.
From Jericho, they could hear the
sound of the flutes. From Jericho,
they could hear the sound of the
cymbals. From Jericho, they could
hear the sound of song. From
Jericho, they could hear the sound of
the shofar. Some even say they could
even hear the voice of the High
Priest when he uttered the Name on
the Day of Atonement.

TALMUD

39. Harp Awakens the King

בבלי ברכות ג: / *Talmud Bavli Berakhot 3b*

כנור היה תלוי למעלה ממטתו של דוד, וכיון שהגיע חצות לילה בא רוח צפונית ונושבת בו ומנגן מאליו, מיד היה עומד ועוסק בתורה עד שעלה עמוד השחר.

A harp was hung above the bed of [King] David, and when midnight arrived, a wind from the north would blow on it, and it would make a melody, all on its own. He awoke at once and delved into Torah until dawn broke.

40. Song Implies Prayer

בבלי ברכות ו. / *Talmud Bavli Berakhot 6a*

במקום רנה שם תהא תפלה

Where there is song, there is prayer.

41. Life Cycle Songs

בבלי ברכות י. / *Talmud Bavli Berakhot 10a*

[דוד המלך ע"ה] דר במעי אמו ואמר שירה, שנאמר: (תהלים קג, א) "ברכי נפשי את ה' וכל קרבי את שם קדשו".

[While King David] resided in his mother's womb, he broke into song, as it was said, "My soul, bless God, and all that is within me, [bless] His holy name" (Psalms 103:1).

(continued)

יצא לאויר העולם ונסתכל בכוכבים
ומזלות ואמר שירה, שנאמר: (תהלים
קג, כ-כא) "ברכו ה' מלאכיו גברי כח
עושי דברו לשמע בקול דברו ברכו
ה' כל צבאיו" וגו'. ינק משדי אמו
ונסתכל בדדיה ואמר שירה, שנאמר:
(תהלים קג, ב) "ברכי נפשי את ה'
ואל תשכחי כל גמוליו"...נסתכל ביום
המיתה ואמר שירה

Once he emerged into the open air, and he gazed at the stars and the constellations, he broke into song, as it was said, "Angels, bless God! You creatures of might and power, who fulfill God's word, who listen for the sound of God's word, the whole host, bless God" (Psalms 103:20–21). When he suckled from his mother's breasts and gazed at them, he broke into song, as it was said, "My soul/throat, bless God, and do not forget all of God's kindness" (Psalms 103:2)…He looked upon his day of death and broke into song.

42. Hannah Prays Silently

בבלי ברכות לא. / *Talmud Bavli Berakhot 31a*

יאמר רב המנונא: כמה הלכתא
גברוותא איכא למשמע מהני קראי
דחנה: (שמואל א א, יג) "וחנה היא
מדברת על לבה" מכאן למתפלל צריך
שיכוין לבו. "רק שפתיה נעות" מכאן
למתפלל שיחתוך בשפתיו. "וקולה לא
ישמע" מכאן שאסור להגביה קולו
בתפלתו.

Rav Hamnuna said, "How many great laws can be learned from these verses on Hannah! 'And Hannah spoke from her heart' (1 Samuel 1:13)—from here, praying requires a focusing of heart/mind. 'Only her lips moved'—from here, praying has distinct mouthing of words (*lit.* cutting with one's lips). 'And her voice was not heard"—it is not allowed to raise one's voice in prayer [i.e. during the *Amidah*]."

43. Music Restores a Person's Mind

בבלי ברכות נז: / *Talmud Bavli Berakhot 57b*

שלשה משיבין דעתו של אדם אלו הן
קול ומראה וריח

Three things restore a person's mind: sound, sight, and smell.

44. Roof Splits when Praising God!

בבלי פסחים פה: / *Talmud Bavli Pesahim 85b*

כזיתא פסחא והלילא פקע איגרא.

[There were so many people that] each person only got an olive-sized piece of the Paschal lamb, and their *Hallel* burst the roof!

45. Song, Divine Inspiration, Song...

בבלי פסחים קיז. / *Talmud Bavli Pesahim 117a*

"לדוד מזמור" מלמד ששרתה עליו
שכינה ואחר כך אמר שירה.

"To David, a Psalm," intimates that the *Shekhinah* (Divine presence) rested upon him, and afterward, he sang a song.

"מזמור לדוד" מלמד שאמר שירה
ואחר כך שרתה עליו שכינה.

"A Psalm of David" intimates that he first sang his song, and afterwards, the *Shekhinah* [came] and rested on him.

46. Music Brings Joy and *Shekhinah*

בבלי פסחים קיז. / *Talmud Bavli Pesahim 117a*

...שאין השכינה שורה לא מתוך עצלות, ולא מתוך עצבות, ולא מתוך שחוק, ולא מתוך קלות ראש, ולא מתוך דברים בטלים, אלא מתוך דבר שמחה של מצוה. שנאמר (מלכים ב ג, טו) "ועתה קחו לי מנגן והיה כנגן המנגן ותהי עליו יד ה'".

The *Shekhinah* does not come to dwell out of laziness, sadness, mockery, mindless fun, or meaningless matters, but rather from the joy of the *mitzvah*, as it was said, "Now, find a musician; and when the musician played, the hand of God rested on him" (2 Kings 3:15).

47. The Largest Amen: Alexandria

בבלי סוכה נא: / *Talmud Bavli Sukkah 51b*

תניא, רבי יהודה אומר: מי שלא ראה דיופלוסטון של אלכסנדריא של מצרים לא ראה בכבודן של ישראל. אמרו: כמין בסילקי גדולה היתה, סטיו לפנים מסטיו, פעמים שהיו בה (ששים רבוא על ששים רבוא) כפלים כיוצאי מצרים [פעמים שהיו שם ששים רבוא כיוצאי מצרים ואמרי לה כפלים כיוצאי מצרים], והיו בה שבעים ואחת קתדראות של זהב כנגד שבעים ואחד של סנהדרי גדולה, כל אחת ואחת אינה פחותה מעשרים ואחד רבוא ככרי זהב.

It was taught: Rabbi Yehudah said, "Anyone who did not see Dyoploston in Alexandria, Egypt, has not seen the glory of Israel." They said, "It was like a great basilica, a colonnade within a colonnade. Sometimes there were (1,200,000 people) double the amount that left Egypt! There were seventy-one golden thrones, matching the seventy-one in the great Sanhedrin, each one made from no less than twenty-one *kikars* of gold.

(continued)

ובימה של עץ באמצעיתה, וחזן
הכנסת עומד עליה והסודרין בידו.
וכיון שהגיע לענות אמן הלה מניף
בסודר, וכל העם עונין אמן.

A wooden dais was in the middle of it all, and the congregation's *hazzan* would stand on it with flags in his hand. When he reached [the time for the community] to answer 'Amen!' he would raise the flag aloft, and all the people would answer 'Amen!'"

ולא היו יושבין מעורבין, אלא זהבין
בפני עצמן, וכספין בפני עצמן, ונפחין
בפני עצמן, וטרסיים בפני עצמן,
וגרדיים בפני עצמן. וכשעני נכנס שם
היה מכיר בעלי אומנתו ונפנה לשם,
ומשם פרנסתו ופרנסת אנשי ביתו.

However, they did not all sit mixed together. Rather, the goldsmiths sat by themselves, the silversmiths by themselves, the blacksmiths by themselves, the metal-weavers by themselves, and the wool-weavers by themselves. When a poor person entered, they would recognize their colleagues and turn there, and it was from them that their family's and their own charitable sustenance would come.

48. Curved Shofar: To Twist our Minds

בבלי ראש השנה כו: / *Talmud Bavli Rosh Hashana 26b*

מר סבר: בראש השנה כמה דכייף
איניש דעתיה טפי מעלי, וביום
הכפורים כמה דפשיט איניש דעתיה
טפי מעלי

One sage suggested: on Rosh Hashanah, the more one twists one's mind, the better is one's prayer, but on Yom Kippur, the more one straightens out one's mind, the better is their prayer.

49. The Honest, Primeval Sound of the Shofar

בבלי ראש השנה כז: / *Talmud Bavli Rosh Hashanah 27b*

תנו רבנן: ...ציפהו זהב, במקום
הנחת פה פסול, שלא במקום הנחת
פה כשר. ציפהו זהב מבפנים פסול.
מבחוץ, אם נשתנה קולו מכמות
שהיה פסול, ואם לאו כשר.

Our Rabbis taught (in a *baraita*):...
If [the shofar] was coated with gold
[in the place where you put your
mouth], it is not kosher. But if not
in that place, then it is kosher. If its
insides were coated with gold, then
it is not kosher. [If] the outside
[was coated], if it changes its sound
at all, then it's not kosher, but if
not, then it's fine.

ניקב וסתמו, אם מעכב את התקיעה
פסול, ואם לאו כשר...

If it was pierced and then plugged,
if it hinders the sound, then it is not
kosher, but if not, then it's fine...

הניח שופר בתוך שופר, אם קול
פנימי שמע יצא, ואם קול חיצון
שמע לא יצא.

If a shofar is installed inside of
another shofar: if the inner one's
sound can be heard, then it exempts
[one's obligation], but if only the
outer one can be heard, then it does
not exempt.

הפכו ותקע בו לא יצא. אמר רב פפא:
לא תימא דהפכיה כבתונא, אלא
שהרחיב את הקצר וקיצר את הרחב...

If it was reversed and blown, it does
not exempt. Rav Papa commented,
"[The *baraita*] did not mean turning
it inside out like a shirt but rather
widening the narrow part and
contracting the wide part..."

(continued)

If pieces of shofars were glued together, it is not kosher…If any amount was added to it, whether of its own material or not, it is not kosher.

דיבק שברי שופרות פסול. תנו רבנן: הוסיף עליו כל שהוא, בין במינו בין שלא במינו פסול.

If it was pierced and then plugged, it is not kosher, whether of its own material or not. Rabbi Natan said, "If its own material was used, then it is kosher, but not if different material was used."

ניקב וסתמו, בין במינו בין שלא במינו פסול. רבי נתן אומר: במינו כשר, שלא במינו פסול...

If its sound is thin or thick or raspy, it is kosher; all of the shofar's [own] sounds are kosher.

היה קולו דק או עבה או צרוד כשר, שכל הקולות כשירין [בשופר]

50. Talmud's Prayer Leader

תענית טז.-טז: / Talmud Bavli Ta'anit 16a–b

One only descends before the Ark if one is a regular. (Who is a regular?) Rabbi Yehudah says, "One who is burdened and has little save [the results] of labor in the fields, whose house is empty, whose history is pleasant, who is humble [lit. "low-kneed"], and pleasing to the community.

אין מורידין לפני התיבה אלא אדם הרגיל (איזהו רגיל)? ר' יהודה אומר מטופל ואין לו ויש לו יגיעה בשדה וביתו ריקם ופרקו נאה ושפל ברך ומרוצה לעם

(continued)

ויש לו נעימה וקולו ערב ובקי לקרות בתורה ובנביאים ובכתובים ולשנות במדרש בהלכות ובאגדות ובקי בכל הברכות כולן...

[Someone] who has a lyrical and sweet voice, who is knowledgeable in reading from the Torah, Prophets, and Writings, who can read from the *midrash*, laws, and lore, and who is expert in all blessings…"

היינו מטופל ואין לו היינו ביתו ריקם אמר רב חסדא זהו שביתו ריקם מן העבירה:

Don't "burdened and has little" and someone "whose house is empty" [mean the same thing]? Rav Hisda said, "This is one whose house is empty from sin."

51. Study Torah with Melody

בבלי מגילה לב. / *Talmud Bavli Megillah 32a*

אמר ר' יוחנן כל הקורא בלא נעימה ושונה בלא זמרה עליו הכתוב אומר (יחזקאל כ, כה) "וגם אני נתתי להם חוקים לא טובים" וגו'.

Rabbi Yohanan said, "Anyone who reads [Torah] without a melody or recites [Mishnah] without a tune, it's about them that Scripture says, 'I have also given them laws that are not good' (Ezekiel 20:25)."

תוספות שם: והשונה בלא זמרה. שהיו רגילין לשנות המשניות בזמרה לפי שהיו שונין אותן על פה וע"י כך היו נזכרים יותר:

Tosafot's commentary there: "*One who recites [mishnah] without a tune*"—It was common to recite *mishnayot* to a tune, since they recited them orally, which increased their memorability.

52. *Trop* Elucidates Torah

בבלי מגילה ג. / *Talmud Bavli Megillah 3a*

דכתיב (נחמיה ח, ח) "ויקראו בספר תורת האלהים מפורש ושום שכל ויבינו במקרא" - "ויקראו בספר תורת האלהים" זה מקרא "מפורש" זה תרגום ו"שום שכל" אלו הפסוקין "ויבינו במקרא" אלו פיסקי טעמים, ואמרי לה אלו המסורת שכחום וחזרו ויסדום.

As it is written "And they read in the book, God's instruction, with interpretation; and they gave the sense to understand the reading" (Nehemiah 8:8). *"They read in the book, God's instruction"* is the Torah, *"with interpretation"* is the Targum (vernacular, Aramaic translation), *"and they gave the sense"* is the division of verses, and *"to understand the reading,"* is the *trop*. They said: this is the tradition of the text that had been forgotten and was re-established.

53. Sensitivities about Singing after Suffering

בבלי מגילה י: / *Talmud Bavli Megillah 10b*

אין הקדוש ברוך הוא שמח במפלתן של רשעים.

The Holy Blessed One does not rejoice at the downfall of the wicked.

ואמר רבי יוחנן: מאי דכתיב (שמות יד, כ) "ולא קרב זה אל זה כל הלילה"? בקשו מלאכי השרת לומר שירה, אמר הקדוש ברוך הוא: מעשה ידי טובעין בים ואתם אומרים שירה?

Rabbi Yohanan said, "Why is it written, 'Each one did not come close all night long?' (Exodus 14:20). The ministering angels wanted to sing a song, but the Holy Blessed One said, 'The work of My hands are drowning in the sea, and you want to sing?!'"

54. C(h)ord of Compassion,
for those who Sing [Torah] at Night

בבלי חגיגה יב:, עבודה זרה ג: / *Talmud Bavli Hagigah 12b, Avodah Zarah 3b*

אמר ריש לקיש: כל העוסק בתורה בלילה הקב"ה מושך עליו חוט של חסד ביום, שנאמר: (תהלים מב, ט) "יומם יצוה ה' חסדו ובלילה שירו עמי".

Reish Lakish said, "Anyone occupied with Torah study at night, the Holy Blessed One extends a loveline to them in the day, as it is said, 'By day, God commends His love, and by night His song is with me' (Psalms 42:9)."

מה טעם יומם יצוה ה' חסדו? משום דבלילה שירו עמי.

Why is it the day that God's love is commended? Because at night, His song is with me.

55. Angels Sing, Angels Silent

בבלי חגיגה יב: / *Talmud Bavli Hagigah 12b*

מעון שבו כיתות של מלאכי השרת שאומרות שירה בלילה וחשות ביום מפני כבודן של ישראל

In their dwelling place, choirs of ministering angels sing songs at night but are silent by day, out of respect for Israel

רש"י שם: וחשות - מפני כבודן של ישראל שמקלסין ביום:

Rashi's commentary: Silent…out of respect for Israel, who sing praises [to God] in the day.

56. The Singing *Mikveh*

בבלי חגיגה יד. / *Talmud Bavli Hagigah 14a*

כל יומא ויומא נבראין מלאכי
השרת מנהר דינור ואמרי שירה
ובטלי...המלאכים מתחדשין בכל יום
ומקלסין להקב"ה והן חוזרין לנהר
אש שיצאו ממנו ושוב האלהים
מחדשן ומחזירן כשם שהיו בראשונה

Day after day the ministering angels are created anew from the river Dinur, and they sing praises and are then destroyed...The angels are renewed every day and sing to the Holy Blessed One, and then return to the River of Fire from which they came. And soon God comes back and renews them and returns them to what they were originally

57. Moses' Call and Response

בבלי סוטה ל: / *Talmud Bavli Sotah 30b*

תנו רבנן, בו ביום דרש רבי עקיבא:
בשעה שעלו ישראל מן הים נתנו
עיניהם לומר שירה, וכיצד אמרו
שירה? כגדול המקרא את הלל והן
עונין אחריו ראשי פרקים, משה
אמר (שמות טו, ב) "אשירה לה'" והן
אומרים "אשירה לה'", משה אמר "כי
גאה גאה" והן אומרים "אשירה לה'"

Our Rabbis taught: on that day, Rabbi Akiva expounded, "When the people of Israel emerged from the Red Sea, they felt an urge (*lit.* cast their eyes) to sing; how did they render their song? "Like an adult who leads [the congregation] in the *Hallel*, and they respond after him with the leading words. [According to this reading] Moses sang: 'I will sing to God,' and they responded, 'I will sing to God!' Moses sang: 'God has the power," and they responded, 'I will sing to God!' (Exodus 15:2)."

(continued)

רבי אליעזר בנו של רבי יוסי הגלילי אומר: כקטן המקרא את הלל והן עונין אחריו כל מה שהוא אומר, משה אמר "אשירה לה'" והן אומרים "אשירה לה'", משה אמר "כי גאה גאה" והן אומרים "כי גאה גאה"

Rabbi Eliezer son of Rabbi Yose the Galilean says, "Like a minor who reads the *Hallel* [for a congregation], and they repeat after him all that he says. [According to this reading] Moses sang: 'I will sing to God,' and they responded, 'I will sing to God!' Moses sang, 'God has the power,' and they responded, 'God has the power!'"

רבי נחמיה אומר: כסופר הפורס על שמע בבית הכנסת, שהוא פותח תחילה והן עונין אחריו.

Rabbi Nehemiah declares, "Like a school-teacher who recites the *Sh'ma* in the Synagogue, he opens, and they respond after him."

58. Singing Embryos

בבלי סוטה ל:-לא. / *Talmud Bavli Sotah 30b-31a*

היה רבי מאיר אומר: מנין שאפילו עוברים שבמעי אמן אמרו שירה? שנאמר: (תהלים סח, כז) "במקהלות ברכו אלהים ה' ממקור ישראל". (והא לא חזו! אמר רבי תנחום: כרס נעשה להן כאספקלריא המאירה וראו).

Rabbi Meir would say, "From where [in the Torah] do we know that even fetuses in their mothers' wombs sang [at the splitting of the Red Sea]? [From here,] as it was said, 'Bless God in gatherings, God from the source of Israel' (Psalms 68:27)."(But they could not see [the *Shekhinah*]! Rabbi Tanhum said, "[Their mothers'] stomach became like a clear lens, and they could see.")

59. The Destructive Force of Music

אמר רב: אודנא דשמעא זמרא תעקר

Rav said, "The ear that hears a song should be ripped off."

אמר רבא: זמרא בביתא חורבא בסיפא...

Rava said, "A song in the home is ruin, in the end."…

אמר רב הונא: זמרא דנגדי ודבקרי שרי דגרדאי אסיר

Rav Huna said, "Sailors' and field-workers' songs are permitted, but the weavers' is not allowed."

רב הונא בטיל זמרא קם מאה אווזי בזוזא ומאה סאה חיטי בזוזא ולא איבעי. אתא רב חסדא זליזיל ביה איבעאי אווזא בזוזא ולא משתכח

When Rav Huna abolished singing, one hundred geese were priced at a *zuz* and one hundred *se'ah* of wheat were priced at a *zuz* [very low prices], but demand dropped off. Rav Hisda came and dismissed him, and geese were in such high demand [and priced] at one for a *zuz*, but they had flown off the shelves.

אמר רב יוסף: זמרי גברי ועני נשי פריצותא זמרי נשי ועני גברי כאש בנעורת...

Rav Yosef said, "When men sing and women join in, it is debauchery. When women sing and men join in, it is like lit tinder."…

(continued)

אמר ר' יוחנן: כל השותה בארבעה
מיני זמר מביא חמש פורעניות
לעולם שנאמר (ישעיה ה, יא-יב)
"הוי משכימי בבקר שכר ירדפו
מאחרי בנשף יין ידליקם והיה כנור
ונבל תוף וחליל ויין משתיהם ואת
פועל ה' לא יביטו" מה כתיב אחריו?
(ישעיה ה, יג) "לכן גלה עמי מבלי
דעת" שגורמין גלות לעולם "וכבודו
מתי רעב" שמביאין רעב לעולם
"והמונו צחה צמא" שגורמין לתורה
שתשתכח מלומדיה (ישעיה ה, טו)
"וישח אדם וישפל איש" שגורמין
שפלות לשונאו של הקב"ה ואין איש
אלא הקדוש ב"ה שנאמר (שמות טו,
ג) "ה' איש מלחמה" "ועיני גבוהים
תשפלנה" שגורמין שפלות של
ישראל.

Rabbi Yohanan said, "Anyone who drinks to [the playing of] the four kinds of musical instruments brings five different kinds of punishment to this world. As it is said, 'Oy to those who arise early in the morning to chase drink and get lit with wine till late at night. At their feasts, there are harps and lyres, drums and flutes, and wine, but they do cannot recognize the work of God, they don't see the act of His hands' (Isaiah 5:11–12). "What comes right after? 'Thus my people were exiled, ignorant' (Isaiah 5:13), bringing exile to the world! 'Its honored citizens dying of hunger,' bringing famine to the world! 'Its masses parched with thirst,' causing Torah to be forgotten by its students. 'A mortal is bowed, a person is humbled,' bringing lowliness God's enemies. For 'person' means God, as it is said, 'God is a person of war' (Exodus 15:3). 'And the lofty's eyes are lowered,' causing the lowliness of Israel.

(*continued*)

ומה כתיב אחריו? (ישעיה ה, יד)
"לכן הרחיבה שאול נפשה ופערה פיה
לבלי חק וירד הדרה והמונה ושאונה
ועלז בה".

"And what is written right after?
'Therefore, Hell has stretched its
gullet and opened its mouth beyond
measure. Down goes their glory,
and their tumult, and their noise,
and those that celebrate with them'
(Isaiah 5:14)."

60. The Full Price of Injuring Someone's Ears

בבלי בבא קמא פה: / *Talmud Bavli Bava Kamma 85b*

אמר רבא: קטע את ידו נותן לו דמי
ידו...שיבר את רגלו נותן לו דמי
רגלו...סימא את עינו נותן לו דמי
עינו...חירשו נותן לו דמי כולו.

Rava said: if he cut off [another's]
arm, he must pay him for the value
of the arm...if he broke [the other's]
leg, he must pay him for the value
of the leg...if he put out [another's]
eye he must pay him for the value of
his eye...but if he deafened him, he
must pay for the value of the whole
of his being.

רש"י שם: חירשו - אין ראוי לכלום.

Rashi's commentary: *"If he deafened
him"*—Because he wouldn't be fit for
anything.

61. Singing in Two Worlds

בבלי סנהדרין צא: / *Talmud Bavli Sanhedrin 91b*

כל האומר שירה בעולם הזה זוכה
ואומרה לעולם הבא

All who sing in this world will merit
to sing in the world to come

62. Ezekiel: Bones Stood up and Sang

בבלי סנהדרין צב: / *Talmud Bavli Sanhedrin 92b*

דתניא, רבי אליעזר אומר: מתים
שהחיה יחזקאל עמדו על רגליהם,
ואמרו שירה ומתו.

It was taught: Rabbi Eliezer said,
"The dead revived by Ezekiel stood
on their feet, sang a song, and died."

מה שירה אמרו? "ה' ממית בצדק
ומחיה ברחמים".

What song did they sing? "God
brings death in justice and revives in
mercy."

63. Hezekiah: The One Who Didn't Sing

בבלי סנהדרין צד. / *Talmud Bavli Sanhedrin 94a*

ביקש הקדוש ברוך הוא לעשות
חזקיהו משיח, וסנחריב גוג ומגוג.
אמרה מדת הדין לפני הקדוש ברוך
הוא: רבונו של עולם! ומה דוד מלך
ישראל שאמר כמה שירות ותשבחות
לפניך לא עשיתו משיח, חזקיה
שעשית לו כל הנסים הללו ולא אמר
שירה לפניך תעשהו משיח?!...

The Holy Blessed One wanted to
make [King] Hezekiah the Messiah,
and Sennacherib Gog and Magog.
The Attribute of Judgment came
before the Holy Blessed One and
said, "Master of the universe! If
David, King of Israel, who sang
so many songs and praises before
You, You did not make Messiah,
Hezekiah, for whom You performed
all these miracles but sang before
You not one song, You'll make him
Messiah?!"...

(continued)

מיד פתחה הארץ ואמרה לפניו: רבונו
של עולם, אני אומרת לפניך שירה
תחת צדיק זה, ועשהו משיח. פתחה
ואמרה שירה לפניו שנאמר (ישעיהו
כד, טז) "מכנף הארץ זמרת שמענו
צבי לצדיק" וגו'.

Right away, the Earth opened and said, "Master of the universe, I will sing before You a song instead of this righteous man, if You make him Messiah." The Earth then opened and sang before God, as it was said, "From the Ends of the Earth we have heard songs, the beauty of the righteous..." (Isaiah 24:16).

אמר שר העולם לפניו: רבונו של
עולם, צביונו עשה לצדיק זה!

The Prince of the Universe said, "Master of the Universe, [the Earth] has fulfilled [Your desired] praise for the righteous!"

יצאה בת קול ואמרה: רזי לי רזי לי.

The divine echo (bat kol, lit. daughter of a voice) broke out and said, "My secret, my secret!"

אמר נביא: אוי לי, אוי לי, עד מתי.

The prophet said, "Oy...oy...until when [must we wait]?"

64. Assyrian Army Dies from Hearing Celestial Song

בבלי סנהדרין צה: / Talmud Bavli Sanhedrin 95b

רבי יצחק נפחא אמר: אזנים גלה
להם, ושמעו שירה מפי חיות ומתו,
שנאמר (ישעיהו לג, ג) "מרוממתך
נפצו גוים".

Rabbi Yitzhak the Smith said, "[The Assyrians'] ears were exposed, and they heard the song of the hayyot (life angels) and died. As it is said, "From Your lifting songs, the nations disintegrated" (Isaiah 33:3).

65. Korah's Sons "Didn't Die;" They Were Singing in the Underworld

בבלי סנהדרין קי. / *Talmud Bavli Sanhedrin 110a*

(במדבר כו, יא) "ובני קרח לא מתו", תנא, משום רבינו אמרו: מקום נתבצר להם בגיהנם, וישבו עליו ואמרו שירה.

"But the children of Korah did not die" (Numbers 26:11). It is taught that in the name of our teacher, it was said: a place was dug out for them, in *Gehenna* (Hell), where they would sit and sing.

66. God Glides Around Listening to the Songs of the Angels of Life

בבלי עבודה זרה ג: / *Talmud Bavli Avodah Zarah 3b*

ובליליא מאי עביד? איבעית אימא: מעין יממא ואיבעית אימא: רוכב על כרוב קל שלו ושט בשמונה עשר אלף עולמות...ואיבעית אימא: יושב ושומע שירה מפי חיות, שנאמר: (תהלים מב, ט) "יומם יצוה ה' חסדו ובלילה שירו עמי".

What does God do at night? You could say just as what is done in the day. Or: God rides a lissome cherub, gliding through eighteen thousand worlds...Or you could say God sits and listens to the song of the *hayyot*, as it is said, "By day, God commends His love, and by night His song is with me" (Psalms 42:9).

67. Cows Straighten Up and Sing

בבלי עבודה זרה כד: / *Talmud Bavli Avodah Zarah 24b*

(שמואל א' ו, יב) "וישרנה הפרות בדרך על דרך בית שמש" וגו'

"The cows went straight (*vayisharnah*) on the path to Beth Shemesh..." (1 Samuel 6:12).

(continued)

מאי וישרנה? אמר ר' יוחנן משום ר' מאיר: שאמרו שירה. ורב זוטרא בר טוביה אמר רב: שישרו פניהם כנגד ארון ואמרו שירה.

But what does *vayisharnah* [really] mean? Rabbi Yohanan said, in the name of Rabbi Meir, that they sang a song (*shirah*). And Rav Zutra bar Tuviah said that Rav said, "They straightened (*yishru*) themselves before the Ark and sang a song (*shirah*)."

68. Musical Instruments from an Idolized Animal?

בבלי עבודה זרה מז. / *Talmud Bavli Avodah Zarah 47a*

בעי רב פפא: המשתחוה לבהמה... קרניה מהו לחצוצרות? שוקיה מהו לחלילין? בני מעיה מהו לפארות?

Rav Papa asked, "If an animal is worshipped...May its horns be used for shofars? May its thigh-bones be used for flutes? May its guts be used for harp strings?"

אליבא דמאן דאמר עיקר שירה בכלי לא תיבעי לך דודאי אסיר, כי תיבעי לך אליבא דמאן דאמר עיקר שירה בפה, בסומי קלא בעלמא הוא ומייתינן, או דלמא אפילו הכי אסיר? תיקו.

According to the one who believes that the essence of song is in its instrumentation, it is clear that these are forbidden, but what about the one who believes that the essence of song is in the mouth? If the purpose of the instruments is only to sweeten the sound, even then is it forbidden? It stands [unanswered].

69. Jacob's Angel Needed to Get to His First Time Singing!

בבלי חולין צא: / *Talmud Bavli Hullin 91b*

ויאמר שלחני כי עלה השחר, אמר לו: גנב אתה, או קוביוסטוס אתה, שמתיירא מן השחר? אמר לו: מלאך אני, ומיום שנבראתי לא הגיע זמני לומר שירה עד עכשיו...

"[The angel] said, 'Let me go, the dawn is coming!'" (Genesis 32:27). [Jacob] said to [the angel], "Are you a thief or a gambler, that you're afraid of the dawn?" [The angel] responded, "I am an angel, and from the day I was created, my time to sing [before God] had not arrived until today."

70. Angels Wait to Sing

בבלי חולין צא. / *Talmud Bavli Hullin 91a*

...אמר רב חננאל אמר רב: שלש כתות של מלאכי השרת אומרות שירה בכל יום, אחת אומרת קדוש, ואחת אומרת קדוש, ואחת אומרת קדוש ה' צבאות. מיתיבי: חביבין ישראל לפני הקדוש ברוך הוא יותר ממלאכי השרת, שישראל אומרים שירה - בכל שעה, ומלאכי השרת אין אומרים שירה אלא - פעם אחת ביום...ואין מלאכי השרת אומרים שירה למעלה, עד שיאמרו ישראל למטה

Rav Hananel said that Rav said, "Three groups of ministering angels sing a song each day, one says, 'Holy,' one says, 'Holy,' and one says, 'Holy is the Lord of Hosts.'" They retorted objected: beloved is Israel before the Holy One, more than all of the ministering angels, since Israel sings a song every period, while the angels only sing once a day! ...The angels do not sing a song above until Israel sings below.

71. Cracks of Holiness: The Simple Flute and the Broken Cymbal

בבלי ערכין י: / *Talmud Bavli Arakhin 10b*

תנו רבנן: אבוב היה במקדש, חלק
היה, דק היה, של קנה היה, ומימות
משה היה, צוה המלך וציפוהו זהב
ולא היה קולו ערב, נטלו את צפויו
והיה קולו ערב כמות שהיה.

Our Rabbis taught: there was a flute in the Temple which was smooth, subtle, made of reed, and from the days of Moses. The King commanded that it be covered in gold leaf, but it made its sound no longer sweet. After they removed the overlay, it returned the sweetness of its sound, like it was before.

צלצול היה במקדש, של נחושת היה,
והיה קולו ערב, ונפגם, ושלחו חכמים
והביאו אומנין מאלכסנדריא של
מצרים ותקנוהו, ולא היה קולו ערב,
נטלו את תיקונו והיה קולו ערב כמות
שהיה.

There was a cymbal in the Temple, made of bronze, whose sound was sweet. It was cracked, and Sages sent for skilled workers from Alexandria, Egypt, who repaired it, but its sound was no longer sweet. They removed the repair, and its sweet sound returned, as it was before.

72. The *Magreifah*: One Thousand Notes

בבלי ערכין י:־י״א. / *Talmud Bavli Arakhin 10b-11a*

מגריפה היתה במקדש, עשרה נקבים
היו בה, כל אחד ואחד מוציא עשרה
מיני זמר, נמצאת כולה מוציאה מאה
מיני זמר.

In the Temple was the *magreifah*, which had ten tone holes, and each one made ten kinds of music, resulting in one hundred types of music.

(continued)

במתניתא תנא: היא אמה וגבוה
אמה, וקתא יוצא הימנה ועשרה
נקבים היו בה, כל אחד מוציא מאה
מיני זמר, נמצאת כולה מוציאה אלף
מיני זמר.

It was taught in a *baraita*: it was a cubit [long] and a cubit high. A chanter emerged from it, with ten tone holes, each one emitting one hundred kinds of music, resulting in one thousand different kinds of music.

אמר רב נחמן בר יצחק, וסימניך:
מתניתא גוזמא.

Rav Nahman bar Yitzhak said, "It's a mnemonic to remember: the *baraita* exaggerates." [*Matnita Guzma* = *MaGreifa*]

73. Song Carries Torah

בבלי ברכות נז: / *Talmud Bavli Berakhot 57b*

ותנא מייתי לה מהכא: (במדבר ז, ט)
"ולבני קהת לא נתן כי עבודת הקדש
עליהם בכתף ישאו", ממשמע שנאמר
בכתף, איני יודע שישאו? מה תלמוד
לומר ישאו? אין ישאו אלא לשון
שירה, וכן הוא אומר: (תהילים פא, ג)
"שאו זמרה ותנו תוף", ואומר: (ישעיה
כד, יד) "ישאו קולם ירונו" וגו'.

The tanna brought a proof from here: "But to the children of Kehat, [Moses] gave nothing, because on them was holy work, lifted on their shoulders" (Numbers 7:9). Since it already said, "on their shoulders," don't I know that they were lifting? What does "lifted" teach? "Lifting" means singing, as it is said, "Raise a song and bring the beat" (Psalms 81:3), and it says, "Lift up their voices and sing" (Isaiah 24:14)!

74. Talmud's Prooftexts: Music Essential to Worship

תלמוד ערכין יא. / *Talmud Bavli Arakhin 11b*

אמר רב יהודה אמר שמואל: מנין
לעיקר שירה מן התורה?...

Rav Yehudah said that Shmuel said, "Where can we find in the Torah that the essence [of worship] is song?"...

רב מתנה אמר, מהכא: (דברים כח,
מז) "תחת אשר לא עבדת את ה'
אלהיך בשמחה ובטוב לבב", איזו
היא עבודה שבשמחה ובטוב לבב?
הוי אומר: זה שירה...

Rav Matnah said, "From here: 'Since you did not serve YHVH your God in joy and good-heartedness…' (Deuteronomy 28:47). What is this joyful and good-hearted service? Let one say: it is song…"

חזקיה אמר, מהכא: (דברי הימים א
טו, כב) "וכנניהו שר הלוים במשא
יסור כי מבין הוא", אל תיקרי יסור
אלא ישיר.

Hezekiah said, "From here: 'And Chananiah, the chief (*sar*) of the Levites, was the conductor of song (*masa yasur*), for he understood' (1 Chronicles 15:22). Do not read 'withdraw' (*yasur*) but rather 'sing' (*yashir*)."

בלווטי אמר ר' יוחנן, מהכא: (במדבר
ד, מז) "לעבוד עבודת עבודה", איזהו
עבודה שצריכה עבודה? הוי אומר: זו
שירה.

Balvati [said that] Rabbi Yohanan said, "From here: 'To do the work of service…' (Numbers 4:47). What is this service that needs work? Let one say: it is song."

רבי יצחק אמר, מהכא: (תהלים פא,
ג) "שאו זמרה ותנו תף כנור נעים
עם נבל".

Rabbi Yitzhak said, "From here: 'Carry a song and take up a drum, a lovely lyre with a harp' (Psalms 81:3)."   (continued)

רב נחמן בר יצחק אמר, מהכא:
(ישעיה כד, יד) "המה ישאו קולם
ירונו בגאון ה' צהלו מים".

Rav Nahman bar Yitzhak said,
"From here: 'They lifted up their
voice and sang with joy; for God's
glory, they shouted from the sea'
(Isaiah 24:14)."

ותנא מייתי לה מהכא: (במדבר ז, ט)
"ולבני קהת לא נתן כי עבודת הקדש
עליהם בכתף ישאו", ממשמע שנאמר
בכתף, איני יודע שישאו? מה תלמוד
לומר ישאו? אין ישאו אלא לשון
שירה, וכן הוא אומר: (תהילים פא, ג)
"שאו זמרה ותנו תוף", ואומר: "ישאו
קולם ירונו" וגו'.

A reciter derived it from here: "To
the children of Kehat, [Moses] gave
nothing [no carts, oxen], since the
holy work was upon them, raised
on their shoulders" (Numbers 7:9).
It is implied from it having said,
"on their shoulders;" wouldn't I
know that they're carrying?! What
is the Torah teaching [by the word]
"raised?" "Raised" means "singing."
Thus it says, "Carry a song and take
up a drum," (Psalms 81:3) and it says,
"They lifted their voice and sang with
joy…"

חנניא בן אחי רבי יהושע אמר,
מהכא (שמות יט, יט) "משה ידבר
והאלהים יעננו בקול", על עסקי קול.

Hananiah nephew of Rabbi
Yehoshua said, "From here: 'Moses
spoke, and God answered him with a
voice' (Exodus 19:19). [This means]
with matters of the voice."

רב אשי אמר, מהכא: (דברי הימים
ב ה, יג) "ויהי כאחד למחצצרים
ולמשוררים להשמיע קול אחד".

Rav Ashi said, "From here: 'It came
to pass that when the trumpeters
and singers were as one, sounding
one voice' (2 Chronicles 5:13)."

(*continued*)

רבי יונתן אמר, מהכא: (במדבר יח, ג) "וְלֹא יָמוּתוּ גַם הֵם גַם אַתֶּם", מה אתם בעבודת מזבח, אף הם בעבודת מזבח

Rabbi Yonatan said, "From here: 'So they will not die, not them, and not you' (Numbers 18:3). Just as you [sing] at the altar's service, they, too, [sing] at the altar's service."

75. Two Cymbals, United...

תלמוד ערכין יג. / *Talmud Bavli Arakhin 13a*

מִשְׁנָה...אֵין פּוֹחֲתִין מִשְּׁתֵּי חֲצוֹצְרוֹת, (וּמוֹסִיפִין עַד לְעוֹלָם). (אֵין פּוֹחֲתִין) מִתִּשְׁעָה כִנּוֹרוֹת, וּמוֹסִיפִין עַד לְעוֹלָם. וְהַצְּלְצָל לְבָד:

Mishnah: ...[In the Temple service,] there were never fewer than two trumpets, (and they could be added to infinity). (There were never fewer) than nine harps, and they could be added to infinity. But there was only a sole cymbal.

גְּמָרָא. וְצִלְצָל לבד. מנא הני מילי? אמר רב אסי, דאמר קרא: (דברי הימים א טז, ה) "וְאָסָף בַּמְצִלְתַּיִם"... מצלתים תרי הוו! כיון דחדא דחדא עבידתא עבדי וחד גברא עביד בהו, קרי להו חד.

Gemara: "...but there was only a sole cymbal"—From where do we know this? Rav Asi said that it was the Scripture that said, "Assaf sounding the cymbals..." (1 Chronicles 16:5). "Cymbals..." that implies there were [at least] two! Since they worked as one, and one person played them, they were called one.

76. Transhistorical Harps of Increasing Sizes

תלמוד ערכין יג: / Talmud Bavli Arakhin 13b

רבי יהודה אומר: כנור של מקדש של שבעת נימין היה, שנאמר: (תהלים טז, יא) שובע שמחות [את] פניך, אל תיקרי שובע אלא שבע. ושל ימות המשיח שמונה, שנאמר: (תהלים יב, א) "למנצח על השמינית", על נימא שמינית של עולם הבא עשר, שנאמר: (תהלים צב, ד) "עלי עשור ועלי נבל עלי הגיון בכנור", ואומר: (תהלים לג, ב-ג) "הודו לה' בכנור בנבל עשור זמרו לו שירו לו שיר חדש"!

Rabbi Yehudah said, "The Temple's harp had seven strings, as it was said, 'Your presence is joy saturated (*sova*)' (Psalms 16:11). Don't read 'saturated' (*sova*) but rather 'seven' (*sheva*)! But the harp of the Messianic Age will have eight! As it was said, 'For the conductor, on the eighth' (Psalms 12:1), that is, on the eighth string. But the harp of the World to Come will have ten! As it was said, 'With the ten-stringed instrument and with the lyre...' (Psalms 92:4). And it says, 'Praise God with the harp, sing to God with the ten-stringed lyre. Sing to God a new song!'" (Psalms 33:2–3).

77. Children in the Levite Choir

תלמוד ערכין יג: / Talmud Bavli Arakhin 13b

משנה: אֵין הַקָּטָן נִכְנָס לָעֲזָרָה לַעֲבוֹדָה אֶלָּא בְּשָׁעָה שֶׁהַלְוִיִּם אוֹמְרִים בַּשִּׁיר, וְלֹא הָיוּ אוֹמְרִים בְּנֵבֶל וְכִנּוֹר אֶלָּא בַפֶּה, כְּדֵי לִיתֵּן תֶּבֶל בַּנְּעִימָה.

Mishnah: Minors were not allowed to enter the sanctuary, for service, except when the Levites sang. They joined into the [music of the] harps and lyres with their voices alone, to add zest to the tune.

(continued)

רַבִּי אֱלִיעֶזֶר בֶּן יַעֲקֹב אוֹמֵר, אֵין עוֹלִין לַמִּנְיָן, וְאֵין עוֹלִין לַדּוּכָן, אֶלָּא בָּאָרֶץ הָיוּ עוֹמְדִין, וְרָאשֵׁיהֶן בֵּין רַגְלֵי הַלְוִיִּם, וְצַעֲרֵי הַלְוִיִּם הָיוּ נִקְרָאִין...

Rabbi Eliezer ben Ya'akov said, "They did not count for the quorum, nor did they stand on the platform but rather on the ground, with their heads between the legs of the Levites. They were called the Levites' afflicters…"

[גמרא:] תנא: וסועדי הלוים היו נקראין. ותנא דידן? כיון דהני קטין קלייהו והני עב קלייהו, הני מקטטי והני לא מקטטי, קרי להו צערי.

[*Gemara:*] It was taught: they were called the Levites' helpers. But our *mishnah*? [They were called afflicters because] some people have high voices and some low. [The youths] could sing high, but the [Levites] were not able to. So, they were called afflicters.

78. Songs Balance Earth's Inner Chaos

ירושלמי סנהדרין נב: / *Talmud Yerushalmi, Sanhedrin 52b*

וכן את מוצא בשעה שבא דוד לחפור תימליוסים של בית המקדש חפר חמש עשר מאוין דאמין ולא אשכח תהומא ובסופא אשכח חד עציץ ובעא מירמיתיה. אמר ליה: לית את יכיל, אמר ליה: למה, אמר ליה: דנא הכא כביש על תהומא.

And so you find that in the moment that David came to dig the foundations of the *Beit HaMikdash* (Temple) he dug down fifteen hundred cubits and didn't find the *tehom*, but in the end, he found a single teapot and wanted to throw it. It said to him, "You can't [throw me]." David said, "Why not?" It said, "I'm here to hold down the *tehom*."

(continued)

אמר ליה: ומן אימת את הכא, אמר ליה: מן שעתא דאשמע רחמנא קליה בסיני אני ה' אלהיך רעדת ארעא ושקיעת ואנא יהיב הכא כביש על תהומא. אף על גב כן לא שמע ליה. כיון דרימיה סליק תהומא ובעא מטפא עלמא...התחיל דוד אומר שירה שיר המעלות שיר למאה עולות על כל מאה אמה היה אומר שירה אף על גב הוה סופה מתחנקה.

David said, "And since when have you been here?" It said, "From the moment that the Compassionate One's voice was heard at Sinai proclaiming, 'I am YHVH your God,' the land trembled and sank and I was put here to restrain the *tehom*." Even so, David didn't listen to it. He threw it away, and the *tehom* started rising and threatened to flood the world…So David started to sing songs—the [Fifteen songs beginning] *Shir HaMa'alot*… and for each song he sang, the *tehom* receded back to its original position."

MIDRASH

79. Divine Silence at Giving of Torah

שמות רבה כט, ט / *Exodus Rabbah 29:9*

אמר ר' אבהו בשם ר' יוחנן כשנתן
הקב"ה את התורה צפור לא צווח עוף
לא פרח שור לא געה אופנים לא
עפו, שרפים לא אמרו קדוש קדוש,
הים לא נזדעזע, הבריות לא דברו,
אלא העולם שותק ומחריש ויצא
הקול "אנכי ה' אלהיך"

Rabbi Abahu said in the name of
Rabbi Yohanan, "When God gave
the Torah, no bird called, no fowl
flew, no cow mooed, the *ofanim*
didn't fly, the *serafim* did not say
"Holy, holy!" the tide did not turn,
humans said not a word, but rather,
the whole world fell silent and
quieted. A voice emerged, "I am
YHVH your God."

80. Ear Gives Life

דברים רבה י, א / *Deuteronomy Rabbah 10:1*

כך מאתים וארבעים ושמונה איברים
שבאדם הזה על ידי האוזן כולן חיין
מניין שנא' (ישעיה נה, ג) "שמעו
ותחי נפשכם".

There are 248 major body parts, but
it is through the ear that they all
live...as it says, "listen and you will
be alive" (Isaiah 55:3).

81. Melody Given to Moses with Torah

מכילתא יתרו יט, יט / *Mekhilta Yitro 19:19*

(שמות יט, יט) "משה ידבר והאלהים
יעננו בקול"...והיה הקב"ה מסייעו
בקולו ובנעימה שהיה משה שומע בו
היה משמיע את ישראל

"Moses spoke, and God answered
him with a voice" (Exodus 19:19)...
The Holy Blessed One helped
[Moses] by sharing His divine
voice—and the melody that Moses
heard, he repeated to Israel.

82. The Ten Songs of Struggle and Freedom

א מכילתא מסכתא דשירה / *Mekhilta Shirah 1*

"This song" (Exodus 15:1)—But is it really just one song? Are there not ten songs?

(שמות טו, א) "את השירה הזאת."
וכי שירה אחת היא והלא עשר
שירות הן?

The first was sung in Egypt, as it was said, "You will have a song like a night a feast is made holy" (Isaiah 30:29).

הראשונה שנאמרה במצרים שנא'
(ישעיה ל, כט) "השיר (הזה) יהיה
לכם כליל התקדש חג" וגו'.

The second was at the [Reed] Sea, as it was said, "Then Moses sang" (Exodus 15:1).

השנייה על הים שנאמר (שמות טו,
א) "אז ישיר משה".

The third was at the well [in the desert], as it was said, "Then Israel sang" (Numbers 21:17).

השלישית על הבאר שנאמר (במדבר
כא, יז) "אז ישיר ישראל".

The fourth was sung by Moses [near the end of his life], as it was said, "Moses concluded writing all the words of this song" (Deuteronomy 31:24).

הרביעית שאמר משה שנאמר
(דברים לא, כד) "ויהי ככלות משה
לדבר את כל דברי השירה הזאת".

The fifth was sung by Joshua, as it was said, "Then Joshua spoke before God on the day God delivered…" (Joshua 10:12).

החמישית שאמר יהושע שנאמר
(יהושע י, יב) "אז ידבר יהושע לפני
ה' ביום תת ה'" וגו'.

The sixth was sung by Deborah and Barak, as it was said, "Then sang Deborah and Barak ben Avinoam…" (Judges 5:1).

הששי שאמרה דבורה וברק שנאמר
(שופטים ה, א) "ותשר דבורה וברק בן
אבינועם".

(continued)

The seventh was sung by David, as it was said, "David spoke to God the words of this song…" (2 Samuel 22:1).

השביעית שאמר דוד שנאמר (שמואל ב כב, א) "וידבר דוד לה' את דברי השירה הזאת."

The eighth was sung by Solomon, as it was said, "A Psalm, a song for the dedication of David's house." (Psalm 30:1) […]

השמינית שאמר שלמה שנאמר (תהלים ל, א) "מזמור שיר חנוכת הבית לדוד" (...)

The ninth was sung by Jehoshaphat, as it was said, "Jehoshaphat counseled with the people and stationed those to sing for God and praise the beauty of the Holy, as they exited before the army, saying 'Praise God…Whose love is eternal.'" (2 Chronicles 20:21)…

התשיעית שאמר יהושפט שנאמר (דביא הימים ב כ, כא) "ויועץ יהושפט ויעמד משוררים לה' מהללים בהדר' קדש בצאתו לפני החלוץ אומר הודו לה' [...] כי לעולם חסדו"...

The tenth will be in the coming future, as it was said, "Sing to God a new song, and praise to the ends of the earth" (Isaiah 42:10).

העשירית לעתיד לבא שנאמר (ישעיה מב, י) "שירו לה' שיר חדש תהלתו מקצה הארץ"...

83. Jehoshaphat Didn't Sing "*Ki Tov (Is Good)*"

מכילתא מסכתא דשירה א / *Mekhilta Shirah 1*

התשיעית שאמר יהושפט שנאמר (דברי הימים ב כ, כא) "ויועץ יהושפט ויעמד משוררים לה' מהללים בהדרת קדש בצאתו לפני החלוץ אומר הודו לה' כי לעולם חסדו." ומה נשתנית הודיה זו מכל ההודיות שבתורה שבכל ההודיות שבתורה נאמר" הודו לה' כי טוב כי לעולם חסדו" ובזו לא נאמר? אלא כביכול לא היתה שמחה לפניו על אבדן של רשעים.

Jehoshaphat[1] sang the ninth [song], as it was said, "Jehoshaphat took counsel and set up those to sing for God and praise the beauty of the Holy, as they exited before the army, saying 'Praise God…One Whose love lasts forever'" (2 Chronicles 20:21). Why did he change this praise from the other iterations of this praise in the Torah, as in all those instances, it was said, "Praise God, for God is good, One Whose love lasts forever" but in this case, it was omitted? Rather, as it were, [because] God is not made happy by the destruction of the wicked.

84. Perek Shirah—the Whole Universe Sings

פרק שירה, פרק א / *Perek Shirah, Chapter 1*

שָׁמַיִם אוֹמְרִים: (תהלים יט, ב) "הַשָּׁמַיִם מְסַפְּרִים כְּבוֹד אֵל וּמַעֲשֵׂה יָדָיו מַגִּיד הָרָקִיעַ":

אֶרֶץ אוֹמֶרֶת. (תהלים כד, א) "לְדָוִד מִזְמוֹר לַה' הָאָרֶץ וּמְלוֹאָהּ תֵּבֵל וְיֹשְׁבֵי בָהּ":

The skies sing: "The skies describe the glory of God; the work of God's hands testify the heavens" (Psalms 19:2).

The earth sings, "A song of David, the earth is God's and all that fills it, the world and those dwelling on it" (Psalms 24:1).

(continued)

---

[1] The fourth king of Judah. See 1 Kings 22:1–50; 2 Kings 3; 2 Chronicles 17:1–21:3.

ואומר. (ישעיהו כד, טז) "מִכְּנַף הָאָרֶץ
זְמִרֹת שָׁמַעְנוּ צְבִי לַצַּדִּיק":

גַּן עֵדֶן אוֹמֵר. (שיר השירים ד, טז)
"עוּרִי צָפוֹן וּבוֹאִי תֵימָן הָפִיחִי גַנִּי
יִזְּלוּ בְשָׂמָיו יָבֹא דוֹדִי לְגַנּוֹ וְיֹאכַל פְּרִי
מְגָדָיו":

גֵּיהִנֹּם אוֹמֵר. (תהילים קז, ט) "כִּי
הִשְׂבִּיעַ נֶפֶשׁ שֹׁקֵקָה וְנֶפֶשׁ רְעֵבָה מִלֵּא
טוֹב":

מִדְבָּר אוֹמֵר. (ישעיהו לה, א) "יְשֻׂשׂוּם
מִדְבָּר וְצִיָּה וְתָגֵל עֲרָבָה וְתִפְרַח
כַּחֲבַצָּלֶת":

שָׂדוֹת אוֹמְרִים. (משלי ג, יט)
"ה' בְּחָכְמָה יָסַד אָרֶץ כּוֹנֵן שָׁמַיִם
בִּתְבוּנָה":

And it says: "From the ends of the earth we have heard songs, the beauty of the righteous" (Isaiah 24:16).

The Garden of Eden sings, "Wake up, North wind, and come, South! Blow on my garden, make the spices flow. Let my beloved come to his garden and eat his delicious fruits" (Song of Songs 4:16).

Hell (Gehenom) sings, "God has quenched the thirsty throat (nefesh), filled with good the hungry spirit" (Psalms 107:6).

The desert sings, "The desert and arid land will celebrate; the wilderness will rejoice and blossom like a lily" (Isaiah 35:1).

The fields sing, "God established the land with wisdom, instituted the heavens with understanding" (Proverbs 3:19).

(continued)

יָמִים אוֹמְרִים. (תהלים צג, ד) "מִקֹּלוֹת מַיִם רַבִּים אַדִּירִים מִשְׁבְּרֵי יָם אַדִּיר בַּמָּרוֹם ה'":

The waters sing, "When God's voice moves the many waters in heaven, it thunders, and the mist rises from the ends of the earth. God makes the rain and lightning, brings the wind out from where it is kept" (Jeremiah 51:16).

מַיִם אוֹמְרִים. (ירמיה נא, טז) "לְקוֹל תִּתּוֹ הֲמוֹן מַיִם בַּשָּׁמַיִם וַיַּעַל נְשִׂאִים מִקְצֵה אָרֶץ בְּרָקִים לַמָּטָר עָשָׂה וַיּוֹצֵא רוּחַ מֵאֹצְרֹתָיו":

The oceans sing, "More than the thunder of the many waters, mightier than the waves of the sea, is God mighty in heaven" (Psalms 93:4).

נְהָרוֹת אוֹמְרִים. (תהלים צח, ח) "נְהָרוֹת יִמְחֲאוּ כָף יַחַד הָרִים יְרַנֵּנוּ":

The rivers sing, "Let the rivers clap their hands, and, as one, the mountains sing for joy!" (Psalms 98:8).

מַעְיָנוֹת אוֹמְרִים. (תהלים פז, ז) "וְשָׁרִים כְּחֹלְלִים כָּל מַעְיָנַי בָּךְ":...

The wellsprings sing, "Singers and dancers [say], 'All my wellsprings are in You!'" (Psalms 87:7).

85. Mythical Harp and Shofars Born at Beginning of Time

פרקי דרבי אליעזר, כא / *Pirkei D'Rabbi Eliezer 21*

ר' חנניא בן דוסא אומר אותו האיל שנברא בין השמשות לא יצא ממנו דבר לבטלה אפרו של איל הוא יסוד על גבי המזבח הפנימי גידי האיל אלו עשרה נבלים של כנור שהיה דוד מנגן בהם עורו של איל הוא אזור מתניו של אליהו ז"ל

Rabbi Hanina ben Dosa said, "The ram that was created at twilight [on the sixth day of creation], nothing that came from it was wasted. Its ashes became the base on top of the inner altar; its sinews became the ten strings on the harp David played; its skin became Elijah's kilt,

(continued)

as it was said, "…He was a hairy man[, girded with leather around his loins]" (2 Kings 1:8); its horns: the left one was blown at Mount Sinai, as it was said, "And when they blow the shofar long and loud…" (Joshua 6:5), and the right one, bigger than the left, will one day be blown in the future to come, as it was said, "And on that day, a Great Shofar will be blown, and God will be ruler over the whole world" (Isaiah 27:13).

שנאמר (מלכים ב א, ח) "איש בעל שער" וכו' קרניו של איל של שמאל שתקע בו בהר סיני שנאמר (יהושע ו, ה) "ויהי במשוך בקרן היובל" ושל ימין שהיא גדולה משל שמאל שהוא עתיד לתקוע בה לעתיד לבא שנאמר (ישעיה כז, יג) "והיה ביום ההוא יתקע בשופר גדול והיה ה' למלך על כל הארץ"

86. Music Entices Dinah

פרקי דרבי אליעזר, לח / *Pirkei D'Rabbi Eliezer 38*

When Jacob came to the land he possessed, in the land of Canaan, he was bitten by a snake. And who was the snake? It was Shechem ben Hamor.[2] When [Dinah,] Jacob's daughter, would sit in the tents and would not go out, what did Shechem do? He brought young women who would play their drums right outside, and Dinah went out to see the local musical women. And he kidnapped her and slept with her, and she conceived and gave birth to Osnat.[3]

וכשבא יעקב לארץ אחוזתו שבארץ כנען נשכו הנחש. ואי זה הוא הנחש, זה שכם בן חמור. שהיתה בתו של יעקב יושבת אוהלים ולא היתה יוצאה לחוץ, מה עשה שכם בן חמור, הביא נערות משחקות חוצה לו מתופפות ויצאה דינה לראות בבנות הארץ המשחקות ושללה ושכב עמה, והרתה וילדה את אסנת

---

[2] For the story of Dinah's kidnapping, see Genesis 34.
[3] Osnat became Joseph's wife in Egypt.

87. Dancing to the Golden Calf, to Imitate Egyptian Ritual

פרקי דרבי אליעזר, מד / *Pirkei D'Rabbi Eliezer 44*

וכשקבלו ישראל את התורה רצה
לומר עשרת הדברות לאחר ארבעים
יום שכחו את אלהיהם ואמרו לאהרן
המצריים היו נושאין את אלהיהם
ומשוררין ומזמרין לפניו ורואין אותו
לפניהם (שמות לב, א) "קום עשה לנו
אלהים אשר ילכו לפנינו"...

When Israel received the Torah,
that is, the ten utterances, after forty
days, they forgot their God and said
to Aaron, "The Egyptians would
carry [out] their gods and play
music and sing before it, everyone
beholding it before them. 'Get up
and make us a god who will go
before us...'" (Exodus 32:1).

88. Bad End for Those Who Don't Sing

פסיקתא רבתי כה, ג / *Pesikta Rabbati 25:3*

דבר אחר בקולך, שאם היה קולך
נאה והיית יושב בבית הכנסת עמוד
וכבד ה' בקולך.

Another interpretation [of] "With
your voice"—If you have a sweet
voice, and you are sitting in the
synagogue, get up and praise God
with your voice!

חייא בן אחותו של רבי אליעזר
הקפר היה קולו נאה, והיה אומר לו
חייא בני עמוד וכבד את ה' ממה
שחננך.

Hiyya, the son of Rabbi Eliezer
HaKappar's sister had a lovely voice,
and he would say to him, "Hiyya, my
son, stand and glorify God with that
which you have been gifted."

(continued)

נבות היה קולו נאה והיה עולה לירו־
שלים, והיו כל ישראל מתכנסים לש־
מוע קולו, פעם אחת לא עלה, והעידו
עליו אותם העדים בני בליעל ונאבד
מן העולם, מי גרם לו, על שלא עלה
לירושלים בראיה לכבד את ה' ממה
שחננו

Navot had a sweet voice and would travel to Jerusalem, and all of Israel would gather to hear him. Once, he did not come, and those worthless people testified against him, and he was wiped from the world.[4] What caused it? Since he did not go up to Jerusalem for the appearance offering, honoring God with what he has been graced.

89. Joshua: "Sun, Be Silent"

מדרש תנחומא, אחרי־מות ט / *Midrash Tanhuma, Aharei Mot 9*

משעה שהשמש זורח עד שעה שהוא
שוקע אין קלוסו של הקב"ה פוסק
מפיו שנא' (מלאכי א, יא) "ממזרח
שמש ועד מבואו", וכן את מוצא
בשעה שעמד יהושע ועשה מלחמה
בגבעון מה כתיב שם (יהושע י, יב)
"אז ידבר יהושע לה' ביום תת ה'
את האמורי לפני בני ישראל ויאמר
לעיני ישראל שמש בגבעון דום" וגו'

From the time the sun rises to when it sinks, the praise of the Holy Blessed One does not cease from its mouth, as it was said, "From the shining of the sun to when it sets…" (Malachi 1:11). Similarly, you find that when Joshua stood and made war with Gibeon, what was written there? "Then Joshua spoke to God on the day God delivered the Amorites before the Children of Israel and said, in the full sight of Israel, 'Sun be silent, still (*dom*) in Gibeon…'" (Joshua 10:12).

(continued)

---

[4] See 1 Kings 21, especially v. 13.

בקש יהושע לשתק את החמה אמר
לו: שמש בגבעון דום לא אמר עמוד
אלא דום למה אמר לו דום שכל זמן
שהוא מקלס יש בו כח להלך דמם
עמד, לכך אמר לו יהושע שיעמוד
שנאמר שמש בגבעון דום,

Joshua sought to silence the sun. It says, "Sun, be silent," not 'stand still' but rather, 'be silent'. Why did he say "be silent?" Since, every moment the sun praises [God], it has the strength to move, but when it is silenced, it stands still. Thus, Joshua, in saying, "sun, be still," told it to stop.

אמר לו השמש ליהושע: יהושע וכי
יש קטן אומר לגדול ממנו דום אני
נבראתי ברביעי ובני אדם נבראו
בששי ואתה אומר לי דום

The sun said to Joshua, "Joshua, can a little one tell it's greater to be still? I was created on the fourth day, and humans were created on the sixth, and you're telling me to be still?!"

אמר לו יהושע: בן חורין שהוא קטן
ויש לו עבד זקן אינו אומר לו שתוק,
ואברהם אבי הקנה לו הקב"ה שמים
וארץ שנאמר (בראשית יד, יט) "ברוך
אברם לאל עליון קונה שמים וארץ",
ולא עוד אלא שנשתחוה השמש לפני
יוסף שנאמר (בראשית לז, לט) "והנה
השמש והירח" וגו', הוי שמש בגבעון
דום,

Joshua replied, "Can't a free little one who has an elder servant tell him to be silent? And the Holy Blessed One granted (hikneh) my ancestor Abraham the heavens and the earth, as it was said, 'Blessed be Abraham, of God most high, Creator (koneh) of heavens and earth' (Genesis 14:19). Further, the sun bowed before Joseph, as it was said, 'Behold, the sun and the moon…bowed before me' (Genesis 37:9). So, 'sun, be still in Gibeon!'"

אמר לו השמש: וכי אתה גוזר עלי
שאדום, אמר לו: הן,

The sun replied, "So, you're ordering me to be still?" "Yes."

(continued)

אמר לו: וכיון שאני שותק מי יאמר
קלוסו של הקב"ה. אמר לו דום אתה
ואני אומר שירה בעבורך שנאמר "אז
ידבר יהושע לה'" ואין אז אלא שירה
שנאמר (שמות טו, א) "אז ישיר
משה"

"And when I am silent, who will sing
praises for the Holy Blessed One?"
Joshua replied, "You be still, and I will
sing in your place," as it was said, "Then
Joshua spoke to God," and there is no
"then" without song, as it was said,
"Then Moses sang…" (Exodus 15:1).

90. Shofar Signals Good Times

תנא דבי אליהו זוטא, כב / *Tanna D'Vei Eliyahu Zuta 22*

ר' יהושע בן קרחה אומר לא נברא
שופר אלא לטובה, שבשופר ניתנה
תורה [בסיני] לישראל, שנאמר
(שמות יט, יט) "ויהי קול השופר",
ובשופר נפלה חומת יריחו, שנאמר
(יהושע ו, כ) "ויהי כשמוע (שופר)
[העם את קול השופר] ויריעו (כל)
העם", ובשופר עתיד הקב"ה לתקוע
בשעה שמגלה (משיחנו) [את
המשיח], שנאמר (זכריה ט, יד) "וה'
אלהים בשופר יתקע", ובשופר עתיד
הקב"ה לתקוע בשעה שמכנס גליות
ישראל למקומן,

Rabbi Joshua ben Korhah said, "The
shofar was created only for good,
since the Torah was given [at Sinai]
with [the accompaniment of] the
shofar, as it was said, 'And with the
sound of the shofar [growing louder
and louder, Moses spoke, and God
answered him with a voice]' (Exodus
19:19). And with the shofar did the
walls of Jericho fall, as it was said,
'And when the people heard the
sound of the shofar, the entire people
shouted' (Joshua 6:20). And in the
future, at the time of the revelation
of the Messiah, will the Holy Blessed
One blow the shofar, as it was said,
YHVH God will blow the shofar…'
(Zechariah 9:14). And with a shofar
will the Holy Blessed One gather in
the exiles of Israel to their place,

(continued)

שנאמר (ישעיה כז, יג) "והיה ביום
ההוא יתקע בשופר גדול" [וגו'] לכך
נאמר (ישעיה נח, א) "כשופר הרם
קולך".

as it was said, 'And it will be, on that day, [that God] will blow the Great Shofar, [and those that were lost will return]' (Isaiah 27:13). Thus is it said: 'Raise your voice like a shofar' (Isaiah 58:1)."

91. Shofar Moves God to Mercy

פסיקתא דרב כהנא כג, ג / *Pesikta d'Rav Kahana 23:3*

יהודה בר נחמן בשם ריש לקיש פתח
(תהלים מז, ו) "עלה אלהים בתרועה"
וג'. בשעה שהקב"ה עולה ויושב על
כסא הדין בדין הוא עולה, דכתיב
(שם) "עלה אלהים בתרועה". ובשעה
שישראל נוטלין שופרות ותוקעין
הקב"ה עומד מכסא דין ויושב על
כסא רחמים, דכתיב (שם) י"י בקול
שופר, ומתמלא עליהם רחמים
ומרחם עליהם והופך להם מידת הדין
למידת רחמים. אימתי, (ויקרא כג,
כד) "בחדש השביעי".

Yehudah bar Nahman, in the name of Reish Lakish, opened, "God (*Elohim*)[5] rises with trumpet blasts" (Psalms 47:6)—When the Holy Blessed One arises and sits on the throne of judgment, He rises in judgment, as it is written, "God rises with trumpet blasts." But when Israel takes up shofars and blows, the Holy Blessed One gets up from the throne of judgment and sits on the throne of compassion/mercy, as it is written, "YHVH,[6] with the sound of the shofar", which fills God up with compassion for them, to be compassionate with them, transforming the quality of judgment into compassion. When? "In the seventh month (Tishrei)" (Leviticus 23:24).

---

[5] In Rabbinic texts, the name Elohim can refer to God's aspect of judgment.

[6] The name YHVH, however, can refer to God's compassion.

92. Levites Jump Into the Fire with Instruments

פסיקתא רבתי (איש שלום) כו / *Pesikta Rabbati, 26*

When the priests and Levites saw that the Temple was burning, they took their harps and trumpets and jumped into the fire to burn.

כשראו הכהנים והלוים שנשרף בית המקדש נטלו את הכינורים ואת החצוצרות ונפלו באש ונשרפו.

93. Instruments Hidden

(אהרון ילינק, בית המדרש, מסכת כלים ט (עמ' 90 / *Massekhet Kelim (Medieval Jewish Midrash), ed. Jellinek, 88–91, Mishnah 9*

All [of the Temple's utensils and instruments] were watched over and stored away under the eye of Zedekiah. They were kept kosher in case they fell, God forbid, into the hands of a trouble-maker, an enemy of Israel, since these utensils/instruments were only provided due to [God's] desire for Israel. They were stored away by Baruch and Zedekiah, so the "kosher ones"[7] would not use them, God forbid, and they are kept until the day that Israel returns to its former place and takes up again the honor and eternal glory, when the Son of David emerges, and the silver and gold are revealed to him, when all of Israel gathers and ascends with a complete ascent to Jerusalem, amen.

הכל צפונים וגנוזים בעין צדקיה שהיו הכשרים בסוד שיפלו חס ושלום ביד צר שהיה שונא לישראל שכלים הללו אין משתמשין בהם אלא לרצון על ישראל והיו גנוזים אותם ברוך וצדקיה שהכשרים לא ישתמשון בהם חס ושלום והטמינום עד היום שישובו ישראל לקדמותן ויקחו כבוד ויקרת עולם כשיצא להם איש דוד בן דוד שמו ויתגלה לו הכסף והזהב כשיתקבצו כל ישראל ויעלו עלייה שלימה לירושלים אמן.

---

[7] This appears to be a euphemism, meaning not the "kosher ones" but the "treyf ones."

94. Frog Scolds David

ילקוט שמעוני, תהלים קנ, סוף / *Yalkut Shimoni, (13th c., Germany), Psalm 150, end*

אמרו על דוד המלך: בשעה שסיים
ספר תהלים זחה דעתו עליו אמר
לפניו רבונו של עולם כלום יש דבר
בעולם שאמר שירה כמותי, נזדמנה
לו צפרדע אחת אמרה לו אל תזוח
דעתך עליך שאני אמרת שירה יותר
ממך, ועל כל שירה ושירה שאני
אומרת אני ממשלה עליה שלשת
אלפים משל...

It is said of David the King: when
he finished his Book of Psalms, he
became full of pride, and he said to
the Master of the World, "There is
no one in the world who can sing
praises like me!"…A frog suddenly
appeared and said to him, "Don't be
so arrogant! I sing more praises than
you, and each of my songs yields
three thousand parables…"

95. Singing After Miracles

ילקוט שמעוני בשלח רמז רנד / *Yalkut Shimoni, B'Shallah 254*

לא כל שרוצה לומר שירה אומר
שירה אלא כל מי שנעשה לו נס
ואומר שירה בידוע שמוחלין לו על
כל עונותיו ונעשה בריה חדשה...

Not everyone who wants to sing a
song can sing a song, but anyone
who has experienced a miracle
and subsequently sings a song, all
their sins will be forgiven and they
become a new creature.

96. Serah's Serenade Heals Jacob

ספר הישר, פרשת ויגש / *Sefer HaYashar* (16th c., Italy), *Parashat VaYigash*

וישב מצרימה ובני יעקב הלכו ארצה
כנען בשמחה ובטובה אל יעקב
אביהם: ויבואו עד גבול הארץ ויאמרו
איש אל רעהו מה נעשה בדבר הזה
לפני אבינו: כי אם נבוא אליו פתאום
ונגד לו הדבר ויבהל מאד מדברינו
ולא יאבה לשמוע אלינו:

They returned from Egypt, and the children of Jacob went to Canaan, in joy and gladness, to Jacob, their father. They came to the border of the land, saying to each other, "How should we relate what happened to our father? If we come to him suddenly and recount what happened, he will be so shocked that he won't be able to bear hearing [more] from us."

וילכו להם עד קרבם אל בתיהם
וימצאו את שרח בת אשר אשר
יוצאת לקראתם והנערה טובה עד
מאד וחכמה ויודעת לנגן בכנור:
ויקראו אליה ותבא אליהם ותשק
להם ויקחוה ויתנו לה כנור אחד
לאמר: בואי נא לפני אבינו וישבת
לפניו והך בכנור ודברת ואמרת
כדברים האלה לפניו:

So, they kept traveling until close to their homes and found Serah bat Asher,[8] who was coming out to greet them. This young woman was exceptionally wise, and she knew how to play a harp. They called to her, and she came and kissed them. They took her with them, gave her a harp, and said, "Please go to our father, sit before him, play this harp, and speak these words to him…"

(*continued*)

---

[8] A granddaughter of Jacob, a child of Asher, mentioned in 1 Chronicles 7:30. As in this example, she becomes the heroine of legends.

ויצוו אותה ללכת אל ביתם ותקח
הכנור ותמהר ותלך לפניהם ותבוא
ותשב אצל יעקב: והיטיב הכנור ותנגן
ותאמר בנועם דבריה יוסף דודי חי
הוא וכי הוא מושל בכל ארץ מצרים
ולא מת:

They directed her to go to their
home, take her harp, and hurry
back to them, to come and sit before
Jacob. The harp was lovely as she
played and said, with soothing
speech, "Beloved Joseph is alive,
ruling over the whole of Egypt. He
did not die!"

ותוסף ותנגן והדבר כדברים האלה
וישמע יעקב את דבריה ויערב לו:
וישמע עוד בדברה פעמים ושלש
ותבא השמחה בלב יעקב מנועם
דבריה ותהי עליו רוח אלהים וידע
כי כל דבריה נכונה: ויברך יעקב את
שרח בדברה הדברים האלה לפניו
ויאמר אליה בתי אל ימשול מות בך
עד עולם כי החיית את רוחי:

She continued to play, saying these
things; Jacob [was able to] hear
her words, a sweetness for him. He
heard her words again, then a third
time, and joy entered his heart due
to the gratifying nature of her words.
The spirit of God came upon him,
and he knew all her words were
true. Jacob blessed Serah with these
words [of his own], "My daughter,
death will never rule over you,
eternally, for you have revitalized my
spirit."

MEDIEVAL

97. Shofar Calls us to Awaken and Act

רמב"ם, משנה תורה, הלכות תשובה ג, ד / *Rambam (Maimonides, b. 1135, Spain), Mishneh Torah, Laws of Repentance 3:4*

אף על פי שתקיעת שופר בראש
השנה גזירת הכתוב רמז יש בו כלו־
מר עורו ישינים משנתכם ונרדמים
הקיצו מתרדמתכם וחפשו במעשיכם
וחזרו בתשובה וזכרו בוראכם

Even though [the reason] the shofar is blown on Rosh Hashanah is because of a biblical mandate, it still has a hint at some meaning, as if it says, "Wake up, you sleepers from your slumber! Get up from your nap, nappers! Sift through your actions and return with repentance (*teshuvah*)! Remember your Creator!"

98. Instrumental Music Forbidden After the Temple's Destruction

רמב"ם, משנה תורה, הלכות תעניות ה, יד / *Rambam, Mishneh Torah, Laws of Fasts 5:14*

וכן גזרו שלא לנגן בכלי שיר. וכל
מיני זמר וכל משמיעי קול של שיר
אסור לשמוח בהן ואסור לשומען
מפני החורבן.

It was decreed not to play musical instruments. It is forbidden to participate in [the playing of] any kinds of musical instruments or in the making of music as well as to listen to them, due to the destruction [of the Temple].

99. Sound Cannot be Stolen

רמב"ם, משנה תורה, הלכות שופר א:ג / *Rambam, Mishneh Torah, Laws of Shofar 1:3*

שופר הגזול שתקע בו יצא שאין
המצוה אלא בשמיעת הקול אע"פ
שלא נגע בו ולא הגביהו השומע
(יצא) ואין בקול דין גזל

One does fulfill [the mitzvah of
hearing the shofar] if one uses a
stolen shofar, since the *mitzvah* is
in hearing the sound, even though
the hearer never touches it or raises
it up. Sound cannot be stolen [*lit.*
sound has no law of stealing].

100. Music Dissolves Depression

רמב"ם, פירוש על המשנה, שמונה פרקים, פרק ה / *Rambam, Commentary on the Mishnah,*
Eight Chapters, Chapter 5

...וכן אם התעוררה עליו מרה שחורה,
יסירה בשמיעת שירים ומיני נגינות,
ובטיול בגנות ובבניינים נאים,
ובישיבה עם צורות נאות, וכיוצא
בזה ממה שירחיב הנפש, ויסיר דאגת
המרה השחורה ממנה.

Similarly, if melancholy awakens
within you, you can dispel it by
listening to singing and different
kinds of melodies, or by strolling
through gardens or beautiful
buildings, or by sitting with lovely
images, or through other activities
which expand the soul (*nefesh*), and
the anxiety and melancholy will
dissolve.

101. Singing Angels: The Essence of Our Beings

רמב"ם, מורה נבוכים (תרגום אבן טיבון) ב, ו / *Rambam, Guide of the Perplexed, 2:6*[1]

ומה שיחזק אצלך היות הכחות האישיות הטבעיות והנפשיות נקראות מלאכים, אמרם במקומות רבים, ועקרו בבראשית רבה, בכל יום הקב"ה בורא כת של מלאכים אומרים לפניו שירה והולכים להם...

And let it be deeply known to you that the essential powers of humankind and of nature and of the soul are called "angels (*malakhim*)," which are spoken of in many places, and their purpose is explained in Breishit Rabbah, that every day the Holy Blessed One creates a choir/class of angels that say song before Him and then move on.

102. Melodies Ordained from Sinai

ספר חסידים, שב / *Judah the Hasid (b. 1150, Germany), Sefer Hasidim 302*

(דברים יט, יד) "לא תסיג גבול רעך אשר גבלו ראשונים"

שתקנו הנגונים שלא יאמר נגון של תורה לנביאים וכתובים ושל נביאים לתורה ולכתובים ושל כתובים לתורה ונביאים אלא כל ניגון כמו שהוא מתוקן שהכל הלכה למשה מסיני שנאמר (שמות יט, יט) "יעננו בקול".

"Do not move the boundary of your neighbor, which were established previously" (Deuteronomy 19:14).

[Those who preceded us] established melodies, such that one would not use the melody of the Torah with Prophets or Writings, or that for the Prophets with Torah or Writings, or that for the Writings with Torah or Prophets. Rather, each melody is established just so, all a law of Moses stemming from Sinai, as it is said, "God answered him with a voice" (Exodus 19:19).

---

[1] Rambam wrote the Guide of the Perplexed in Arabic, so the Hebrew here is also a translation.

103. *Anim Z'mirot*, the Song of Glory

שִׁיר הַכָּבוֹד (אַנְעִים זְמִירוֹת) / *The Song of Glory (circa. 12th c., Germany)*

אַנְעִים זְמִירוֹת וְשִׁירִים אֶאֱרוֹג. כִּי
אֵלֶיךָ נַפְשִׁי תַעֲרוֹג: נַפְשִׁי חָמְדָה בְּצֵל
יָדֶךָ. לָדַעַת כָּל רָז סוֹדֶךָ:

I will make melodies and spin sweet songs; it is You that my soul thirsts for. My soul yearns for the shade of Your hand, to know all of Your secrets.

מִדֵּי דַבְּרִי בִּכְבוֹדֶךָ. הוֹמֶה לִבִּי אֶל
דּוֹדֶיךָ: עַל כֵּן אֲדַבֵּר בְּךָ נִכְבָּדוֹת. וְשִׁמְךָ
אֲכַבֵּד בְּשִׁירֵי יְדִידוֹת: [...]

Each time I speak of Your glory, my heart moans/sighs after Your love. So I will speak of You in praise, and Your Name will I glorify with songs of love. [...]

שִׁית הֲמוֹן שִׁירַי נָא עָלֶיךָ. וְרִנָּתִי
תִקְרַב אֵלֶיךָ: תְּהִלָּתִי תְּהִי לְרֹאשְׁךָ
עֲטֶרֶת. וּתְפִלָּתִי תִּכּוֹן קְטוֹרֶת:

Amidst this noise, I place my song before You, I bring my song close to You. May my praise be a crown for Your head and my prayer prepared like an incense offering.

תִּיקַר שִׁירַת רָשׁ בְּעֵינֶיךָ. כַּשִּׁיר יוּשַׁר
עַל קָרְבָּנֶיךָ:

May my poor song be made rich in Your eyes, like a song sung over the offerings once made for You.

בִּרְכָתִי תַעֲלֶה לְרֹאשׁ מַשְׁבִּיר. מְחוֹלֵל.
וּמוֹלִיד צַדִּיק כַּבִּיר:

May my blessing ascend to the head of the Sustainer, the Generator, Who delivers the mighty and righteous.

וּבְבִרְכָתִי תְנַעֲנַע לִי רֹאשׁ. וְאוֹתָהּ קַח
לְךָ כִּבְשָׂמִים רֹאשׁ: יֶעֱרַב נָא שִׂיחִי
עָלֶיךָ. כִּי נַפְשִׁי תַעֲרוֹג אֵלֶיךָ:

And for my blessing please nod Your head, apply it to Your head like a perfume. May my words be sweet before You; it is for You my soul thirsts.

104. Refreshing our Songs

ר' דוד קמחי (רד"ק), פירוש על תהלים לג, ג / David Kimhi (Radak, b. 1160, France), Commentary on Psalms 33:3

"שירו לו שיר חדש" (תהילים לג, ג).
חדשו לו שיר תמיד. היטיבו נגן
בתרועה, בפה וביד השתדלו לרנן לו:

"Sing a new song to God" (Psalms 33:3): refresh the melody to the divine, always. Make a beautiful *nigun* that calls out, with your mouth and with your hand try to make joyous music to God.

105. Instruments Awaken the Soul of Wisdom…

ר' דוד קמחי (רד"ק) על תהלים לג, ב / David Kimhi on Psalms 33:2

(תהלים לג, ב) "הודו לה' בכנור", כי
כלי הניגון מעוררים הנפש החחכמה
ועוזרים אותה.

"Praise God with a harp" (Psalms 33:2)—For musical instruments awaken and assist the spirit of wisdom.

106. Prayerful Song is a Ladder

ר' יעקב בן אשר, בעל הטורים על בראשית כח, יב / Jacob ben Asher (d. ca. 1340, Germany), Ba'al HaTurim, on Genesis 28:12

סולם. בגימטריא קול, שקול תפלת
הצדיקים הוא סלם למלאכים לעלות
בו. וכן עלה המלאך בלהב. הקרבן
והתפלה היא העבודה. לכך כל
מי שמתכוין בתפלתו הסלם שלם
בשליבותיו ויכולים לעלות בו.

"Ladder" (*sulam*) has the numerical equivalence (*gematria*) as "voice" (*kol*), since the sound of the prayers of the righteous is a ladder for angels to ascend. Similarly, an angel would climb the flame of a sacrifice, and prayer is [today's] service. Thus, when someone is focused in their prayer, the ladder has a complete set of rungs, and one can climb it.

107. The Bible's Ten Greatest Hits, According to the Ba'al HaTurim

ספר החינוך, מצוה שפב / *Jacob ben Asher, Ba'al HaTurim, on Exodus 15:1*

"יָשִׁיר". י' שִׁיר. שיו"ד שירות יש.
ים, באר (במדבר כא, יז). האזינו
(דברים לב, א). יהושע (י, יב). דבורה
(שופטים ה, א). חנה (ש"א ב, א). דוד
(תהלים יח, א). שלמה (תהלים ל, א).
חזקיה (ישעיה לח, י) ושירה לעתיד
(ישעיה מב, י).

"Sang" (yashir). Ten songs (yod[2] shir). That is, there are ten songs [in the Bible]. [At the:] [Reed] Sea, well (Numbers 21:17), [Moses' farewell song] Ha'azinu (Deuteronomy 32:1), [those of] Joshua (10:12), Deborah (Judges 5:1), Hannah (1 Samuel 2:1), David (Psalms 18:1), Solomon (Psalms 30:1), Hezekiah (Isaiah 38:10), and the song of the future (Isaiah 42:10).

108. Trumpets, and Entering Spiritual Space

ר' יעקב בן אשר, בעל הטורים על שמות טו, א / *Sefer HaHinukh (Anonymous, 13th c.),* Commandment #384

לתקוע בחצוצרות במקדש בכל יום
בהקריב כל קרבן, וכמו כן בשעת
הצרות...

[The 384th commandment is...] To blow the trumpets in the Sanctuary, every day, when each sacrifice is offered, and similarly in times of suffering...

(continued)

---

[2] In *gematria* (Jewish numerology) the letter *yod* equals 10.

From the roots of the commandment: since, at the time of the sacrifice, it was essential for [the priests] to intend their minds, beautifully, in that matter, as it is known that [a priest] is disqualified with certain thoughts. In addition, the sacrifice itself needed complete intentionality, before the Sovereign of All, Who commanded us [to do] it.

משרשי המצוה, לפי שבשעת הקרבן היו צריכין לכוון דעתם יפה בענינו כמו שידוע שהוא נפסל במחשבות ידועות, וגם כן צריך הקרבן כוונה שלמה לפני אדון הכל שציונו עליו,

Similarly, during a time of pain, a person really must intend in supplicating before his Creator, to manifest compassion for him and save him from his suffering. Thus, we are commanded in the blowing of the trumpets in these times.

וגם כן בעת הצרה צריך האדם כיוון גדול בהתחננו לפי בוראו שירחם עליו ויצילהו מצרתו, ולכן נצטוו בתקיעת החצוצרות בעתים אלה.

Since people, due to their material nature, greatly need to be woken up to [attend to] things—for their nature, without awakening, is to be still as if asleep—and nothing awakens one like the sound of song. This is known. And all the more so the sound of trumpets, which have the loudest sound of all musical instruments.

לפי שהאדם מהיותו בעל חומר צריך התעוררות גדול אל הדברים, כי הטבע מבלי מעיר יעמוד כישן, ואין דבר יעוררהו כמו קולות הנגון, ידוע הדבר, וכל שכן קול החצוצרות שהוא הקול הגדול שבכל כלי ניגון.

(continued)

ועוד יש תועלת נמצא בקול
החצוצרות לפי הדומה, מלבד
ההתעוררות אל הכוונה, כי בכח
הקולות יסיר האדם מלבו מחשבת
שאר עסקי העולם ולא יתן לב
באותה שעה כי אם בדבר הקרבן,
ומה אאריך וידוע זה לכל אשר הטה
אוזן לשמוע חצוצרות וקול שופר
בכוונה.

Additionally, there is a benefit found in the trumpets' sound, besides the awakening towards intentionality, for in the power of the sounds, a person will banish from his heart all thoughts regarding the rest of the world and its matters, and will not give his mind over to anything at that time save the sacrifice. But why should I go on, when it is known to any who incline their ear to listen to the trumpet and shofar, with intention.

109. The Complete Wisdom of Music

אברבנאל על שמואל א א, טז / *Abarbanel (1437–1508), on 1 Samuel 1:16*

"יודע לנגן", רוצה לומר שהיה יודע
חכמת הניגון בשלמות, ושהיה שלם
לא לבד בפעל כי אם גם בחכמת
המוז"יקא, וזהו שאמר יודע לנגן...

"Who knows how to sing", that is to say, one who knew the science of song, in completion, who was complete not only in practice but also in the study of music. This is what it means when it speaks of one who knows how to sing

110. *P'sukei D'Zimrah* with a Partner, for Added Safety

ר' חיים בן בצלאל, ספר החיים, ספר סליחה ומחילה, פרק ה, דף קפה / *Hayyim ben Betzalel*

(1530–1588), Sefer HaHayyim, Sefer Selihah uMehilah, ch 5, p. 185

ואנו נוהגים שאין לומר פסוקי דזמרה רק בשנים שזה אומר פסוק אחד וזה אומר פסוק אחד והטעם לפי שעיקר לשון של זמירות הוא מלשון 'וכרמך (ואת) לא תזמר' לפי שהוא מזמר וכורת כל מיני משחיתים הבאים לקטרג על התפלה ע"י הפסוקים הללו לכך לא יאמר אותם ביחידי שמא יבא לידי סכנה. אבל שנים רואים ואינם נזקים.

Our custom is not to say *p'sukei d'zimrah* (verses of song)[3] unless there are [at least] two, one to say this verse, and the other to say the next. The reason [for this custom] is that the essence of the word "songs" (*z'mirot*) is from the [Torah's] words, "And your vineyard, you shall not prune (*tizmor*) [during the Sabbatical year]" (Leviticus 25:4), since one prunes and cuts away all kinds of destructive forces which come to denounce your prayer, by means of these verses. Therefore, one should not say them alone, lest one come to peril. But two can see and are not harmed.

111. Singing Fiery Love Songs to the Holy One

אלעזר אזכרי, ספר חרדים, מצוות לא תעשה ז, נו-נז / *Elazar Azikri* (1533–1600), Sefer

Haredim, "Negative Commandments," 7:56–57[4]

מצות ואהבת את ה' אלהיך שרשה ועיקרה וענפיה...

The commandment "Love YHVH your God" has roots, a core, and branches…

(*continued*)

---

[3] The introductory service in morning prayers.

[4] Azikri is the author of the mystical love song, *Yedid Nefesh*, the first hymn of *Kabbalat Shabbat*. From the selection that follows, in the original source, of other compositions, it seems that the writing of new devotional liturgy was a common practice for him and his partners.

One of its precious branches is when a lover sings, out of the burning desire, a love song before God.

אחד מן הענפים היקרים שבהתלהבות החשק ישיר האוהב שיר ידידות לפניו

So, I present you with a selection of love songs that we have joyfully sung in the community of attending [mystical] comrades.[5] A [song of] pleading, [composed] to fit the tune[6] of "I Will Praise You, God of All Souls"[7] or "Your Gates Open at My Knock."[8] It is in alphabetical order [as follows:]:

לכן אשים לפניך קצת שירי אהבה אשר שרנו בשמחה בחברת חברים מקשיבים. בקשה לחן אגדל[ך] "אלהי כל נשמה" או לחן "שעריך בדפקי יה" [פתחה] והוא על סדר אלפנא ביתא:

"I sing a song before my Creator, in fear. With solemnity, I garb myself in trembling-clothing."[9]

אומר שירה לפני יוצרי באימה. בכובד ראש ואלביש סות חרדה...

---

[5] Here, Azikri refers to the circles of kabbalists living in Safed, in the sixteenth and seventeenth centuries.

[6] Perhaps "tune" (לחן) might have referred to the *maqam*, or mode, of the song.

[7] A *piyut* by medieval commentator, philosopher, and poet Abraham ibn Ezra (1089–1167).

[8] A *piyut* composed by medieval poet and philosopher Solomon ibn Gabirol (c.1021–c.1050).

[9] This poem then continues. See *Sefer Haredim* for the rest.

Mystical

112. Tree-Song Invites to Torah

זוהר א, ז. / *Zohar I:7a*

אזלו, מטו לחד טורא, והוה נטי
שמשא, שרו ענפין דאילנא דטורא
לאקשא דא בדא, ואמרי שירתא, עד
דהוו אזלי, שמעו חד קלא תקיפא
דהוה אמר, בני אלהין קדישין, אינון
דאתבדרו ביני חייא דהאי עלמא,
אינון בוצינין בני מתיבתא, אתכנשו
לדוכתייכו לאשתעשעא במאריכון
באורייתא...

They walked and reached a mountain, as the sun was setting. The branches of the trees on the mountain began to hit one another, singing a song. As they went, they heard one strong voice, saying, "Holy children of the Divine, scattered among the living of this world, lanterns, pupils of the academy, enter your places to delight with your Lord in Torah!"...

113. Melodies Lead the Letters, Like King Leads His Army

זוהר א, טו: / *Zohar I:15b*

(דניאל יב, ג) "והמשכילים יזהירו",
כגוונא דתנועי (נ"א, דטעמי) דמנגני,
ובנגונא דלהון אזלין אבתרייהו אתוון
ונקודי ומתנענען אבתרייהו, כחיילין
בתר מלכיהון, גופא אתוון, ורוחא
נקודי, כלהו נטלי במטלניהון בתר
תנועי (נ"א, טעמי) וקיימי בקיומייהו,
כד נגונא דטעמי נטיל, נטלי אתוון
ונקודי אבתרייהו, כד איהו פסיק
אינון לא נטלין וקיימי בקיומייהו.

"And the enlightened will shine" (Daniel 12:3), like music's movements (*or*: notes). The letters [of the Torah and vowels] follow their melody, oscillating, like soldiers after their king. The letters are body, the vowels are spirit. Their motions follow the movements (*or*: notes) and stand in place. When a melody of Torah notes moves, the letters and vowels follow. When it pauses, they cease and stand in place.

114. Cows Sing When Carrying Torah

זוהר א, קכג.-קכב: / *Zohar I:123a–123b*

רבי יוסי פתח ואמר, (תהלים צח, א) "מזמור שירו לה' שיר חדש כי נפלאות עשה, הושיעה לו ימינו וזרוע קדשו", האי קרא אוקמוהו חבריא דפרות אמרוה, כמה דכתיב (שמואל א ו, יב) "וישרנה הפרות בדרך", מאי וישרנה, דהוו אמרי שירתא חדתא, ומאי שירה? אמרו מזמור שירו לה' שיר חדש כי נפלאות עשה. הכא אית לאסתכלא, דכל מה דברא קב"ה בעלמא כולהו אמרי תושבחן ושירתא קמיה, בין לעילא בין לתתא. ואי תימא דאינהו מגרמייהו אמרי שירתא דא, הכי הוא ודאי, דרזא עלאה איהו, אבל הני ארונא הוה על גבייהו, וכיון דארונא אשתקיל עליהו ושויוה לעילא, אינון שרירו שירתא, דהא כיון דאתנטיל מנייהו ארונא הוו געאן כאורח שאר פרות דעלמא, ולא אמרו שירתא. וודאי ארונא דעל גבייהו עביד לון לזמרא מזמור הא אוקימנא ואתמר...

Rabbi Yosi opened and said, "A song: sing to God a new song, for God has done wonders; whose right hand and holy arm saves" (Psalms 98:1). The fellows have established this verse as speaking about cows, as it is written, "The cows walked straight (*vayisharnah*) on the path" (1 Samuel 6:12). What does "walked straight" mean? That they sang a new song (*shirta*). And which song? They sang, "Sing to God a new song, for God has done wonders!" There is something to contemplate here, since all in the world that the Holy Blessed One has created sings praises and songs before Him, above and below. And if you were to say that they sang this song from themselves, what is true is that it is a great secret. But the Ark was on their backs, and when the Ark weighed down on them, and they were weighed out above (*fig.* "found worthy"), they sang a song, and when the Ark was lifted off of them, they mooed like any other cow in the world, not singing a song. Truly, the Ark on their backs made them to chant a hymn, as is established and declared..

115. Levites "Grasp" Torah

(ירמיה ב, ח) "ותופשי התורה" - מאן אינון תופשי התורה. וכי כהני לאו תופשי התורה נינהו. אלא אלין אינון ליואי דתפשי בכנורות דאתין מסטרא דאורייתא. ואתיהיבת מסטרא דלהון אורייתא.

"And those who take up the Torah" (Jeremiah 2:8)—Who are these, who "take up the Torah"? It is not the priests who take up the Torah.[1] No, it is the Levites who take up harps, which come from the side of the Torah, bringing others from the side that is not the Torah.

116. Holy of Holies: Silence to Song

וקטרא דדהבא זקפא ברגליה. נטיל ג' פסיען וכלהו קיימין בקיומייהו ולא נטלין בתריה נטיל ג' פסיען אחרן אסחר לדוכתיה. נטיל ג' פסיען אסתים עיינין ואתקשר לעילא. עאל לאתר דעאל שמע קול גדפי דכרוביא מזמרין ואקישן גדפין פרישאן לעילא

A golden cord is tied to the leg [of the High Priest].[2] He takes three steps, and all stand in their station and do not follow him. He takes another three steps and turns to his own place. He takes [a final] three steps, closes his eyes, and is connected above. He enters where one enters and hears the sound of the cherubs' wings, singing and beating their wings, stretched out above.

(continued)

---

[1] Earlier in the passage, the priests are identified as those who offer holy words to God. The physical work is left to the Levites.

[2] In kabbalistic symbolism, the priest, as a functionary who facilitates cleansing of sin, is seen as connected to the *sefirah* (divine aspect) of *hesed* (love).

הוה אקטיר קטורת משתככא קול
גדפייהו ובלחישו אתדבקן. אי כהנא
זכי דהא לעילא בחידו אשתכח.
אוף הכא בההיא שעתא נפיק רעוא
דנהורא מתבסמא מריחין דטורי
אפרסמונא דכייא דלעילא ואזלא בכל
ההוא אתר אעיל ריחא בתרי נוקבי
דחוטמיה ואתיישבא לבא כדין כלא
הוא בלחישו ופטרא לא אשתכח תמן.
פתח כהנא פומיה בצלותא ברעותא
בחדוותא וצלי צלותיה. בתר דסיים
זקפין כרובייא כמלקדמין גדפייהו
ומזמרין כדין ידע כהנא דרעותא הוו
ועידן חדוותא לכלא.

When he offers the incense, the sound of the wings fades, and they cleave together in silence. If the priest is pure, and joy is found above, then here, too, at that moment, shines a ray of light, perfumed with the scent of the heavenly mountains of pure balsam, and infuses the entire space. The scent enters his two nostrils and, and his heart is soothed. All is silent, and there is no opening [for the Other Side]. The priest, with desire and ecstasy, opens his mouth in devotion, offering his prayers. When he finishes, the cherubs extend their wings as before and sing. Then the priest knows that it has been accepted, and there is jubilation for all.

117. Four-Part Song Raises Israel from Exile

תקוני זוהר,הקדמה, ג. / *Tikkunei Zohar, Introduction, 3a*

דאינון שיר פשוט ודא י'. שיר כפול
ודא יק. שיר משולש ודא יקו. שיר
מרובע ודא יקוק. בשמא דיקוק סלקא
צלותא דאיהי שכינתא. אורייתא
בנגונא שכינתא בנגונא.

This is a simple song, a *yod*. A doubled song is *yod-hey*. A trebled song is *yod-hey-vav*. A quadrupled song is *yod-hey-vav-hey*. With the Name *yod-hey-vav-hey*, the prayer of the *Shekhinah* ascends. A Torah in song, the *Shekhinah* in song.

(continued)

ישראל סלקין מגו גלותא בנגונא.
הדא הוא דכתיב (שמות טו, א) "אז
ישיר משה ובני ישראל את השירה
הזאת לה'"

Israel will arise from exile with a song. Thus is it written, "Then, Moses and the Children of Israel will sing this song for God…" (Exodus 15:1).

118. Tears and Song: Keys to Divine Palaces

תיקוני זוהר, תיקון חד סר, כו: / *Tikkunei Zohar, Tikkun 11, 26b*

דאית היכלא דדמעה, דלית לה רשו
למפתח אלא בדמעה, ואית היכלא
דנגונא, דלית לה רשו למפתח אלא
בנגונא, ובגין דא דוד מתקרב לההוא
היכלא בנגונא, הדא הוא דכתיב
(שמואל ב ג, טו) "והיה כנגן המנגן",
ואית היכלא דנהורא, דלא מתפתחא
אלא לבר נש דהוה מתעסק בנהורא
דאורייתא:

There is a palace of tears, to which no one can gain entrance except through crying, and there is a palace of song that can be entered only through song. Because of this, David was drawn closest to the palace of song, as it was written, "Now, find a musician, [and when they play, the hand of God will rest on me]" (2 Samuel 3:15). There is also a palace of light that only opens for one who is absorbed in the light of the Torah.

119. World Was Created to Sing to Creator

זוהר חדש, פרשת בראשית, דף רצח / *Zohar Hadash, Bereishit p. 298*

בְּרֵאשִׁית, רַבִּי אֶלְעָזָר פְּתַח, (תהלים
קכ, א) "שִׁיר הַמַּעֲלוֹת אֶל ה' בַּצָּרָתָה
לִי קָרָאתִי וַיַּעֲנֵנִי". שִׁירִים תְּאֵבִים
בָּרָא הַקָּדוֹשׁ בָּרוּךְ הוּא בִּבְרִיאַת שָׁמַיִם
וָאָרֶץ, כְּדֵי לְהַלְּלוֹ וּלְשַׁבְּחוֹ, שֶׁהוּא
יוֹצֵר הַכֹּל.

Bereishit: Rabbi Elazar opened, "'A song of ascents, I called out to God in my pain, and He answered me' (Psalms 120:1). 'Desiring songs' (*shirim t'eivim*) did the Holy Blessed One create, whilst creating the heavens and the earth, to praise and exalt Him, the Maker of all.   *(continued)*

הַשָּׁמַיִם אוֹמְרִים שִׁירָה לְפָנָיו, שֶׁנֶּאֱמַר (תהלים יט, ב) הַשָּׁמַיִם מְסַפְּרִים כְּבוֹד אֵל, וְהָאָרֶץ אוֹמֶרֶת שִׁירָה, שֶׁנֶּאֱמַר (שם צו, א) "שִׁירוּ לַה' כָּל הָאָרֶץ".

The heavens sing before Him, as it is said, 'The heavens tell of God's glory' (Psalms 19:2), and the earth sings its song, as it is said, 'Sing to God, all the earth!' (Psalms 96:1)

וְעוֹד, שֶׁכָּל הָעוֹלָם תָּאֵבִים וּשְׂמֵחִים לְפָאֵר לְיוֹצְרָם, בַּחֲזוֹתָם נִפְלְאוֹתָיו בַּשָּׁמַיִם וּבָאָרֶץ, וְזֶהוּ בְּרֵאשִׁית. עַיֵּין בָּאוֹתִיוֹת וְתִרְאֶה, שִׁי"ר תָּא"ב. כְּלוֹמַר, תָּא"ב לֵאמֹר שִׁי"ר, עַל נִפְלְאוֹתָיו בַּשָּׁמַיִם וּבָאָרֶץ...

"And more: the whole world wants to sing, exults in singing to its Maker, in witnessing God's wonders in the heavens and earth. This is Bereishit, that is to say, it wants (*ta'eiv*) to sing (*sing*) of God's wonders in the heavens and earth."

120. Instrumentalists Direct Hearts Towards Divine

ר' יצחק בן יעקב הכהן, מאמר על האצילות השמאלית / *Isaac ben Jacob HaKohen (13th c., Castille), Treatise on the Left Emanation*[3]

כהן גדול בקדושה וטהרה ביראה וברעדה יודע לכוין כונה שלימה בכל אצילות ואצילות חיצוניים ופנימיים ומשפיע בסוד שרפי קדש ומעלתו כפי הרחקתו וכפי הקרבתו ומתעורר כחו בנועם השיר והתפלה הזכה.

The High Priest, in holiness and purity, fear and trembling, knows how to reach complete intentionality with each and every emanation, inner and outer, and can influence the flow in the secret of the holy Seraphim. His position [with the Divine] accords with his distance or closeness, and his power is awakened with the beauty of song and the purity of prayer.   (*continued*)

---

[3] Retranslated from an article by Moshe Idel, "Conceptualizations of Music in Jewish Mysticism," p. 163.

So do the [Levite] musicians, according to their position and ability, direct their fingers to the hollows and strings of their instruments, awakening a song and a melody, directing their hearts to the Omnipresent. Thus, blessing is aroused, and the *Shekhinah* rests on them, each person according to their work and reach.

וגם המשוררים כפי מעלתם והשגתם מכוונים באצבעותיהם בנקבי הכנורות והנימין המעוררים השיר והניגון מכוונים לבם למקום ואז הברכה מתעוררת והשכינה שורה עליהם איש כפי עבודתו וכפי השגתו

121. God Plays Us Like a Harp

אברהם אבולעפיה, מפתח הרעיון / *Abraham Abulafia[4] (b. 1240, Spain), Mafte'ah HaR'ayon[5]*

It is known that in a hollowed out or pierced space, a sound is heard much more strongly because of the spiritual atmosphere that has entered there, like a harp or other such instruments, which generate sound without any speech, like drafty hallways on high floors, or caverns, or mountains, or bathhouses, or ramshackle houses.

וידוע שהמקום החלול או המנוקב, הקול נשמע בו יותר חזק מפני האויר הרוחני הנכנס בו כמו הכנור והדומים להם מכלי המולידים קול בלא דיבור כלל וכן האצלות העליות הגבוהות והמערות וההרים והמרחצאות והבתים החרבות וכיוצא בהן.

(continued)

[4] Abulafia propounded a version of Jewish mysticism that centralized the attaining of prophecy and of ecstatic, unitive experiences of the Divine.

[5] Ms Heb e 123 (IMHM 24762), 64b. Also found in: Moshe Idel, "Music and Prophetic Kabbalah," Yuval: Studies of the Jewish Music Research Center Vol. IV, ed. Israel Adler & Bathja Bayer (Jerusalem: Magnes Press, 1982), p. 153 (fn. 13).

אוירם חלול, וראה כי נולד מהן
ג"כ קול כקול המדבר ומזה הסוד
תבין מהענין "משה ידבר והאלהים
יעננו בקול" בקולו של משה
שתדע שגוף האדם כלו נקבים נקבים
חלולים חלולים ומזה תבין איך
השכינה שורה בגוף הנקוב החלול
המוליד הדבור.

Their atmosphere is empty/hollow, and sounds are generated like the voice of one speaking. From this one can understand the secret meaning of "Moses spoke and God answered him with a voice," the echo of Moses' own voice! Know that the human body is all holes and hollows, and from this one can understand how the *Shekhinah* dwells in the pierced and hole-y body that can generate sound.

122. Harmonic Healing: Rebalancing the Organs

אברהם אבולעפיה, גן נעול, כט / *Abraham Abulafia, Gan Na'ul, p. 29*[6]

והעד כנור ונבל שמצרפין קולם
ובצרוף הקולות האזנים שומעות
חילוף ותמורה בחבלי אהבה והיתרים
המוכים ביד ימין וביד שמאל הם
מתנועעים מביאים הטעם המתוק
לאזנים. ומהם עובר הקול אל
הלב ומן הלב אל הטחול והשמחה
מתחדשת בינתיים באמצעות תענוג
חילוף הנגונים.

See, when a lyre and harp combine their sound, combining their voices, the ears hear the fluctuation and interchange in the pangs of love, the strings struck by the right hand or left, vibrating, bring a sweet taste to the ears. From the ears, the sound passes to the heart, and from the heart to the guts and joy is renewed between them, through the pleasure of a melody's fluctuation.

---

[6] In Amnon Gross, ed. (Jerusalem, 1999).

123. The Soul's Native Language

מאיר אבן גבאי, עבודת הקודש, חלק ג - התכלית, פרק י / *Meir ibn Gabbai, (b. 1480, Spain),*
Avodat HaKodesh, part 3, ch. 10

בגין דנשמתא אתגזרת מלעילא
מצרור החיים ורגילה בניגונין ובשיר
של מלאכי השרת, ושיר הגלגלים,
עתה בהיותה בגוף ושומעת ניגון אז
מוצאה נחת רוח, ונהנית כפי מה
שהיתה רגילה בהיותה דבקה ביסודה
בנועם קול הגלגלים ומרבוי ההנאה
והערבות ראויה לשרות עליה רוח
אלהים כפי הנהגתה ביסודה הראשון
עד כאן:

The soul was carved above, from the knot of life, regularly surrounded by the melodies and song of the angels of service, and the song of the cosmos. Now that the soul is in the body, and it hears a melody, it finds ease of spirit, taking pleasure in what it was once regularly surrounded by, cleaving to the bedrock of the melody of the cosmic voice. From this great pleasure and sweetness, it is fitting for the spirit of God to rest on it, because of its primordial comportment.

124. All Prophets Needed Music, Except Moses

מאיר אבן גבאי, עבודת הקודש, חלק ד - סתרי תורה, פרק כג / *Meir ibn Gabbai, Avodat*
HaKodesh, part 4, ch. 23

לא הוצרך כל ימיו עליו השלום
לשום התעוררות ממיני הניגונים
להשרות עליו רוח נבואה כי לא
נסתלק מעליו כלל ותמיד היה מוכן
ועומד אין לו מונע מצד עצמו
כלל, לפי שאין בכחו למעלה שום
הסתלקות רוח ושפע אורה ולזה היה
בדוגמא ההיא,

All his days, [Moses] never required any stimulation from any kind of *nigun* (melody) to invoke the spirit of prophecy, for it never withdrew from him at all, always at the ready, from his side, never refraining at all, as, in his supernal power, there is no withdrawal of spirit or the flow of [divine] light, and this was his paradigm.

(continued)

מה שאין כן בשאר הנביאים ע"ה
שיצטרכו למיני הניגון לעורר עליהם
הרוח ולהשרות עליהם הנבואה וכמו
שכתוב (שמואל א י, ה) "ופגעת חבל
נביאים ירדים מהבמה ולפניהם נבל
ותף וחליל וכנור והמה מתנבאים",
וכתיב (מלכים ב ג, טו) "ועתה קחו
לי מנגן והיה כנגן המנגן ותהי עליו
יד ה'":

This was not the case with the rest of the prophets, peace be upon them, who needed *nigunim* (melodies) to awaken the spirit and invoke prophecy upon them, as it is written, "You will encounter a band of prophets descending from the high place, before them a lute, drum, and flute, and harp, and they will be prophesying" (1 Samuel 10:5) and, "Now, get me a musician, and as he plays a melody, the hand of God will be on him" (2 Kings 3:15).

125. Singing to "Fix the Candle"

מאיר אבן גבאי, עבודת הקודש, חלק ד, פרק כד / *Meir ibn Gabbai, Avodat HaKodesh, part 4, ch. 24*

וכתיב (תהלים ל, יג) "למען יזמרך
כבוד ולא ידום ה' אלהי לעולם
אודך." אמר דוד למען יזמר וישורר
לך הכבוד סוד הכלה, על כן אודך אני
לעולם בלי הפסק כדי שגם הכבוד
למעלה לא ידום.

It is written, "so my heart will sing to you and not be silent, oh! YHVH, my God, I will praise you forever" (Psalms 30:13). David spoke so he could croon and sing to You, the Glory, the secret of the Bride. "I will praise You forever without cessation so that the Glory above will not be silent either."

(continued)

"What will be aroused above accords with what I arouse below, as it is written, 'Awake, my glory! Awake, lyre and harp! I will awake the dawn'" (Psalms 57:9), which is the secret of the harp of David's that played itself.

In the chapter "From When?"[7] it says that a harp was suspended above David's bed, and when midnight struck, a northern wind would blow and [the harp] would start to play." Its secret is that it is the community of Israel[8] that sings, and She is the harp of David. [The Hebrew word for "harp" (*kinor*, כנור) can be broken into] *kaf-vav* (twenty-six)[9] and *nun-reish* (ner, lamp), a secret that forever burns and sways to unite above. The blue light in the flame yearns and sways upward to fuse with white light, and when it is integrated and united one in another, behold it becomes complete, the union of the Bride with her Beloved from the sweetness of the song.

(continued)

כי כפי מה שאני מעורר למטה
יתעורר למעלה, וכתיב (תהלים נז, ט)
"עורה כבודי עורה הנבל וכנור אעירה
שחר", והוא סוד כנור דוד המנגן
מאליו:

ובפרק מאימתי כנור היה תלוי
למעלה ממטתו של דוד, וכיון שהגיע
חצות לילה רוח צפונית מנשבת בו
והיה מנגן מאליו, והסוד על כנסת
ישראל שהיא המשוררת והיא כנור
דוד כנור כ"ו נ"ר היא סוד הדולקת
ומתנועעת תמיד להתייחד למעלה
אור התכלת שבנר משתוקק ומתנועע
להתחבר למעלה עם האור הלבן,
וכשנכלל ומתיחד זה בזה הרי נעשה
ונשלם כנ"ור ייחוד הכלה עם דודה
מתוך נועם שיריה

---

7 The first chapter of Masechet Berakhot, and the entire Talmud.

8 This is a phrase that means the *Shekhinah*. The whole of the community of Israel is seen as an earthly correlate to God's presence.

9 This number corresponds to the numerical value of the four letter name of God, YHVH.

ולזה אינה נותנת דמי לה (תהלים
פג, ב) "אלהים אל דמי לך אל תחרש
ואל תשקוט" והתעוררות השמחה
בא אליו מרוח צפון בחצות לילה
בסוד (שיר השירים ב, ו) "שמאלו
תחת לראשי" והוא מנגן מאליו
בהתעוררות ההוא, ודוד שהוא
דוגמתה למטה אמר חצות לילה
(תהלים קיט, סב) "אקום להודות לך",
והכל כדי לעורר עליה רוח ממרום
ולבער כל מיני חוח וקוצים מסביב
הכרם.

This is not available to one who is silent. "Don't be silent, God. Don't be mute, and don't be quiet, God" (Psalms 83:2). The awakening of joy comes upon one from the North wind[10] at midnight, in the secret of "His right hand[11] is under my head" (Song of Songs 2:6), and [the harp] plays in this awakening, and David, who is the [*Shekhinah*, who is the Harp's] paradigm below, at midnight says, "I rise to praise you" (Psalms 119:62). All is in order to awaken upon Her a spirit from the heights and to burn up all kinds of prickles and thorns from around the vineyard.

כי דוד אין לו חיים מעצמו זולת מה
שהניח לו אדם הראשון סוד נעלם,
ולזה צריך לעורר בכל מיני ניגון
להמשיך רוח הקדש וחיים ממקור
החיים למדתו,

For David's life was not his own but was rather the secret concealed and left to him by the Primordial Adam. Towards this, he had to awaken all kinds of *nigunim*/melodies to draw down the spirit of holiness and life from the Source of Life to his own measure.

(*continued*)

---

[10] The direction north corresponds to the *sefirah* of *gevurah*, which means strength and refers to God's aspect of judgment.

[11] The right side, however, corresponds to the *sefirah* of *hesed*, Divine love. If one's orientation faces east, then the right side is south (*hesed*), and the left side is north (*gevurah*). When they come together and join as one, what results is balance. In Kabbalah, unity is not a single element, alone, but rather the joining of opposites in harmony.

So, the top quality of a musician is if they know how to awaken voice and breath and speech and to draw down Divine desire to one's world, and how to burn up all wicked spirits from there.

ועל זה ראש מעלותיו יודע נגן לעורר קול ורוח ודבור ולהמשיך הרצון לעולמו ולבער כל רוח רעה משם,

This is how he would play before Saul, turning away the negative spirit that terrorized him. For when David's harp began to play through the secret of arousal, which comes from the north side, and the beloved with shining eyes craves to come to Her, saying to Her, "Let me hear Your voice, for Your voice is sweet…" (Song of Songs 2:14). It sweetens the two lovers in the secret of their solitude.

ולזה היה מנגן לפני שאול וסר מעליו הרוח הרעה ההיא המבעתתו, כי בהיות כנור דוד מנגן מאליו בסוד ההתעוררות ההוא הבא אליו מצד צפון והידיד אור עיניה משתוקק ובא אליה, ואומר לה (שיר השירים ב, יד) "השמיעני את קולך כי קולך ערב ממתיקים" השני דודים סוד לבדם

Behold those notorious kings, who ruled the land of Edom,[12] passed away. "[A heart knows the bitterness of its spirit,] so no stranger can be involved with its joy" (Proverbs 14:10). This is the exemplum of David below, a knowing musician, specifically knowing how to arouse the holy spirit and destroy the spirit of negativity.

הנה המלכים אשר נועדו ומלכו בארץ אדום עברו (משלי יד, י) "ובשמחתם לא יתערב זר", ודוגמא זו דוד למטה נגן יודע ודאי לעורר רוח הקדש ולבער רוח רעה,

(continued)

---

[12] These seven mythic kings first appear in Genesis 36:31, who ruled before the advent of Israel's monarchy. In the Zohar's Idra Rabba, these kings are understood as primordial sources of judgment, signifying God's abandoned first attempt to create the cosmos strictly through the principle of justice.

כי הוא תקן הנר להאיר ומלא אחרי
ה' מלא והשלים ולזה זכה למלכות
הוא ובניו לעולם.

For he repaired the lamp to shine
and fully follow after God, fully and
completely. And if was for this that
he was worthy of the kingship,[13] him
and his descendants, forever and ever.

126. Melodies Ride High Above Letters

ר' משה קורדוברו, פרדס רמונים, שער כט, פרק הר / *Moses Cordovero (b. 1522 Tzfat), Pardes Rimonim, Gate 29, Ch. 5*

האותיות הם נפש והנקודות הרוח
לנפש שהם האותיות. והטעמים
הם נשמה לרוח שבנפש...והנקודות
רוכבות על האותיות כרוכב על הסוס
ולרוב דקותם יותר מהאותיות אינם
חונים בעצם בגשמות האות אלא
בהברתם שהיא אחר הזכרת האות....
והטעם נמצאהו שאינו נוגע באות
כלל אלא רוכב על הניקוד שהיא
הברה נעלמת וצריך האדם לדקדק
בזה מעצמו כי אין בכתיבה לבארו
אלא מפה לפה.

...the letters are the animus (*nefesh*),
the vowels are the spirit (*ru'ah*) to
the animus, which is the letters,
and the accents/cantillation are
the soul (*neshamah*) of the spirit
of the animus...The vowels ride on
the letters, like a rider on a horse,
but their subtlety, which is greater
than the letters', cannot dwell in
the material substance of letters
but rather in their echoes, which
follows the letter's articulation...
The cantillation does not come into
contact with a letter but rather rides
on top of the vowels, the hidden
echo. One must bring great attention
to this from oneself, since it cannot
be explained in writing, only mouth
to mouth.

---

[13] King David is associated with the *sefirah* of *malkhut* (sovereignty), another name for the *Shekhinah*.

HALAKHIC

127. Broken Singing

ר' ישעיהו הורוביץ, שני לוחות הברית, מסכת תמיד, פרק נר מצוה, סו / *Isaiah Horowitz (b. 1565, Prague), Sh'nei Luhot HaBrit, Massekhet Tamid, Perek Ner Mitzvah §66*

מב: אמרו רז"ל (בבא מציאה נט, א): כל השערים ננעלו חוץ משערי דמעה. על כן יעורר אדם עצמו ויראה שתפילתו תהיה בדמעה...ואף אם לפעמים אינו בוכה ממש, יהיה קול דברים שמדבר בתפילתו יהיה בקול נמוך ומשבר כאילו היה בוכה.

Our Rabbis said: all gates are closed except the gates of tears (Talmud Bavli Bava Metzi'a 59a). Thus, one must awaken oneself and see that one's prayers are tearful...Even if sometimes one cannot truly bring oneself to tears, one's voice during prayer, in vocalizing the words, should still be humble and broken, as though one were crying.

128. *Mitzvah* to Sing

בית יוסף על טור, אורח חיים 53 / *Beit Yosef on Tur, Orah Hayyim 53*

מי שקולו ערב מצוה לכבד ה' בהונו: ועל זה נענש נבות:

Whoever has a sweet voice, it is a *mitzvah* to honor God with your gift. This is why Navot was punished.[1]

---

[1] Naboth the Jezreelite (see 1 Kings 21) was the owner of a vineyard desired by King Ahab, who, in partnership with Queen Jezebel, put Naboth to death. See #128.

129. Who is Fit to Be a Prayer Leader?

שולחן ערוך, אורח חיים נג, ד-ה / *Shulhan Arukh, Orah Hayyim 53:4–5*

שליח צבור צריך שיהיה הגון. ואיזהו הגון, שיהא ריקן מעבירות, ושלא יצא עליו שם רע, אפלו בילדותו, ושיהיה ענו ומרצה לעם, ויש לו נעימה, וקולו ערב, ורגיל לקרות תורה נביאים וכתובים:

A prayer leader must be fitting. Who is "fit?" One who is free of sin; who has never had a poor reputation, even in their youth; who is humble and appealing to the community; who has a lyrical and sweet voice; and who regularly reads Torah, Prophets, and Writings.

אם אין מוצאין מי שיהיה בו כל המדות האל, יבחרו הטוב שבצבור בחכמה ובמעשים טובים:

If such a person, with all these characteristics, cannot be found, then choose the wisest and most virtuous member of the community.

הגה: ואם היה כאן עם הארץ זקן, וקולו נעים, והעם חפצים בו, ובן י"ג שנה המבין מה שאומר, ואין קולו נעים, הקטן הוא קודם:

Gloss:[2] If there were an unlearned elder, who had a lovely voice, and people wanted him, but there were also a thirteen year-old child who understands what he says, but his voice is not so nice, the child is preferable.

---

[2] Authored by Moses Isserles, to provide Ashkenazic alternatives to the main body text. Entitled *HaMappah*, the "tablecloth" for Joseph Caro's "set table" (*Shulhan Arukh*).

130. *Shaliah Tzibur:* Focus on the Public's Prayer

שולחן ערוך, אורח חיים נג, יא / *Joseph Caro, Shulhan Arukh, Orah Hayyim 53:11*

שליח ציבור שמאריך בתפלתו כדי
שישמעו קולו ערב...אם הוא מחמת
ששמח בלבו על שנותן הודאה להשם
יתברך בנעימה תבא עליו ברכה...
והוא שיתפלל בכובד ראש ועומד
באימה וביראה...

A communal prayer leader who extends his prayer so others hear his beautiful voice...if it is out of the joy of his heart to praise the Blessed Name with a lovely melody, a blessing should come to him! This is if he prays with seriousness, in fear and awe...

אבל אם מכוין להשמיע קולו ושמח
בקולו הרי זז מגונה...

But if a prayer leader is just trying to have people hear his own voice, and is rejoicing in the mere quality of his voice—this is a travesty.

ומכל מקום כל שמאריך בתפלתו לא
טוב עושה מפני טורח הצבור:

Generally, anyone who extends prayer [i.e. to show off] is not doing something good, since it becomes a burden for the community

131. Limiting the Prohibitions Against Music

שולחן ערוך, אורח חיים תקס, ג / *Shulhan Arukh, Orah Hayyim 560:3*

וכן גזרו שלא לנגן בכלי שיר וכל
מיני זמר וכל משמיעי קול של שיר
לשמח בהם:

It was decreed that one should not play musical instruments or any kind of music, or ever lift one's voice in song in celebration [due to the destruction of the Temple].

(continued)

הגה: ויש אומרים, דווקא מי שרגיל בהם, כגון המלכים שעומדים ושוכבים בכלי שיר או בבית המשתה.

Gloss: Some say that this only applies to those used to [music-making], like kings who sit and stand accompanied by a band, or in a tavern.

ואסור לשומעם, מפני החורבן. ואפילו שיר בפה על היין אסורה, שנאמר: (ישעיה כד, ט) "בשיר לא ישתו יין". וכבר נהגו כל ישראל לומר דברי תשבחות או שיר של הודאות וזכרון חסדי הקדוש ברוך הוא על היין.

It is forbidden to listen to them because of the destruction [of the Temple]. Even a capella music over wine is forbidden, as it was said, "They do not drink wine with song…" (Isaiah 24:9). [However,] all of Israel has the custom of singing praises or songs of gratitude and remembrance of the kindness of the Holy Blessed One over wine.

הגה: וכן לצורך מצווה, כגון בבית חתן וכלה, הכל שרי.

: Similarly, for the sake of a *mitzvah*, as in the home of newlyweds, all is permitted.

132. "Don't Change the Melodies of Your Community"

שולחן ערוך, אורח חיים תריט / *Moses Isserles, Gloss on Shulhan Arukh, Orah Hayyim, 619*

ואל ישנה אדם ממנהג העיר אפילו בניגונים או בפיוטים שאומרים שם (מהרי"ל)

A person should not change the [liturgical] custom of the city, even in the melodies or poems that are used there ([based on ruling of] Maharil)

(continued)

ר' ישראל מאיר הכהן (החפץ
חיים), משנה ברורה, שם: אפילו
בניגונים. כי עי"ז מבלבל דעת הקהל

Israel Meir Kagan (*Hofetz Hayyim*), Mishnah Berurah, commentary there: "Even in the melodies…"—Because, through this, one will confuse the communal consciousness.

133. Symphony of Differences

ר' יחיאל מיכל אפשטיין, ערוך השולחן, חושן משפט, הקדמה / *Yehiel Mikhal Epstein (1829 -1908, Lithuania), Arokh HaShulhan, Hoshen Mishpat, Introduction*

וכל מחלוקת התנאים והאמוראים,
והגאונים והפוסקים באמת, למבין
דבר לאשורו - דברי אלקים חיים
המה, ולכולם יש פנים בהלכה.
ואדרבה: זאת היא תפארת תורתינו
הקדושה והטהורה. וכל התורה כולה
נקראת "שירה", ותפארת השיר היא
כשהקולות משונים זה מזה, וזהו
עיקר הנעימות. ומי שמשוטט בים
התלמוד - יראה נעימות משונות בכל
הקולות המשונות זה מזה.

All the differences between the *Tanna'im, Amora'im, Ge'onim,* and *Poskim*,[3] if we are to really understand the matter truly, are all words of the living God, each is a facet of *halakhah*. On the contrary, that is the beauty of our holy and pure Torah. The entire Torah is called a song, and a song is beautiful when all of its voices differ one from another; this is the essence of its polyphonic pleasantness (*ne'imot*). Anyone who swims about in the sea of the Talmud can see the harmony in all of the voices differing from each other [but yet coexisting].

---

[3] The term *Tanna'im* referes to rabbinic sages who flourished from the first century to the third century CE; *Amora'im* are the sages who followed, until the 5th–6th centuries; *Ge'onim* are authorities around 7th–11th centuries; by *Poskim* he means later medieval rabbinic authorities.

HASIDIC

134. Don't Have Too Much Fun with Music

משנה ברורה, אורח חיים תקס, ג / *Israel Meir Kagan, Mishnah Berurah, Orah Hayyim 560:3*

"[In the home of newlyweds,] all is permitted"—This means [music,] whether a capella or with instruments, even over wine, as long as there is not idle chatter. Still, one should not have too much fun.

הכל שרי - פירוש, בין בפה ובין בכלי ועל היין, רק שלא יהא בה ניבול פה. ומכל מקום אין לשמוח ביותר.

135. Songs Open the Larger World of Mystery

ר' נועם אלימלך מליז'ענסק, נועם אלימלך, הוספות ליקוטי שושנה / *Elimelekh of Lizhensk, (b. 1717, Galicia) No'am Elimelekh, Addenda Likkutei Shoshanah*

"I will open my riddle with a harp" (Psalms 49:5)—This means: with this, too, can I enact my service, that is, with a harp, as above, or with songs and praises can I open another, grander world that is above this plane of existence, which is called "my riddle," for a riddle is a matter too great to hear/understand with ears alone.

(תהלים מט, ה) "אפתח בכינור חידתי", פירוש וגם זאת אפעל בעבודתי באמת שעל ידי הכנור כנ"ל, דהיינו בשירות ותשבחות אני פותח על ידם עוד עולם גדול שהוא למעלה ממדרגה הזאת והוא הנקרא חידתי: כי חידה הוא דבר היותר גדול מדבר שיכול לשמוע באזנים...

136. Singing to Ease Death of Egyptians

שמן הטוב, ער' נתן נטע נ"י קראנענבערג (פיעטרקב, תעס"ה), עמ' 7 / *Shmelke of Nikolsburg (b. 1726, Galicia), as quoted in Shemen haTov, ed. Nosn Nete Cronenberg (Piotrkov, 1905), p. 7*

בש"ס סנהדרין (לט:) ולא קרב זה אל
זה כל הלילה בקשו מלאכי השרת
לומר שירה. אמר הקדוש ברוך הוא
מעשי ידי טובעין בים ואתם אומרים
שירה.

In Sanhedrin (39b), [it says,] "'And no one came close to each other all night…' (Exodus 14:20). [To celebrate the downfall of the Egyptians at the Red Sea,] the ministering angels wanted to sing a song. The Holy Blessed One said [to them], 'The work of My hands are drowning in the sea, and you want to sing a song?!'"

דהיינו שמלאכי השרת בקשו לומר
שירה כדי שישמעו מצרים נעימות
הקול שלהם ויצאו נשמתם...וטעם
הדבר כי בספר דברי שאול, פרשת לך
לך ידוע שיש כח בשיר לעורר כל כך
עד כלות הנפש

The [true reason the] ministering angels wanted to sing was so the Egyptians would hear their sweet voices, and their souls could leave [in peace]…The reason for this [can be found] in *Divrei Sha'ul*,[1] in his commentary on *Lekh Lekha*: it is known that there is power in song to bring so much awakening such that the soul cannot take it.

(continued)

---

[1] A book of Torah commentary by Joseph Saul Nathanson, a nineteenth century Polish rabbi. Though he was not Hasidic himself, he had good relations with Hasidic rabbis, even providing approbations for some of their books.

וכבר כותבי סופרי הקורות שלפעמים
בנסעם על הים שמעו ב"א
שמשוררים בקול נעים להפליא. ואם
לא המלחים שהיו מקישים בתופים
למען לא ישמעו קולם אז היו מתים
מפני המתיקות]

Chroniclers have written about this, that sometimes, when traveling by sea, [sailors] have heard sirens singing with voices of overwhelming beauty, and if the sailors did not bang their drums to drown out the sound, they would die from the sweetness.

אמר הקדוש ברוך הוא מעשי ידי
טובעין בים כלומר שהמצריים טבעו
את מעשי ידי שהם ישראל בים.
דהיינו שהשליכו אותם ליאור. וצריך
אני להפרע מהם מדה כנגד מדה
שיטבעו בים, ואתם אומרים שירה,
היינו אתם רוצים להמיתם בשירה:

The Holy Blessed One said, "The work of My hands are drowning in the sea," meaning, the Egyptians drowned the work of My hands, the Israelites, in the sea, that is, they threw them into the Nile. Thus, I need to punish them measure for measure, so that they drown in the sea, too. "And you are singing a song?!" That is, you want to [subvert My justice and] have them die by a song?

137. Second Singer Makes the Song

ר' פנחס מקורץ, מדרש פנחס, חלק א', צ-צא / *Pinhas of Koretz (b 1728, Russia), Midrash Pinhas, vol. 1 (Lvov, 1872), §90–91*

(צ) אמר שטוב לאדם לישן עם בניו
הקטנים, שהוא בסוד, אתדבקות רוחא
ברוחא, והוא טוב לחלומות.

90. He said that it is good for a person to snuggle with their small children, which [actualizes] the secret meaning of uniting, soul to soul, and this is good for dreams.

(continued)

גם אמר שלפעמים, כשאדם מנגן ואי
אפשר לו להרים קול. וכשבא איש
לעזור ורים את קולו, גם הוא יכול
להרים את קולו, הוא גם כן מסוד:
אתדבקות רוחא ברוחא...

He also said that sometimes, when a person sings, he cannot raise his voice. But when someone comes to help and sings strongly, this in turn gives the first person the ability to raise his own voice [to match]. This is of the secret significance of uniting, soul to soul...

(צא) (משנה אבות א, ו) "וקנה לך
חבר" הוא כי יש סוד זיווגים בפה
והענין כי לפעמים שאדם לומד ואינו
מבין כלל וכשהוא מדבר עם חבר טוב
(וכופל הדברים) הוא בסוד התדבקות
וכו' אזי היא בסוד הלידה ונתרץ כל
הקושיות

91. "And acquire a friend for yourself" (Pirkei Avot 1:6)—There is a mystical secret of coupling by mouth. Sometimes, when a person is studying but does not understand at all, when he speaks with a good friend (and reviews matters), through the secret of cleaving [to another, to God], they partake of the mystical secret of birth, and all their difficulties are solved.

138. Taste of Torah

ר' מנחם נחום מטשערנאבל, מאור עינים, פרשת חקת / *Menahem Nahum of Chernobyl*
(c.1730–1797), Me'or Einayyim, Parshat Chukat

לכך נקרא הטעמים של הנגינות
טעמים מפני שהן עדיין בבחינה
שאפשר להשיג ולתת טעם אף שהם
דבר גבוה

This is why the notes of the [Torah's] melodies are called *te'amim* (tastes, reasons), since they are still within the bounds in which one is able to grasp and provide meaning, even if they are very very.

(continued)

אבל הפנימיות נקרא אי"ן שאין לו
טעם ותפיסה וצריך הלומד לדבק
באור הנשפע מבחינות אי"ן ואז
בודאי מחזירו למוטב מאחר שנדבק
פנימיותיו באור פנימיות התורה
נעשה כסא להשראתו יתברך השורה
בהתורה ושופע בתוכה ואף שצריך
בעת לימודה להבין מה שלומד
ולהטעים בכדי שיבין הטעם. מכל
מקום צריך גם כן להאמור בכדי
שיהא שלימות הגמור...

But their interiority is called *Ayin*
("no-thing"),[2] since it cannot be
grasped and has no reason. Thus,
one learning must cleave to the
flowing light from the aspect of nothing. Then, one will be returned
to the good, since what is inside
you has cleaved to the light inside
the Torah, which becomes a seat in
which the Blessed One is infused,
Who dwells in the Torah and flows
within it. Even one who, while
studying Torah, needs to understand
what one is learning and chants it
in order to understand its reason.
Even so, one must always state that
one does this so that there will be
complete wholeness.

139. "If I Could Sing, I'd…"

אמרי פנחס השלם, עניינים שונים, מעלת הנגינה / *Pinhas Shapiro of Koretz (d. 1790), Imrei
Pinhas, Miscellany, "The Worth of Song"*

ב' הרב בעיר שיש מנגנים יש מוחין
חדשים.

In the Rabbi's words: a city
that has musicians has renewed
consciousness.

(*continued*)

---

[2] This term refers to the infinite source of being that is the most radical description of God
offered by Kabbalah. The infinite (*Ein Sof*) is also called no-thing (*Ayin*) because it transcends
any definition or limit.

If only I could sing, then I would be the downfall of the wicked. For, when the Holy Blessed One flows into this world, they are unable to receive the manifold light, that is, the light of consciousness. Like a stalking wolf, and all other foul creatures, they specifically go about in darkness, because they are blinded by the light. Their downfall comes down to this.

In the Rabbi's words, who abundantly praised the worth of song. "If I were a singer, I would take on traveling from city to city, praying in each and every synagogue." It was also heard in his name, that he said, "If I were a singer, I would not allow You to live up in the heavens. No, You would be forced to live with us, here. It was to God that he said this.

And he said, may his candle shine, in the name of the *siddur* of the Maharil,[3] that the Ari described how lofty the level of a prayer leader who could sing beautifully and become connected with the whole community, because of the song, becoming connected to God, raising everyone to God.   (*continued*)

אם הייתי יכול לזמר בודאי היה מפלה גדולה לרשעים, כי כשממשיכין הקב"ה בזה העולם, והם אינם יכולים לקבל רוב אור וכמדומה שאמר אור המוחין, כמ"ש זאב אורב וכל הדברים טמאים הם הולכים דוקא בחושך והאור הנ"ל מסמא עיניהם, ומחמת זה יש להם מפילה גדולה.

ב' הרב שקילס מאד מעלת הנגינה, ואם הייתי מנגן הייתי מקבל עלי לנסוע מעיר לעיר ולהתפלל בבתי כנסיות. גם שמע בשמו ז"ל שאמר אם הייתי מנגן לא הייתי מניח לדור אותך בעליונים אלא היית מוכרח לדור עמנו בכאן, ולהשי"ת אמר כן.

ואמר הוא נ"י בשם סידור מהרי"ל שהביא מהאר"י, מה שזכה למדרגה עליונה בעבור שהיה ש"ץ והיה מנגן יפה ונתקשרו כל הצבור עמו בעבור הנגינה והוא נתקשר אל השי"ת והעלה את כולם להשי"ת.

---

[3] Judah Leib of Zaklikov, a major disciple of Elimelekh of Lizhensk, the Noam Elimelekh.

אמר לבנו כשיזמר יזמר דברים של
זמירות, כי הקול הוא הוי(ה) הדיבור
הוא אד(ני) והוא יחוד...

He said to his son, that when you
sing the words of a song, the voice is
HaVaYaH,[4] the words are *Adonai*,[5]
and you are the unity.

140. Ascent from One Essence to Another

ר' שניאור זלמן מליאדי, תורה אור על בראשית ד, כ-כא / *Shneur Zalman of Liadi (b. 1745,
Russia), Torah Or on Genesis 4:20–21*

יבל הוא היה אבי יושב אהל ומקנה.
ושם אחיו יובל הוא היה אבי כל
תופש כנור ועוגב.

"Yaval, he was the father of all who
dwelled in tents and had cattle. And
his brother's name was Yuval, who
was the father of all who take up a
harp and pipe" (Genesis 4:20–21).

הנה ארז"ל כל בעלי השיר יוצאין
בשיר כו'. (משנה שבת ה, א)

Our Rabbis, of blessed memory,
said, "[On Shabbat,] all leashed
(*ba'alei hashir*) animals go out on a
leash (*shir*)" (Mishnah Shabbat 5:1).

פי' שכל בחי' העלאה ממהות למהות
כמו מג"ע התחתון לג"ע העליון
וכדומה הוא ע"י השיר שהוא בחי'
בטול היש

This means that any ascent from
one essence to another, like from
the lower Gan Eden[6] to the upper
Gan Eden[7] or similar, is by means
of song (*shir*), which is an aspect
of the nullification of what is (*bitul
ha-yeish*).   (*continued*)

---

[4] The four-letter name of God, referring to the divine masculine.

[5] Referring to the divine feminine, the *Shekhinah*.

[6] This term refers to the *sefirah* of *malkhut* (sovereignty), the divine emanation closest to manifest reality, another name for the *Shekhinah*.

[7] This refers to *binah*, the cosmic Mother, from which all reality flows. Her sharing of a symbolic name with the *Shekhinah* implies their relationship, as Mother and Daughter.

As it is known, one cannot to change from one state of being to another unless one state of being becomes nothing,[8] then it can become something else, with a surplus of blessing. As an allegory, a seed planted in the earth must rot in the ground first and only afterward can sprout and produce many seeds. Similarly, above, for souls and angels to ascend to greater comprehension, they must first attain the state of nullifying being as well as their prior comprehension, and afterward can ascend to greater comprehension. This is an aspect of the central pillar between the lower Gan Eden and the upper, which is the essence of nullification.

This is the meaning of "all leashed animals (*ba'alei shir*) go out" of their prior comprehension and are drawn to ascend above by means of song (*shir*). When sacrifices were offered, there had to be a song as well, since the nature of sacrifice is the ascent, from below to above, of an aromatic fragrance, which needs song, that is, the aspect of nullification, so it can rise.

וכנודע שלא יוכל להתהוות מיש ליש אא"כ נעשה היש תחילה בחי' אין אז יוכל להתהוות ממנו יש אחר בתוס' ברכה. כמשל הגרעין הנזרע בארץ שצריך להיות נרקב בארץ ואח"כ יכול לצמוח מזה הרבה גרעיני'. וכמו"כ למעלה בנשמות ומלאכים כדי שיהיה לו עלייה בתוספת השגה צריך מקודם להיות בבחי' בטול היש והשגה ראשונה שהיה לו ואח"כ יוכל לעלות השגה יותר גדולה וזהו בחי' עמוד שבין ג"ע התחתון לג"ע העליון הוא בחי' בטול כנ"ל

וזהו כל בעלי השיר יוצאין בהשגתם ונמשכים לעלות למעלה ע"י השיר ולכן בשעת הקרבת הקרבן היה צריך להיות ג"כ שיר כי ענין הקרבנות הוא העלאה ממטה למעלה אשה ריח ניחוח וצריך לזה ג"כ בחי' שיר בחי' בטול כנ"ל שיוכל להתעלות...

---

[8] As in note 2 above, this refers to becoming like the No-thing of the Divine Infinite.

...וזהו ענין יובל אבי כל תופש כנור
כו' פי' יובל לשון הולכה שמוביל
וממשיך למעלה ע"י כנור ועוגב בחי'
שיר כנ"ל שע"י השיר הוא העלייה
יוצאין בשיר כו'.

This is the meaning of "Yuval… father of all who take up a harp and pipe…" "Yuval" implies a movement that mobilizes (*movil*) and draws above through the harp and pipe, aspects of music, and it is by means of song that one can go out and up.

141. The Deaf Man and the Divine Dance

משה חיים אפרים מסודילקוב, דגל מחנה אפרים, פרשת יתרו / *Moshe Hayyim Ephraim of Sudylkov (b. 1748, Poland), Degel Mahaneh Efraim, Parshat Yitro*

"וכל העם רואים את הקולות" וגו'
(שמות כ, טו).

"And the entire people saw the sounds…" (Exodus 20:15)

יש לפרש בזה על דרך ששמעתי
משל מן אא"ז זללה"ה שהיה אחד
מנגן בכלי זמר יפה מאוד במתיקות
ועריבות גדול ואותם שהם שומעים
זה לא יכלו להתאפק מגודל
המתיקות והתענוג עד שהיו רוקדים
כמעט עד לתקרה מחמת גודל
התענוג והנעימות והמתיקות וכל מי
שהיה קרוב יותר והיה מקרב עצמו
לשמוע הכלי זמר היה לו ביותר
תענוג והיה רוקד עד מאוד

It is possible to interpret this verse by means of a parable from my sainted grandfather (the Ba'al Shem Tov), whose memory should be a blessing: once, a person played an instrument so beautifully and with such sweetness that those who heard it, due to the sweetness and pleasure of the music, were not able to restrain themselves and almost danced themselves up to the ceiling, because of its great pleasure, delight, and sweetness. Everyone who was nearby and brought themselves closer to hear the instrument had such great pleasure and really began to dance.

In the midst of this, a deaf man entered the room. He could not hear the sweet sound of the musical instrument, but he could see people really dancing, which, to his eyes, looked like they were going insane. He said in his heart, "What is this joy?!" But, in truth, if he were wise and understood that it was due to the great pleasure and delight of the sound of the musical instrument, then he, too, would have danced.

The meaning of the parable is clear, and we can use it to interpret "the entire people saw the sounds." The Blessed Name caused the Divine Light to appear to them, which they apprehended as one. When they witnessed the great joy of the angelic hosts in rapture (Talmud Bavli Shabbat 88b), they understood that it was due to the sweetness and delight of the light of the holy Torah, and they pushed themselves to hear the sound of the Torah even though it was as if they were partially deaf, since they could not hear the sounds.

ובתוך כך בא אחד חרש שאינו שומע כלל הקול של כלי זמר הערב רק ראה שאנשים רוקדים עד מאוד והם בעיניו כמשתגעים ואומר בלבו כי לשמחה מה זו עושה ובאמת אילוהיה הוא חכם וידע והבין שהוא מחמת גודל התענוג והנעימות קול של כלי זמר היה הוא גם כן רוקד שם.

והנמשל מובן, ויש לפרש בזה וכל העם רואים את הקולות היינו שה' יתברך הופיע על כולם כאחד אור אלוהותו שהשיגו יחד כולם כשראו גודל השמחה כי מלאכי צבאות ידודון ידודון וכו' (שבת פ"חב) הבינו שהוא מחמת מתיקות ונעימות אור התורה הקדושה ודחקו עצמם לשמוע קול התורה אף על פי שהיו קצת חרשים מכבר שלא היו שומעים את הקולות

(continued)

הכל נעשו פקחין ועיינין פקוחין היה
להם שהיו רואים החדוה והשמחה
הגדולה הבינו שהוא בודאי את
הקולות היינו נעימות ועריבות הקול
של תורה אף על פי שהם לא השיגו
זה נעימות התורה הבינו על ידי
השמחה שהוא בודאי מגודל נעימות
התורה ולכך דחקו עצמם לשמוע
הקול ממש אולי ישיגו ויבינו נעימות
אור התורה.

They made themselves sharp-sighted, with eyes wide open, so they could see the exuberance and great joy, which really were the sounds, the delight and sweetness of the sound of the Torah, even though they could not apprehend the delight of the Torah itself, they understood, in [witnessing] this joy, that it was surely due to the great delight of the Torah, and therefore pushed themselves to really hear the sound, so that maybe they could apprehend and understand the delight of the Torah's light.

והמשכיל יבין:

The enlightened will understand.

142. Spontaneous Ecstasy

ר' דוב בער שניאורי, האדמו"ר האמצעי, קונטרס ההתפעלות / *Dov Ber Schneuri of Lubavitch (the Mittler Rebbe, 1773–1827), Tract on Ecstasy*

ותחלה יש להבין מהות התפעלו'
הניגון שהוא בחי' התפעלות פתאומי'
דוקא בלתי בחירה ורצון שכלי כלל,
והוא התפעלות מורגשת ובלתי
מורגשת בעצמו מצד שאינה באה
מצד עצמו לכוין לעשות התפעלות
כ"א ממילא ומאליו בלתי נודע לו.

First, we must understand the substance of the *nigun's* ecstasy, a spontaneous ecstasy without the mind's choosing or intention at all. The ecstasy itself is both felt and not felt since it does not come of its own accord in order to wreak/bring about ecstasy but rather immediately, from an unknown cause beyond itself.

(continued)

Since it is as if one does not feel it at all, nor, at that moment, does it become known, ecstasy is insensate in its substance, but still it is felt. This can be understood through an example of spontaneous ecstasy we have observed, when a person, after hearing a piece of good news, in great joy, is brought to ecstasy, or other similar cases. Clearly, this ecstasy is felt in this person's heart, wreaking forceful movements from beyond, resulting in a feeling of satisfaction. This occurred completely without choice or intention, wholly caused from beyond.

A sign of this is when one cannot sense themselves at all, if in ecstasy, feeling it in their heart but knowing nothing of it at all. The truth of this ecstasy is from the fact of the good thing to which one's spirit is connected.

ומפני שזהו כאלו אינו מרגיש ונודע לו כלל באותה שעה ממש זהו הנק' העדר הרגשת עצמו בזה כלל, אבל מ"מ התפעלות מורגשת הוא. ויובן זה ע"ד דוגמא ממה שאנו רואים בהתפעלות פתאומית שאדם מתפעל [בשמחה] רבה בהגיע לו איזה בשורה טובה וכה"ג, שבודאי מורגשת התפעלות זאת בלבו עד שיעשה תנועות חזקות מאליו וממילא והוא הסיפוק בידיו כידוע, והוא בלתי בחירה ורצון כלל וכלל רק ממילא ומאליו מספק,

והוא האות על היות שאיננו מרגיש בעצמו כלל אם מתפעל הגם שמורגש' בלבו אבל כאלו אינו יודע מזה כלל, והוא להיות שההתפעלו' הוא אמיתי' רק מצד עצם הדבר הטוב שנפשו קשור [בו].

143. The Cantor: A Visionary

ר' נחמן מברסלב, ליקוטי מוהר"ן, ג / *Nahman of Breslov (1772–1810, Ukraine), Likkutei Moharan I, 3*

...לכך נקרא המנגן חזן מלשון חזון, היינו לשון נבואה, כי לוקח הנגינה מאתר דנביאים ינקין.

Thus, the cantor is called a *hazzan*, from the language of vision (*hazon*), that is the language of prophecy, because he snatches the song from the place where prophets suckle.[9]

144. Hidden Spirit on David's Harp

ר' נחמן מברסלב, ליקוטי מוהר"ן ח, ט / *Nahman of Breslov, Likkutei Moharan I, 8:9*

רוח צפונית המנשבת בכנור של דוד(ברכות ג' ע"ב)...כנור של דוד היה של חמש נימין, כנגד חמשה חומשי תורה. ורוח צפון שהיתה מנשבת בו, הוא בחי' ורוח אלקים מרחפת על פני המים הנ"ל. כי רוח צפון, הוא בחי' הרוח הצפון בלבו של אדם, שהוא בחי' הרוח חיים.

"A northern wind blew on the harp of David," (Talmud Bavli Berakhot 3b)...David's harp had five strings, like the five books of the Torah. "The North wind blew..." This is associated with/related to "the spirit of God hovered on the face of the waters" (Genesis 1:2). The northern wind (*ru'ah hatzafon*) is the spirit hidden (*ru'ah hatzafun*) in the heart of each person, and this is the spirit of life.

---

[9] The *sefirot* of *netzah* (victory) and *hod* (majesty).

145. Gathering Goodness, Composing *Nigun*

ר' נחמן מברסלב, ליקוטי מוהר"ן נד, ו / *Nahman of Breslov, Likkutei Moharan I, 54:6*

וזה שמנגן ביד על הכלי, הוא מקבץ
ומלקט ביד את הרוח טובה, רוח
נבואה, מתוך עצבות רוח. וצריך
להיות יודע נגן, שידע לקבץ וללקוט
ולמצוא חלקי הרוח אחת לאחת,
כדי לבנות הניגון, היינו השמחה.
היינו לבנות הרוח טובה, רוח נבואה,
שהוא היפך עצבות רוח. כי צריך
לעלות ולירד בידו על הכלי שמנגן,
כדי לכוין לבנות השמחה בשלימות:
וכשהנביא שומע זה הניגון מהיודע
נגן, אזי מקבל ממנו רוח נבואה,
שקיבץ זה בידו מתוך העצבות רוח.
וזה, (שמואל א טז, טז) וניגן בידו
וטוב לך.

One who plays a musical instrument by hand, gathers in, with that hand, and collects a spirit of goodness, a spirit of prophecy, from the midst of a sadness of spirit. One must understand music to gather in, collect, and locate the parts of spirit, one by one, to compose a *nigun* (melody)—and the same goes for the joy—that is, to compose a spirit of goodness, a spirit of prophecy, the opposite of a sadness of spirit. One must bring one's hands up and down on the musical instrument to focus one's attention and compose joy in fulness. When the prophet hears this *nigun* from one who [truly] knows this *nigun*, the prophet receives from them a spirit of prophecy, gathered by hand from the midst of a sadness of spirit. This is [the meaning of] "He plays by hand, and you will be well" (1 Samuel 16:16).

146. The Prayer Leader, the Melody, and Finding the Good in People

ר' נחמן מברסלב, ליקוטי מוהר"ן, רפב / *Nahman of Breslov, Likkutei Moharan I, 282*

דע כי צריך לדון את כל אדם לכף
זכות, ואפילו מי שהוא רשע גמור,
צריך לחפש ולמצוא בו איזה מעט
טוב, שבאותו המעט אינו רשע, ועל
ידי זה שמוצא בו מעט טוב, ודן אותו
לכף זכות, עי"ז מעלה אותו באמת
לכף זכות, ויוכל להשיבו בתשובה...

"Know that you must judge each person with the benefit of the doubt" (Pirkei Avot 1:6). Even with someone [who seems] entirely wicked, you must search out in them and find a tiny bit of good, since in that tiny bit, they are not wicked. And if you can find in them a bit of good, you can judge them with charity, and bring them, truly, to the side of merit, and even bring them to *teshuvah*...

וכן צריך האדם למצוא גם בעצמו...
וכן יחפש וילקט עוד הנקודות טובות,
ועי"ז נעשין נגונים...בחי' מנגן בכלי
זמר, שהוא בחי' שמלקט הרוח
טובה מן הרוח נכא העצבות רוח
ע"ש. [והכלל כי נגינה דקדושה היא
גבוה מאד מאד כידוע, ועיקר הניגון
נעשה, ע"י בירור הטוב מן הרע,
שע"י שמבררין ומלקטין הנקודות
טובות מתוך הרע, עי"ז נעשים נגונים
וזמירות, ע"ש היטב]...

Similarly, each person must find this [goodness] even in oneself... search out and collect other points of goodness, and through this process, they will become *nigunim* (melodies), which is the secret of playing a musical instrument...the essence of plucking good spirit from a depressed spirit, the spirit of sadness. (It is true that the song of holiness is so very high, as is known, and the essence of this *nigun* comes from the elicitation of the good from the bad. It is by eliciting the points of goodness from the bad that *nigunim* and songs come about)...   (continued)

And know that one who can make these *nigunim*, collecting points of goodness that are found within each and every Jew, even the sinners of Israel, it is only this person that can lead a community in prayer. The prayer leader is called a "messenger of the community" (*shaliah tzibur*), which means that they must be sent by the entire community, that they are able to gather in every point of goodness from each member of those praying, each point included within the prayer leader standing and praying with all of this goodness. This is the messenger of the community…

This means judging each person with charity, even the unserious and the wicked, striving to search out and seek to find in everyone points of goodness, from which you can make melodies…

ודע שמי שיכול לעשות אלו הנגונים, דהיינו ללקט הנקודות טובות שנמצא בכל אחד מישראל, אפילו בהפושעי ישראל כנ"ל, הוא יכול להתפלל לפני העמוד, כי המתפלל לפני העמוד, הוא נקרא שליח ציבור, וצריך שיהיה נשלח מכל הציבור, דהיינו שצריך שיקבץ כל נקודה טובה שנמצא בכ"אמה מתפללין, וכל הנקודות טובות יהיו נכללין בו, והוא יעמוד ויתפלל עם כל הטוב הזה, וזהו שליח ציבור ...

דהיינו שיכול לדון את כל אדם לכף זכות, אפילו את הקלים והרשעים, כי משתדל לחפש ולבקש למצוא בכולם נקודות טובות כנ"ל, שעי"ז נעשין נגונים כנ"ל...

147. The Song of the Grasses

ר' נחמן מברסלב, ליקוטי מוהר"ן תנינא, סג / Nahman of Breslov, Likkutei Moharan II, 63

דַּע, כִּי כָל רוֹעֶה וְרוֹעֶה יֵשׁ לוֹ נִגּוּן מְיֻחָד לְפִי הָעֲשָׂבִים וּלְפִי הַמָּקוֹם שֶׁהוּא רוֹעֶה שָׁם, כִּי כָל בְּהֵמָה וּבְהֵמָה יֵשׁ לָהּ עֵשֶׂב מְיֻחָד, שֶׁהִיא צְרִיכָה לְאָכְלוֹ. גַּם אֵינוֹ רוֹעֶה תָּמִיד בְּמָקוֹם אֶחָד.

For each and every shepherd has his own unique *nigun* (melody), according to the blades of grass and the place in which he shepherds, as each kind of animal has its own particular grass, which it needs to eat. Additionally, a shepherd cannot stay in one place forever.

וּלְפִי הָעֲשָׂבִים וְהַמָּקוֹם שֶׁרוֹעֶה שָׁם, כֵּן יֵשׁ לוֹ נִגּוּן. כִּי כָל עֵשֶׂב וָעֵשֶׂב יֵשׁ לוֹ שִׁירָה שֶׁאוֹמֵר, שֶׁזֶּה בְּחִינַת פֶּרֶק שִׁירָה, וּמִשִּׁירַת הָעֲשָׂבִים נַעֲשֶׂה נִגּוּן שֶׁל הָרוֹעֶה. וְזֶה סוֹד מַה שֶׁכָּתוּב (בְּרֵאשִׁית ד, כ-כא): "וַתֵּלֶד עָדָה אֶת יָבָל, הוּא הָיָה אֲבִי יֹשֵׁב אֹהֶל וּמִקְנֶה; וְשֵׁם אָחִיו יוּבָל, הוּא הָיָה אֲבִי כָּל תֹּפֵשׂ כִּנּוֹר וְעוּגָב". כִּי תֵכֶף כְּשֶׁהָיָה בָּעוֹלָם רוֹעֶה מִקְנֶה, הָיָה תֵכֶף כְּלֵי זֶמֶר כַּנַּ"ל.

According to the grass and the place where he shepherds, there is his *nigun*. Each and every blade of grass has its own song that it sings, its aspect of the Song of the World (*Perek Shirah*), and from the song of the grass is made the shepherd's song. This is the secret of what is written, "Ada gave birth to Yaval, who was the father of all who dwelled in tents, with flocks. His brother's name was Yuval, who was the father of those of took up the harp and pipe" (Genesis 4:20–21). As soon as there was, in the world, a shepherd of flocks, there were musical instruments.

וְעַל כֵּן דָּוִד הַמֶּלֶךְ, עָלָיו הַשָּׁלוֹם,
שֶׁהָיָה "יֹדֵעַ נַגֵּן" (שְׁמוּאֵל א טז, יח)
עַל כֵּן הָיָה רוֹעֶה (שָׁם) כַּנַּ"ל. [גַּם
מָצִינוּ בַּאֲבוֹת הָעוֹלָם כֻּלָּם, שֶׁהָיוּ רוֹעֵי
מִקְנֶה.]

Thus, King David, peace be upon him, who "knew to make music" (1 Samuel 16:18), was also a shepherd [and, as we have found, the ancient ancestors were shepherds as well].

(יְשַׁעְיָה כד, טז) "מִכְּנַף הָאָרֶץ זְמִרֹת
שָׁמַעְנוּ", הַיְנוּ שֶׁזְּמִירוֹת וְנִגּוּנִים
יוֹצְאִים מִכְּנַף הָאָרֶץ, כִּי עַל יְדֵי
הָעֲשָׂבִים הַגְּדֵלִים בָּאָרֶץ נַעֲשֶׂה נִגּוּן
כַּנַּ"ל. וְעַל יְדֵי שֶׁהָרוֹעֶה יוֹדֵעַ הַנִּגּוּן,
עַל יְדֵי זֶה הוּא נוֹתֵן כֹּחַ בְּהָעֲשָׂבִים.
וַאֲזַי יֵשׁ לַבְּהֵמוֹת לֶאֱכֹל. וְזֶה בְּחִינַת
(שִׁיר הַשִּׁירִים ב, יב) "הַנִּצָּנִים
נִרְאוּ בָאָרֶץ, עֵת הַזָּמִיר הִגִּיעַ"; הַיְנוּ
שֶׁהַנִּצָּנִים גְּדֵלִים בָּאָרֶץ עַל יְדֵי הַזֶּמֶר
וְהַנִּגּוּן הַשַּׁיָּךְ לָהֶם כַּנַּ"ל.

"We have heard songs from the ends of the earth" (Isaiah 24:16). The songs and *nigunim* were emerging from the ends of the earth! Because of the grass that grows from the land did the *nigun* emerge, and because the shepherd knows the song, they can endow the grass with energy, and then there is [sustenance] for the animals to eat. This is the meaning of, "Blossoms have appeared in the land, the season of pruning/singing (*zamir*) has come" (Song of Songs 2:12). That is, the blossoms grow in the earth because of the songs and *nigunim* that belong to them.

148. Musical Yoke of Torah

ר' נחמן מברסלב, ליקוטי מוהר"ן תנינא, לא / *Nahman of Breslov, Likkutei Moharan II, 31*

על ידי הנגינה, אדם ניכר אם קבל
עליו עול תורה.

By means of making music, a person can know if they truly have taken on the yoke of Torah.

(continued)

וסימן, בכתף ישאו (במדבר ז), ודרז"ל
(ערכין יא) אין ישאו אלא לשון
שירה, שנאמר שאו זמרה ותנו תוף.
ומקרא זה נאמר במשא בני קהת,
שהיו נושאים בכתף את הארון, היינו
בחי' עול תורה:

A sign: "Raised on their shoulders" (Numbers 7:9), which the Rabbis interpreted, "There is no 'raising' but singing, as it is said, 'Raise a song and bring the beat' (Psalms 81:3)" (Talmud Bavli Arakhin 11a). This verse is said regarding the lifting of the children of Kehat, who carried the ark on their shoulders, a manifestation of the yoke of Torah.

149. Song Rooted in Silence

ר' נחמן מברסלב, ליקוטי מוהר"ן סד, ה / *Nahman of Breslov, Likkutei Moharan I, 64:5*

כי כל השירות, בין לעולם הזה בין
של לעתיד לבא, הוא רק אצל משה,
שהוא בחינות שתיקה שזכה לזמר
ששייך לאמונה העליונה על הכל,
ששם נכללין כל הזמירות, כי כולם
נמשכים ממנה...

All songs, whether of this world or the one of the future to come, are only by means of Moses, who is the aspect of silence, who merited to sing since all songs are related to that elevated faith, which includes all songs, all are drawn from it…

150. Melody of the Land of Israel

ר' נחמן מברסלב, ליקוטי מוהר"ן תנינא, סג / *Nahman of Breslov, Likkutei Moharan II, 63*

דַּע, כִּי יַעֲקֹב אָבִינוּ, כְּשֶׁשָּׁלַח אֶת
בָּנָיו עֲשֶׂרֶת הַשְּׁבָטִים לְיוֹסֵף, שָׁלַח
עִמָּהֶם נִגּוּן שֶׁל אֶרֶץ יִשְׂרָאֵל. וְזֶה סוֹד:
(בְּרֵאשִׁית מג, יא) "קְחוּ מִזִּמְרַת הָאָרֶץ
בִּכְלֵיכֶם" וְכוּ'

Know that when Jacob our ancestor sent his sons, ten tribes, to Joseph, he sent with them the *nigun* (melody) of the land of Israel. Its secret [connection] is: "Take from the land's bounty (*zimrat ha'aretz*, i.e. the native produce of the land), in your vessels…" (Gen. 43:11).   *(continued)*

This refers to the song and melody he sent, through [his other sons] to Joseph. It goes along with Rashi's interpretation, "'From the bounty' (zimrat), this is the language of 'song' (zemer)..." Jacob our ancestor, even though he did not know the one [he sent his sons to parley with] was Joseph but only what the "tribes" recounted to him regarding Joseph's behavior, [Jacob] sent a melody appropriate to such an official, according to what he had heard from his sons regarding [Joseph's] bearing and behaviour. Jacob, by means of a melody, sought to impact [Joseph] according to what he needed, and thus sent the melody of the land of Israel.

Thus, he said to his sons, "Take from the bounty (zimrat) of the land, into your vessels (k'leikhem)," that is, they took the essence of its nigun, the essence of the land's melody (zimrat ha'aretz), with their instruments (keilim). "Bring down a gift for him, a bit of balm, a bit of honey, aromatic gum, resin, pistachio, and almonds..." (Genesis 43:11).

בְּחִינַת זֶמֶר וְנִגּוּן שֶׁשָּׁלַח עַל יָדָם לְיוֹסֵף. וּכְמוֹ שֶׁפֵּרֵשׁ רַשִׁ"י: "מִזִּמְרַת" לְשׁוֹן זֶמֶר וְכוּ'...יַעֲקֹב אָבִינוּ, אַף שֶׁלֹּא הָיָה יוֹדֵעַ אָז שֶׁהוּא יוֹסֵף, רַק כְּפִי מַה שֶּׁסִּפְּרוּ לוֹ הַשְּׁבָטִים הַנְהָגוֹתָיו שֶׁל יוֹסֵף, שָׁלַח לוֹ נִגּוּן הַשַּׁיָּךְ לְשַׂר כְּמוֹתוֹ, כְּפִי מַה שֶּׁשָּׁמַע מִבָּנָיו דְּרָכָיו וְהַנְהָגוֹתָיו, כִּי יַעֲקֹב רָצָה לִפְעֹל אֶצְלוֹ עַל יְדֵי הַנִּגּוּן מַה שֶּׁהָיָה צָרִיךְ, עַל כֵּן שָׁלַח לוֹ אוֹתוֹ הַנִּגּוּן שֶׁל אֶרֶץ יִשְׂרָאֵל.

וְזֶהוּ שֶׁאָמַר לְבָנָיו: "קְחוּ מִזִּמְרַת הָאָרֶץ בִּכְלֵיכֶם"; הַיְנוּ שֶׁיִּקְחוּ בְּחִינַת הַנִּגּוּן הַנַּ"ל, שֶׁהוּא בְּחִינַת זִמְרַת הָאָרֶץ כַּנַּ"ל, בַּכֵּלִים שֶׁלָּהֶם. "וְהוֹרִידוּ לָאִישׁ מִנְחָה, מְעַט צֳרִי וּמְעַט דְּבַשׁ, נְכֹאת וָלֹט, בָּטְנִים וּשְׁקֵדִים."

(continued)

הֵם בְּחִינַת מִשְׁקוֹלוֹת וּמִדּוֹת הַנִּגּוּן, כִּי
הַנִּגּוּן נַעֲשֶׂה מִגִּדּוּלֵי הָאָרֶץ כַּנַּ"ל.

These are kinds and types of melody, since a melody is made from what grows from the land.

151. Lift of a *Nigun*

ר' נחמן מברסלב, שיחות הר"ן, רעג / *Nahman of Breslov, Sihot HaRan 273*

אמר: טוב להאדם להרגיל את עצמו
שיוכל להחיות את עצמו עם איזה
נגון, כי נגון הוא דבר גדול וגבוה
מאד מאד ויש לו כח גדול לעורר
ולהמשיך את לב האדם להשם
יתברך. ואפילו מי שאינו יכול לנגן,
אף על פי כן בביתו ובינו לבין עצמו
יוכל להחיות את עצמו באיזה נגון
כפי שיוכל לזמר אותו. כי מעלת
הנגון אין לשער.

It's good for a person to accustom himself to reviving himself with a *nigun*, because *nigun* is a powerful and mighty tool, and it has the great strength to awaken a person and point his heart towards the Blessed Name. And even one who doesn't know how to play music [or sing out loud], can sing to himself and through that revive himself. For the "lift" of a *nigun* cannot be measured.

152. Prophet is Instrument Played by the Divine

ר' עוזיאל מייזליש, תפארת עוזיאל, דרוש ליום ב של ראש השנה / *Uziel Meisels (18th c. Eastern Europe), Tif'eret Uziel, Sermon for the Second Day of Rosh HaShanah*

מה ששמעתי גם כן ממורי ורבי...
דוב בער (המגיד ממזריטש)...על פי
(מלכים ב ג, טו) "והיה כנגן המנגן
ותהי עליו רוח אלקים".

What I also heard from my teacher and master...Dov Ber (the Maggid of Mezritsh)...[an interpretation] based on "when [the musician] plays a melody, the spirit [*sic*][10] of God will be on him" (2 Kings 3:15).

(*continued*)

---

[10] The verse in our Tanakh and as elsewhere quoted has "hand of God", not "spirit of God."

Everyone has seen this: when a skilled musician plays, he has ambitions and tries to make his voice sound more beautiful. But this is not the case with the instrument itself, which is silent and has no capacity to have its own ambitions. This is the meaning of "when the musician plays…:" when a musician, that is, a human being, can become "as *if* being played" (בְּנַגֵּן), that is to say, like an instrument played by a musician, having no ambition of its own, then, "the spirit of God will be upon him."

דהנה זה נראה לעיני כל אדם המנגן יפה בעת שמנגן יש לו כמה פניות ומכוין הכל להתפאר בקולו. לא כן הכלי שמנגן בו הוא דומם ובודאי אין יכולת בהכלי לעשות שום פנייה. וזה והיה כנגן המנגן, רצון לומר, אם יהיה המנגן, הוא האדם, כנגן, רצון לומר, כהכלי שמנגן בו שאף לו לא יהיה שום פנייה, אז ותהי עליו רוח אלקים.

153. The Remnants of Song

זאב וואלף מזשיטומיר, אור המאיר, פרשת תצוה / *Ze'ev Wolf of Zhitomir (d. 1800, Poland [modern Ukraine]), Or HaMe'ir, Parashat Tetzaveh*

We say each day, in the words of *Yishtabah*,[11] "God, Who selects songs of melody (*shirei zimrah*), Divine king, eternal life." At first, these words appear challenging, since there is a doubling of words, "song" and "melody." If these were two separate concepts, then it would have appeared, "in song and melody," with the *vav* (for "and") attached to "song."   (continued)

..אנו אומרים בכל יום בסדר ישתבח "הבוחר בשירי זמרה מלך אל חי העולמים," ולכאורה קשה כפל לשון שירה היינו זמרה, ולכל הפחות אם המה שתי בחינות, מהראוי לומר הבוחר בשירה ובזמרה ו' נוסף על השירה.

---

[11] The Yishtabah (יִשְׁתַּבַּח) prayer concludes the daily morning singing of the "Verses of Song" known as *P'sukei D'zimrah*. As all of the singing is coming to a close, we're in a position to listen carefully to the silence after those songs.

ולפי הנזכר יתפרש על נכון, כי
זמרה כמשמעו, ושירה משמעו לשון
שירים...החכם אשר עיניו בראשו
נשאר אצלו מן הזמרה שיריים,
מיראתו לדבר להוציא גדולת לנורא
תהלות פן יגרע, וזה אומנתו לבלום
פיו ולעשות עצמו אלם, ובאמת
יראת ה' היא אוצרו וזה עצם תענוגו
יתברך, ובוחר בשירי זמרה, היינו
מה ששייר מהזמרה מיראתו מפניו
יתברך יותר מהזמרה עצמה.

[However,] It can be interpreted more fittingly if "melody" is as its conventional meaning, and the meaning of "song" (*shir*) is "leftovers" (*shirayim*)...[12] The wise, who has eyes in his head, will be left with the residue of song, because of his reticence to speak to discharge and lessen the magnitude of the Awesome Praised One. His skill is to seal his mouth, making himself mute, for, in truth, his fear of God is his treasure, the essence of God's blessed pleasure, Who selects songs (*shirei*) of melody, that is, what remains (*shiyeir*) from the melody, due to his fear before God, even more from the melody itself.

154. Renewal of a Melody

ר' זאב וואלף מז'יטומיר, אור המאיר, דברים, קהלת / Ze'ev Wolf of Zhitomir, Or HaMe'ir, *Deuteronomy, Ecclesiastes*

ועל פי הדברים האלה בארתי, מה
שנשאלתי במשל נאה בשם הבעש"ט
זלל ה"ה, בלא נמשל,

Regarding these matters, I have explained it according to a lovely parable in the name of the Ba'al Shem Tov, of blessed memory, which I received without its own explication:

(continued)

[12] In Hasidic culture, the term shirayim refers to the sustenance distributed to those gathered from the rebbe's own portion.

Once there was a king who had servant who knew how to make the most beautiful music in the world. The king especially loved one of his melodies, so he commanded that it be played before him in the palace, every day, multiple times a day. So it was done.

As the days passed, the *nigun* (melody) became stale in the musician's eyes; the desire and excitement he once felt was gone. What did the king do to reawaken the excitement and loving desire for the musician? He had it announced every day, each time, that he wanted to hear this *nigun* that was so dear in his eyes, [and each time] a new person from the area would come from the market, who had never heard the *nigun* before. And so it was that when the person from nearby came, he elicited cravings and enthusiasm for the *nigun* anew. The king did this many times. After a while, he sought advice what to do with the servant who knew how to make music, since the king was worried about the strain of inviting a new person from the market each time, in order to bring fresh excitement for the musician.

(continued)

מלך אחד, היה לו איש יודע לנגן בכנור בתכלית היופי, וישרה בעיני המלך ניגון אחד מנגוניו, ואז צוה המלך שינגן לפניו בהיכלו, זה הניגון בכל יום ויום כמה פעמים ביום, וכן עשה.

לימים בא הניגון בעיני המנגן לכלל זקנה, וניטל ממנו החשק והתעוררת כימים ימימה, מה עשה המלך, להכניס התעוררת וחשק האהבה להמנגן, היה קורא בכל יום ובכל פעם, שרצה לשמוע הניגון שישר בעיניו, איש חדש מקרוב בא מהשוק, אשר לא שמע מעולם נגונו, ולהיות שהאיש מקרוב בא, גורם חשקות והתלהבות לנגון מחדש, וכן נהג המלך זמן רב, לימים נתיעץ המלך כדת מה לעשות עוד, עם היודע לנגן, כי טרחא יתירא היה להמלך, להזמין לפניו בכל פעם ופעם איש חדש מהשוק, בכדי ליתן התעוררות מחדש להמנגן.

The advice he received was to blindfold the musician (*lit.* remove the musician's eyes), so he could never see the form of a person again, and every time the king wanted to hear his favorite *nigun* again, he would tell the musician that a new person had come from nearby, who had never heard this *nigun* before, and fresh pleasure would be born in the musician once more.

ועצה היעוצה על זה, צוה לנקר את עיניו של המנגן, לבל יראה לנצח עוד תואר דמות אדם, וכל זמן שעלה ברצונו לשמוע ניגון הישר בעיניו, אמר להמנגן הנה איש חדש בא מקרוב, שלא שמע מעולם נגינה שלך, ואזי נולד אצלו תענוג מחדש...

The questioner asked what meaning emerges from this parable, which came from such a holy mouth.

ושאל השואל, מליצה של המשל היוצא מפי קדוש.

It seems that it is regarding prayer, which is beloved in the eyes of the King of kings, before Whom we, God's people Israel, pray three services, each and every day.

והנראה שזה נאמר על ענין התפלה, אשר ישרה בעיני מלך מלכי המלכים, שאנחנו עמו ישראל יתפללו לפניו, שלש תפלות בכל יום ויום

155. *P'sukei D'Zimrah*: Trimming Away Husks from Our Hearts

ר' זאב וואלף מז'יטומיר, אור המאיר, דברים, ראש השנה / *Ze'ev Wolf of Zhitomir, Or HaMe'ir, Deuteronomy, Rosh Hashanah*

...ועתה תחזה, טרם כל, אנו אומרים פסוקי דזמרה, וחז"ל אמרו (שערי אורה שער א) "למה נקרא פסוקי דזמרה? על שם שמזמרים הקליפות".

Look, first of all, we say *P'sukei D'Zimrah* (Verses of Song), about which our Rabbis of blessed memory said, "Why are they called verses of song (*zimrah*)? Since they pare away (*m'zam'rim*) the husks."[13]

ולכאורה, מי האיש שראה אפילו פעם אחת, קליפות מוטלים לארץ בבית המדרש? אמנם הכונה שמזמר הקליפיות מקרב לבו ועצמותו...

But look: who has ever seen husks left about on the floor of a synagogue? Rather, it really means to pare away (*m'zameir*) the husks from one's heart and soul...

וכמוהו מהזמירות. מזמר בקרבו את הקליפיות ממדות המגונות שמרגיש בעצמו, ואחר כך יתכן לו להתפלל, משמעו לשון התחברות, לייחד פנימיות מחשבתו לרוממות אלהותו, וכשבא לקריאת שמע...אזי נעשה אחדות גמור עם הקדוש ברוך הוא.

And we continue in this through all the hymns (*z'mirot*): we pare away the husks of the negative qualities we feel within us, and afterwards, we are ready to pray, implying connection, uniting the one's inner thoughts to the loftiness of one's divinity. When the recitation of the *Sh'ma* arrives...then, a complete unity with the Holy Blessed One is achieved.

---

[13] Usually, "Our Rabbis of blessed memory" (*Hazal*) refers to the sages of the Talmudic era. In this case, this teaching is from Joseph Gikatilla, a thirteenth century Kabbalist.

156. Jacob Becomes Honest, and Takes the Name "Song"

שפת אמת, ויקרא, פסח, שנת תרנ"ח / *Judah Aryeh Leib Alter (b. 1847, Poland), Sefat Emet,*
Leviticus, Passover, 5658

וישראל כשבאין לדרך הישר אז ישיר
ישראל שיר אל:

And Israel (*YiSRael*), as it comes to
the straight path (*derekh haYaSHaR*),
thereby Israel starts Singing
(*YaSHiR*) a song of God (*SHiR EL*).

157. Cleaning Person's Soul with a *Nigun*

ר' יוסף יצחק שניאורסון, ספר השיחות תרפ"ט, יום שמחת תורה, טז[14] / *Joseph Isaac Schneerson*
(1880–1950), Book of Discourses, 1928, Simhat Torah 16

אין דעם ניגון "קול דודי דופק" איז
דער רבי...אדמו"ר הזקן...מנקה...
סקראָבעט...אַ נשמה, ער נעמט אַראָפּ
אַ סירכא. [...] הוד כ"ק אדמו"ר
האמצעי האָט געזאָגט, אַז דער
טאַטע...אדמו"ר הזקן...האָט געקענט
אַרײַנקריכן בקרבו של חסיד און
אַרויסרײַסן וואָס טויג ניט, מיט
חסידות אָדער מיט אַ ניגון. און דער
ניגון (קול דודי)...מאַנט. ער...הכוונה
על החסיד...זאָגט, וואָס האָסטו
צו מיר...כסוס שאינו רוצה לילך
וכשרוצים להנהיגו שטעלט ער זיך
אויף די פאָרנסטע פיס...

During the *nigun* "My Beloved's
Voice is Knocking" (*Kol Dodi Dofek*),
the Alter Rebbe would scrub out
a soul. He would scrape off its
blemishes! [...] the illustrious holy
priest, the Mittler Rebbe (Dov Ber
Schneuri) [said] that his father, the
Alter Rebbe—Shneur Zalman of
Liadi—could crawl into the inside of
a Hasid and could rip out the good-
for-nothing stuff, either with a Hasidic
teaching, or with a *nigun*. And the
nigun (*Kol Dodi*)—makes a claim.
He—meaning the Hasid—would say,
"What do you want from me?"—like
a horse that does not want to move,
when you want to lead it, it rears up
from its front feet.　　(*continued*)

---

[14] This text is Yiddish in Hebrew characters.

People describe the *nigun* accordingly: in the introduction, [it signifies]— the Divine is God, truly, the living God, the Divine is truth forever. In the following movement: why did the soul descend into the body? As it continues, [it answers]—Because the Holy Blessed One wants a dwelling, even in the lowest of places. The third movement is as souls say, this intention is executed solely through us. The following continuation is the feeling of receiving in that flow. The holy priest, the Rebbe directed us to sing this *nigun* over and over, and each time, he explicated the intention of the *nigun* as above, only in different words, commanding us to seize fast to this *nigun*, with that which is inside it, and to sing it when we gather together, and it will have great impact.

זאָגט מען אים אין דעם ניגון אַזוי: דער ערשטער פאַל...הוי' אלקים אמת הוא אלקים חיים, ואמת ה' לעולם. דער צווייטער פאַל: למה ירדה הנשמה בגוף, דער וויטערדיקער המשך...וויל נתאוה הקב"ה להיות לו דירה בתחתונים. דער דריטער פאַל איז, וואָס נשמות זאָגן, אַז די כוונה פירט זיך אויס נאָר דורך אונז, דער וויטערדיקער המשך איז, דער הרגש המקבל אין דער המשכה. כ"ק אדמו"ר צוה לנגן ניגון זה כמה פעמים ובכל פעם ביאר הכוונה של הניגון ע"ד הנ"ל, רק בתיבות שונות, וצוה לתפוס הניגון היטב עם העניין הפנימי שבו, ולנגנו בזמני התוועדות אנ"ש ויפעול הרבה.

158. *Nigun* is Ladder to the Heavens

ר' קלונמוס קלמן שפירא מפיסצ'נה, צו וזרוז, אות לו / *Kalonymus Kalman Shapira of Piazetsne (b 1889, Poland), Tzav veZeiruz 36*

Sometimes, a person must build ladders to climb to the heavens. A *nigun* (melody) is one of these ladders, specifically when its singing comes from the joy of a *mitzvah*, and with a heart broken open…

האדם צריך לעשות סולמות לעלות על ידיהם לפעמים השמימה, הנגון הוא אחד מהסלמות, ובפרט כשמרננים אחר שמחה של מצוה, ובלב נשבר ...

159. Sing God's Praises, Don't Just Talk

ר' קלנמוס קלמן שפירא מפיסצ'נה, חובת התלמידים, עמ' צח-צט / *Kalonymus Kalman Shapira of Piazetsne, Hovat ha-Talmidim, Torah Prayer and Singing to God, Sec 2, pp. 98–9*

המספר משבחי ד' וגדלותו דומה למי שמספר שיש אור גדול שמאיר במקום פלוני רחוק, והאומר שירה משבחי וגדלות ד' דומה למי שמביא את הנר מהתם להכא, ראיה יתירה של בחינת בני נביאים שבנו התעוררה בו, ובשירתו וברוחו מגלה הוא קצת ממנה.

One who speaks of the praises and glory of God is like one who recounts that there is a great light [like the sun] that shines in a certain place far away. But one who sings a song of praise and glory for God is like one who brings a candle close from far away. This [singing] arouses in him an extra visioning power of the *B'nei Nevi'im* (children of prophets)[15] that is within him, and through his song and spirit it is somewhat revealed.

160. *Nigun* Reawakens Life-inspiration

משה יחיאל אלימלך מלברטוב, מאמר הניגון, עמ' ג / *Moses Yehiel Elimelekh of Levertov, (b 1895, Poland), Ma'amar Nigun, p. 3*

העניין ה"ניגון" הוא עניין התעוררות לעורר רעיון נשגב לנצחון או לשפלות, ומעורר גם את עצם האדם ורעיונותיו העמוקים אשר אינם נגלים לו בלי זה ע"י איזה סיבה.

The meaning of a *nigun* is awakening, to awaken a sublime concept, of triumph or being laid low, and to awaken the essence of humanity and its deep significance that cannot be revealed save by other means.

---

[15] The people of Israel, if not prophets, are at least the children of prophets. See 2 Kings 2:3 and Bavli Pesahim 66a.

161. Singing in Isolation: The Shepherd

'משה יחיאל אלימלך מלברטוב, מאמר הניגון, עמוד ג / *Moses Yehiel Elimelekh of Levertov,*
Ma'amar Nigun, p. 3

דרך הרועים לנגן ביותר משאר בני
אדם, ובפרט אותם הרועים אשר
מרחיקים את עצמם עם המקנה
מישוב בני אדם למקום מרעה
שבע ודשן. כי רוצים שיתעורר בם
אנושיותם ולחזק ולסעד את לבם
עבור געגועיהם לחברה האנושיות
באשר זה עצם האדם כמחז"ל
חברותא או מיתותא ונמצאים המה
בין בהמות וחיות הארץ נבדלים
מישוב בני אדם על כן רוצים לעורר
בם את העצם שלהם.

Shepherds tend to sing more than other kinds of people, specifically when they have taken themselves, with their flock, to a spot for satisfactory grazing, far away from human civilization. They want to awaken their humanity within themselves, to strengthen and care for their heart, due to their longing for personal fellowship, since this is the essence of a human being, as our Rabbis of blessed memory said, "fellowship or death" (Talmud Bavli Ta'anit 23a). They find themselves amidst animals and the beasts of the land, separated from human civilization, and thus they want to awaken their essence, [so they sing].

162. Music Lifts Us Up, Out of Our Worldly Condition

משה יחיאל אלימלך מלברטוב, מאמר הניגון, עמ' ה / *Moses Yehiel Elimelekh of Levertov,*
Ma'amar Nigun, p. 5

...ולזה צוה לקח לו מנגן ובזה אשר
(מלכים ב ג, טו) "והי' כנגן המנגן"
באמצעות זה יתעלה מהמצב העולמי
ובכח וזה "ותהי עליו יד ה'"

...This is why he commanded, "Bring me a musician," since "when the musician played," through this, one is lifted up from one's worldly situation, "the hand of God rested on him" (2 Kings 3:15). *(continued)*

וזהו כענין שאחז"ל (בבמ"ק) "כל הכועס אם נביא נביאתו מסתלקת" כי אלו מדות הגרועים מבטלים ומסתרים את צד הזך שבנפש שבכחה לקבל נבואה וכו' וז"ש אין השכינה שורה לא מתוך עצבות וכו' אלא מתוך שמחה של מצוה כי זה לבדו אשר הורם ואשר הונף מהרגישות הנפשית לבא לידי הטוב הגמור בעודו בחיים חיותו כי הוא מדה אשר לה שלימות מכל צד.

This is just as our Rabbis, of blessed memory, said in many places: "Anyone who becomes angry, if they are a prophet, their prophecy withdraws…" These are the destructive characteristics which negate and sabotage the subtle side of the soul through whose power one can receive prophecy. This is as it was said, "The *Shekhinah* does not rest on one in a downhearted state… but rather from the joy of a *mitzvah*," in this sole state is one lifted up and elevated from the vicissitudes of the spirit to come to complete goodness while still vital and alive, this is a quality *complete* in every side.

163. Uncovering Hidden Inner Beings

משה יחיאל אלימלך מלברטוב, מאמר הניגון, עמ' יז / *Moses Yehiel Elimelekh of Levertov, Ma'amar Nigun, p. 17*

הניגון מעורר הזכרון ואהבה והדביקות אף כי נסתרה באדם עד שהאדם בעצמו לא ירגישה כי נעלמה ממנו בכל זה צפון ועומדת בו ונזכרת על ידי הניגון

The *nigun* awakens the trace of a memory of love and attachment… even when it is hidden in a person, such that they can no longer feel it in themselves, for it has disappeared from them. Even so, it is hidden and still remains to be brought to mind by means of the *nigun*.

164. *Nigun* and the Pleasantness of Torah

משה יחיאל אלימלך מלברטוב, מאמר הניגון, עמ' יט / *Moses Yehiel Elimelekh of Levertov,*
Ma'amar Nigun, p. 19

וזה הוא הענין במ"ש מגילה ל"ב. כל
הנקרא בלא נעימה ושונה בלא זמרה
עליו הכתוב אומר (יחזקאל כ, כה)
וגם אני נתתי להם חוקים לא טובים
וגו' כי זה מורה על שלא הרגיש נועם
התורה ומתיקתה כי לא פעלה בנפשו
כלל שתעורר בו זמרה.

This is the idea in what is written in
Talmud Bavli Megillah 32a, "Anyone
who reads [Torah] without tonality
or recites [Mishnah] without a
tune, this verse applies to them: 'I
have also given them laws that were
not good, etc.' (Ezekiel 20:25)."
This indicates someone who does
not feel the pleasantness of Torah
and its sweetness, for they have
not activated their spirit at all,
awakening it through song.

165. Remaining Tasks in Life...To Sing!

נפלאות היהודי, ער' יהושע העשיל מבית ראקאץ (פיעטרקוב, תרפ"ח) ל / *Niflaoth HaYehudi,*
ed. J. K. K. Rokotz (Pietrkov, 1908) p. 59[16]

פעם אחד, ראה היהודי הקדוש ברוח
קדשו שהמגיד הקדוש מקאזיניץ
זצ"ל הוא חולה בסכנת נפשות וצוה
תיכף על שני אנשיו, א' הנקרא ר'
שמואל יעדלינסקער, והשני הוא
הנקרא ר' שמואל סקשינער, ופקד
עליהם שיסעו לבית המגיד הקדוש
ויהיה עוד בחיים חיותו.

Once, the Holy Jew (Rabbi Jacob Isaac
Rabinowitz of Pshischa) saw, with
his holy spirit of prophecy, that the
holy Maggid of Koznitz was deathly
ill, so he immediately ordered two of
his men, one named Rabbi Samuel
Yedlinsker, and the other named
Rabbi Samuel Sekshiner, to travel to
the house of the holy Maggid while he
still lived. (continued)

---

[16] Found in Louis Newman, *Hasidic Anthology* (New York: Schocken Books, 1963), 65, §9.

There they will take in a Shabbat with the holy Maggid, for they are immensely skilled singers and can, with their songs, restore and return [the Maggid] to this world. Due to [the Holy Jew's] command, they were protected and [smoothly] traveled to Koznitz and came before the holy Maggid, who still lived. He asked them from where they came, and they answered that the Holy Jew had sent them to here. Rabbi Samuel Yedlinsker said that he was able to sing, and the holy Maggid honored him with [leading] Kabbalat Shabbat, and Rabbi Samuel Sekshiner would enhance his leading as a *meshorrer* (harmonizer). When the holy Maggid heard the *nigunim* (melodies) of Kabbalat Shabbat, his health began to improve, more and more with each one. He felt within himself that the *nigunim* were the specific medicine for his illness. Said the holy Maggid, "The Holy Jew saw, in his radiant lens [of prophecy] that I had already walked throughout all realms, but I had not yet been to the world of song. So he sent me these men who could return me to this world, through their *nigunim*."

אז יקבלו שם שבת לפני המגיד הקדוש כי הם היו בעלי מנגנים גדולים ויכלו בהניגונים שלהם לקיימו ולהחזור אותו לזה העולם ותיקף פקודתו הקדושה שמרה רוחם ונסעו לקאזיניץ ויבואו לפני המגיד הקדוש בעודו חיים. וישאל להם מאין באתם? ואמרו שהיהודי הקדוש שלח אותם לכאן. ור' שמואל יעדלינסקער אמר שהוא יכול לנגן. ואז כיבד אותו המגיד הקדוש בקבלת שבת. ור' שמואל סקשינער היה למסייע לו כמשורר. ובעת ששמע המגיד הקדוש הניגונים של קבלת שבת הוטב לו מחוליו ובכל פעם יותר ויותר והרגיש בעצמו שהניגונים המה רפואה בדוקה למחלתו. ואמר המגיד הקדוש שהיהודי הקדוש ראה באספקלריא המאירה שאני הלכתי בכל העולמות, אך בעולם הניגון לא הייתי, ושלח לי השני אנשים האלה שיחזרו אותי לזה העולם בהניגונים שלהם.

166. Carrying Our Burdens with Song

אליעזר שטיינמאן, באר החסידות: הרבנים מפולין, עמ' רז, שאול טויב ממודזיץ. / A story of
Saul Taub of Modhitz (b. 1886), as told by Eliezer Shtainman

במדרש בראשית רבה פרק ו' נאמר:
(במדבר ז, ט) "ולבני קהת לא נתן כי
עבודת הקודש עליהם בכתף ישאו".
מה תלמוד לומר ישאו? אין ישאו
אלא לשון שירה.

In Bereishit Rabbah, chapter 6, it was said: "But 'A reciter derived it from here: 'To the children of Kehat, [Moses] gave nothing [no carts, oxen], since the holy work was upon them, raised on their shoulders' (Numbers 7:9). What is the Torah teaching [by the word] 'raised?' 'Raised' means 'singing.'"

ותמוה הדבר: מה ענין שירה
למשאות הכתף? אלא לומר לך,
כי אף בשעה שהכתף רובצת תחת
עול השעבוד והצרות, צריך לשאת
את הקול בשירות ובזמירות ולקוות
לישועה. וזהו: אין וישאו אלא לשון
שירה.

This is surprising: what does song have to do with lifting atop one's shoulders? Rather, it is saying to you, that even when your shoulder buckles under the yoke of subjugation, and the pain, you have to lift up your voice in melody and song, in hope for salvation. That is it: "Lifting" is the language of song.

על הכתוב ב"במדבר" ח' "נתונין
נתונים המה לי" אומר רש"י: נתונים
למשא, נתונים לשיר. ובתיקוני זוהר,
תיקון כ"א נאמר: אורייתא בניגונתא,
שכינתא בניגונתא, ישראל סלקין מני
גלותא בניגונתא.

Regarding the verse in Numbers 8:16, "They are completely given unto Me," Rashi says: "They are given for lifting, they are given for song." And in the Tikkunei Zohar 21, it is said: "Torah is in song, Shekhinah is in song, Israel is lifted out of exile with song."

167. Reb Zusha's Whistling

ר' זושא מאניפולי, מצוטט בספר אהל אלימלך, ער' אברהם חיים מיכלזאהן, סז:-סח. / *Zusha of Anipoli (c.1730–c.1800), as related in Ohel Elimelekh (Premishlan, 1910), pp. 134–135*

Relatedly, I recall something I heard, when Rabbi Zusha, may his merit protect us, stayed by the holy genius (Rabbi Mordecai Shapiro) of Neskiz, who gave him a room to sleep. After midnight, the elder of Neskiz heard Rabbi Zusha alight from his bed in burning enthusiasm and run around his room, hither and thither. After these sprints, he cried out, "Master of the universe! Behold! I love You, but what can I do [for You]? I can't do anything." Then he ran around again, like before, saying this repeatedly, running again and again, until he said, "Behold! [All] I can do is whistle with my mouth for the sake of the Creator, of the blessed name." And he began to whistle with his holy mouth (in Yiddish, *svishtsen*) with awesome, burning enthusiasm until the elder of Neskiz said to him companion, standing next to him, "Go! Flee from here, or you'll be burned up by the breath of his holy mouth."

אגב אזכיר מה ששמעתי שהר"ר זושא זי"ע היה אצל הגה"ק מנעסכיז ונתן לו חדרו לשינה ואחר חצות לילה שמע הזקן מנעסכיז את הרר"ז שקם ממטתו בהתלהבות ורץ בחדרו אנה ואנה ואחר איזו ריצות צועק רבש"ע! הנני אוהב אותך אך מה אוכל עשות. הלא איני יכול מאומה. ואח"כ רץ שוב כמקדם ואומר כך כמ"פ ורץ כמ"פ עד שאמר הנני יכול שווישצען בפה בעבור הבורא ית"ש. והתחיל לתקוע בפיו הק' (בלשון אידיש שווישצען) בהתלהבות נורא עד שאמר הזקן מנעסכיז לחבירו שעמד אצלו. לכה ונברח מפה שלא ישרפנו בהבל פיו הקדוש.

168. Sing Now, or Inspiration Might Pass

אליעזר שטיינמאן, באר החסידות: הרבנים מפולין, עמ' רפא, מנחם מנדל מקאצק / *A story of the Kotzker Rebbe (1787–1859), as told by Eliezer Shtainman*

כשהמלאכים ביקשו לומר שירה אמר
להם הקדוש ברוך הוא: אז ישיר משה
ובני ישראל תחילה, ואחרי כן אתם.
כך נאמר במדרש.

When the angels asked [God] to sing a song [at the Red Sea,] the Holy Blessed One said to them, "Moses will sing then, and the Children of Israel, and after them, you." Thus is it said in the *midrash*.

הטעם הוא, שהמלאכים מסוגלים
לשיר בכל שעה ורגע. מה שאין
כן בני אדם, הזקוקים להתעוררות
החשק, ואם דוחים את השירה לאחר
זמן עלול להיבטל החשק.

The reason is that the angels were designed to sing, in each hour, each moment. But not people, who need the awakening of desire [to move themselves to sing], and if they put [the song] off, that desire is liable to fade away.

SIDDUR/MAHZOR

169. If Our Mouths Could be Full of Song

שבת שחרית, נשמת / *Shabbat Morning Liturgy, Nishmat*

נִשְׁמַת כָּל חַי, תְּבָרֵךְ אֶת שִׁמְךָ
ה' אֱלֹהֵינוּ...

The soul of all alive, blesses Your Name, YHVH our God...

אִלוּ פִינוּ מָלֵא שִׁירָה כַּיָּם,

Even if our mouths were as full of song as the sea,

וּלְשׁוֹנֵנוּ רִנָּה כַּהֲמוֹן גַּלָּיו,

our tongues with joy as the many waves,

וְשִׂפְתוֹתֵינוּ שֶׁבַח כְּמֶרְחֲבֵי רָקִיעַ,

our lips with praise as the expanse of the sky,

וְעֵינֵינוּ מְאִירוֹת כַּשֶּׁמֶשׁ וְכַיָּרֵחַ,

our eyes shining like the sun and the moon,

וְיָדֵינוּ פְרוּשׂוֹת כְּנִשְׁרֵי שָׁמָיִם,

our hands spread out like eagles' wings,

וְרַגְלֵינוּ קַלּוֹת כָּאַיָּלוֹת,

our legs as swift as gazelles',

אֵין אֲנַחְנוּ מַסְפִּיקִים, לְהוֹדוֹת לְךָ ה'
אֱלֹהֵינוּ וֵאלֹהֵי אֲבוֹתֵינוּ

we still could not satisfy the praises due to You, YHVH our God, God of our ancestors.

170. Renewing the Work of Creation, with Song

שחרית של חול, יוצר אור / *Daily Morning Liturgy, Yotzer Or*

לָאֵל בָּרוּךְ נְעִימוֹת יִתֵּנוּ. לְמֶלֶךְ אֵל
חַי וְקַיָּם זְמִרוֹת יֹאמֵרוּ וְתִשְׁבָּחוֹת
יַשְׁמִיעוּ...

They [the angels] offer songs to the blessed God, to the Ruler, God Who Lives and Is. They sing songs and make praises heard... *(continued)*

הַמְחַדֵּשׁ בְּטוּבוֹ בְּכָל יוֹם תָּמִיד מַעֲשֵׂה
בְרֵאשִׁית.

Who renews the work of creation
with goodness…every day and in
every moment—always.

171. Angels : Singing As One

שחרית של חול, ברכות לפני קריאת שמע / *Daily Morning Liturgy, Blessings Before Sh'ma*

וְכֻלָּם פּוֹתְחִים אֶת פִּיהֶם בִּקְדֻשָּׁה
וּבְטָהֳרָה, בְּשִׁירָה וּבְזִמְרָה, וּמְבָרְכִים
וּמְשַׁבְּחִים...

And all open their mouths, in
holiness and purity, in song and
melody, blessing and praising…

וְכֻלָּם מְקַבְּלִים עֲלֵיהֶם עֹל מַלְכוּת
שָׁמַיִם זֶה מִזֶּה. וְנוֹתְנִים בְּאַהֲבָה רְשׁוּת
זֶה לָזֶה, לְהַקְדִּישׁ לְיוֹצְרָם בְּנַחַת רוּחַ,
בְּשָׂפָה בְרוּרָה וּבִנְעִימָה קְדוֹשָׁה כֻּלָּם
כְּאֶחָד עוֹנִים וְאוֹמְרִים בְּיִרְאָה:

And all accept the yoke of heaven's
kingdom upon themselves, each
from the other, lovingly giving
each other permission to sanctify
their Creator with delight, with
crystal language and sacred song, all
answering as one, speaking with awe:

קָדוֹשׁ, קָדוֹשׁ, קָדוֹשׁ, ה' צְבָאוֹת, מְלֹא
כָל הָאָרֶץ כְּבוֹדוֹ:

"Holy, holy, holy is God of Hosts,
filling the whole world with His
Glory" (Isaiah 6:3).

172. Freedom Shofar

תפילת עמידה לחול / *Weekday Amidah Prayer*

תְּקַע בְּשׁוֹפָר גָּדוֹל לְחֵרוּתֵנוּ

Sound the Great Shofar for our
freedom.

173. Loud and Soft

ונתנה תוקף / *Unetaneh Tokef Prayer*

וּבְשׁוֹפָר גָּדוֹל יִתָּקַע. וְקוֹל דְּמָמָה דַקָּה
יִשָּׁמַע.

And the Great Shofar is sounded,
and the still small voice is heard.

TWENTIETH CENTURY

174. The Metamorphosis of a *Nigun*

י.ל. פרץ, א גילגול פון א ניגון (1922), עמ' ד-ה / I.L. Peretz,

"Metamorphosis[1] of a Nigun," 1922, excerpt p. 4–5, Vilna

דאָס איז ערשט דער גוף פון ניגון; ער
דארף נאָך אַ נשמה! און די נשמה
פון אַ ניגון איז שוין אַ געפיל פון אַ
מענטש: זיין ליבשאַפט, זיין צאָרן,
לייטזעליקייט, נקמה, האַרצבענקעניש,
חרטה, צער, - אַלץ, אַלץ, וואָס אַ
מענטש פילט, קאָן ער אַריינגעבן אין
אַ ניגון און דער ניגון-לעבט...

און אַ ניגון לעבט, און אַ ניגון
שטאַרבט; און מען פאַרגעסט אַ ניגון,
ווי מען פאַרגעסט אַ שוכן-עפר!

יונג און פריש איז ער אַמאָל געוועז,
דער ניגון! מיט פריש לעבן האָט
ער געשפריצעט...מיט דער צייט איז
ער אָפּגעשוואַכט געוואָרען, ער האָט
אָפּגעלעבט זיין צייט און די כוחות
זיינען אים אויסגעגאַנגען...עבר-ובטל
איז ער געוואָרען...דערנאָך איז זיין
לעצטער הויך אַריין אין דער לופט און
ערגעץ פאַרשטיקט געוואָרען - ואיננו!...

נאָר אַ ניגון קען אויפשטיין תחית
המתים...

First there is the body of a *nigun*, but it still needs a soul! And the soul of a *nigun* is, of course, a person's feelings: his love, his rage, his grace, his vengefulness, his heart's longing, his regret, his pain—all, all that a person feels, can he put into a it and the *nigun*—can come to life!...

And a *nigun* lives, and a *nigun* dies; and one forgets a *nigun*, like one forgets someone who has been buried!

Young and fresh it once was, that *nigun*! With fresh life it had burst forth...but with time it became weak, it had lived through its prime, and its energy left it...It was a thing of the past, it was nullified.. Its last breath went into the air, and somewhere quiet it went...and it was no more!

But even a *nigun* can be resurrected...   (continued)

---

[1] In Hebrew, gilgul which refers to the Kabbalistic idea of the soul's reincarnation. It can also refer to transformation.

פלוצים דערמאָנט מען זיך אָן אַלטן
ניגון, ער שװימט פּלוצים אַרױס און
רײסט זיך פֿון מױל אַראָפּ...נישט
װילנדיק, לײגט מען אין אים אַרײן
אַ נײַ געפֿיל, אַ נײַע נשמה, און
כמעט אַ נײַער ניגון לעבט...

Suddenly and old *nigun* is recollected, it bubbles up and springs out of one's mouth…not intentionally, a new feeling infuses it, a new soul (*neshome*), and it is almost a new *nigun* that comes to life…

דאָס איז שױן אַ גלגול פֿון אַ ניגון.

That is indeed a metamorphosis of a *nigun*.

175. Four Levels of Song: Particular Songs, Universal Songs

רב אברהם יצחק הכהן קוק, אורות הקודש, כרך ב, עמ' תמ"ד-תמ"ה / *Abraham Isaac Kook (d. 1935, Jerusalem), Orot HaKodesh, 2:444–445*

יש שהוא שר את שירת נפשו,
ובנפשו הוא מוצא את הכל, את מלא
הסיפוק הרוחני במילואו.

There is one who sings his soul's song, and in it he finds all, the fullness of spiritual satisfaction.

ויש שהוא שר שירת האומה, יוצא
הוא מתוך המעגל של נפשו הפרטית,
שאינו מוצא אותה מרווחבת כראוי,
ולא מיושבת ישוב אידיאלי, שואף
למרומי עז, והוא מתדבק באהבה
עדינה עם כללותה של כנסת ישראל,
ועמה הוא שר את שיריה, מצר
צרותיה, ומשתעשע בתקוותיה, הוגה
דעות עליונות וטהורות על עברה ועל
עתידה, וחוקר באהבה ובחכמת לב
את תוכן רוחה הפנימי.

There is one who sings the song of the nation. It emerges from the circle in the most private part of his soul, since he cannot find it abroad, nor in contemplation of the ideal. He aspires to great heights, cleaving with pure love to the congregation of Israel, completely. And with her he sings her songs, from the pain of her pain, luxuriating in her hopes, crafting lofty and pure thoughts on her past and on her future, digging deep with love and the wisdom of the heart to the innermost interior of her spirit.

(continued)

ויש אשר עוד תתרחב נפשו עד
שיוצא ומתפשט מעל גבול ישראל,
לשיר את שירת האדם, רוחו הולך
ומתרחב בגאון כללות האדם והוד
צלמו, שואף אל תעודתו הכללית
ומצפה להשתלמותו העליונה,
וממקור חיים זה הוא שואב את
כללות הגיונותיו ומחקריו, שאיפותיו
וחזיונותיו.

There is one whose soul will expand until it emerges, spreading beyond the boundary of Israel, to sing humanity's song. Her spirit will continue to expand, taking in the wholeness of the humanity and its majestic form, aspiring to the extent of what it can achieve, envisioning the extent of its coming to fruition. From this life-source, she will draw all her imagining and inquiring, all her hopes and all her dreams.

ויש אשר עוד מזה למעלה ברוחב
יתנשא, עד שמתאחד עם כל היקום
כולו, עם כל הבריות, ועם כל
העולמים, ועם כולם אומר שירה,
זה הוא העוסק בפרק שירה בכל יום
שמובטח לו שהוא בן העולם הבא.

There is one who will reach still further and higher until he unites with all of existence; with all creatures, with all worlds, and with them all he sings a song. This is the one who, on each and every day promised to him, delves deep into the Perek Shirah, a child of the world that is coming.

ויש אשר עולה עם כל השירים הללו
ביחד באגודה אחת, וכולם נותנים
את קולותיהם, כולם יחד מנעימים
את זמריהם, וזה לתוך זה נותן לשד
וחיים, קול ששון וקול שמחה, קול
צהלה וקול רנה, קול חדוה וקול
קדושה.

There is one who ascends in unity along with all these songs, together as one. All contribute their voices, making their melodies together, each infusing the other with energy and life. Sound of joy, sound of delight; sound of celebration sound of exultation; sound of pleasure, sound of holiness.   *(continued)*

שירת הנפש, שירת האומה, שירת
האדם, שירת העולם, כולן יחד
מתמזגות בקרבו בכל עת ובכל שעה.

The song of the soul, the song of the nation, the song of humanity, the song of the universe, all of them blending together inside him, in each and every moment.

והתמימות הזאת במילואה עולה
היא להיות שירת קודש, שירת אל,
שירת ישראל, בעוצם עזה ותפארתה,
בעוצם אמתה וגדלה, ישראל שיר
אל, שיר פשוט, שיר כפול, שיר
משולש, שיר מרובע. שיר השירים
אשר לשלמה, למלך שהשלום שלו.

This perfection, in its wholeness, ascends to be a sacred song, a song of God, a song of Israel, the essence of her power and beauty, the essence of her truth and expanse. Israel, the singer of God, a simple song, a song in counterpoint, a song in three-part harmony, a song in four. The song of songs of Solomon, king of peace.

176. How Do We Sing Praises?

ר' אברהם יצחק קוק, שמונה קבצים, קובץ ה, פד / *Abraham Isaac Kook, Shemoneh Kevatzim*
5:84

כיצד מזמרין זמירות ואומרים
תהילות ותשבחות? בא רוח הנשמה,
והשיגוב אלהי ממלא את הלב, והלב
מרגיש איך שהוא צר מהכיל את
המון רגשותיו, התענוג הקדוש ממלא
כל קרביו.

How does one [come to] make melodies and sing songs of praise? The spirit of your soul comes, and the overwhelmingness of the divine fills the heart. And your heart feels how it is too limited to contain all of its sensations, and holy pleasure suffuses all of its limbs.

(continued)

והשכל הולך ומאיר, מברר לו את
האמת שיש בגודל החזיון, ואת
הזעירות שיש בהקלטתו לעומת
המילוי העליון. והוא מתרומם
מתעלה ומתקדש, והתביעה הפנימית
הולכת ומתגברת בקרבו. מתמלא הוא
עז כברק, ממולא נוגה ומחשכים,
עובר רעיון בקרבו על דבר שפלותיו
לעומת מעמד גודל זה. וכרגע בא
ברק אחר, כולו אור וחסד עליון
ורחמיו, ויעוד הטוב של גיאות ד'
וחזות נועמו, בגודל ופחד, בגבורה
ותפארת, ממלא כל חדרי לב.

Your mind expands and illumines, discerning the truth of the immensity of its vision, yet also its diminution, due to its being copied from a supernal original. It is lifted and ascends and is sanctified, and a compulsion felt inside grows and becomes stronger within, filled with power, like lightning, glow-full but then darkened, as a thought of lowliness passes through your mind running counter to this magnificent state. But another flash of lightning appears, and all is light and love and mercy. The goodness of God's greatness, the envisioning of divine beauty, in immensity and awe, with strength and splendor, is appointed and infuses all chambers of your heart.

הוא עודנו מתחשב, וההרגשה
מתגברת, המחשבה מתאדרת, קוי
חיים הולכים ושוטפים, לא יתנו לו
שקט. עוד הפעם התענוג העליון
דופק, קול דודי הנה הוא זה. קרוא
הוא, והוא מתעורר, פותח פה ברננה,
(תהלים סג ו) "כמו חלב ודשן תשבע
נפשי ושפתי רננות יהלל פי."

It keeps thinking, and the feeling grows. Consciousness becomes one, lifelines radiating continuously, providing no rest. Suddenly, supernal pleasure knocks, the voice of my beloved; He is here! [Your consciousness] is called, it awakes, and your mouth opens with song. "Like the fat and smoke [of the altar], my soul is satiated, my lips sing my mouth's praise" (Psalms 63:6).

(continued)

(תהלים עא, כג) "תְּרַנֵּנָּה שְׂפָתַי כִּי
אֲזַמְּרָה-לָּךְ וְנַפְשִׁי אֲשֶׁר פָּדִיתָ".

"My lips rejoice because I make music for You, and my soul that You saved" (Psalms 71:23).

177. The Nightingale and the Orchestra

משה קליינמאן, אור ישרים (פיעטרקוב, תרפ"ד), כ:-כא. / *Or Yesharim*, ed. *M. Kleinman*, Piotrkov, 1924, pp. 40–41[2]

פעם אחד, התאונן אדם אחד לפני
[ר' משה מלעבוויץ] על קיצור
עבודתו, ורוע מעבדיו, ויש לו עצבות
גדול מזה. אך בזאת יתנחם ויפיג
צערו ויתחזק בשמחה, בהיחשבו
כי הלא נמצא גרועים ממנו. ויאמר
אליו הרוח הקדש (אל הרבי), האם
מעניין כזה יכול האדם לקבל שמחה,
כי נמצא גרועים מאתו, ומאין תדע
זאת כי הוא גרוע ממך, ועוד איך
יכול אדם לחשוב זאת כי נמצא גרוע
ממנו. אך מזאת יבא אדם לשמחה.

Once, a man was *kvetching* before Rav Moshe of Lekovitsh about the brevity of his prayer, and the poor quality of his acts, and how sad this made him. However [the very act of talking about his problems] brought him comfort, his pain/sorrow/suffering faded, and his ability to feel joy was strengthened, for he realized that others were worse off than he. The Holy Spirit said [to the Rebbe], "Can one truly derive joy from realizing that other people are worse? How can one even know who is worse [or better]? How can one make that judgment that someone else is worse off, and from there come to [sincere] joy?"

(continued)

[2] Can also be found in Louis Newman and Samuel Spitz, *Hasidic Anthology: Tales and Teaching of the Hasidim*, p. 155, "Service to God," §65.

This can be compared to a king who had an orchestra, with musicians for each and every kind of instrument, available to play for him at any time. Also, in his palace, there was kept a small bird, a nightingale that trilled and chirped in its cage. The king derived great pleasure from its song, though the bird had no awareness of this at all; it did not know the laws of music theory to sing, [and definitely did not know] more than the masters of music, who are experts in their instruments. But the king's pleasure was to hear its voice, because it is a creature without any consciousness or intelligence, through which it made heard its lovely voice.

So, with a person: does not the Holy Blessed One have bands and bands replete with multitudes of angelic charioteers who exalt and glorify [God] with speech crystal clear and lovely [tone], with celebration and song, melodious exultation…Still, the Holy Blessed One receives such pleasure from the human being, an imperfect creature, in an ugly body, seemingly so much [worse] than the hosts of [perfect] angels above.

למלך שיש לו להקת מנגנים הפורטים על כל מיני כלי זמר, ומנגנים לפניו בכל עת, ונמצא גם בהיכלו צפור אחת קטנה בכלוב, צפורת הזמיר המנגנת ומפצפצת בכלובה, אשר מקבל המלך תענוג מהצפור הקטנה אשר אין לה שום דעת, ואינה יודעת איך להנעים על פי תנועות חוקי השיר, יותר מכל הבעלי כלי זמר הבקיאים החכמת הניגון. וזה תענוג המלך לשמוע קולה, יען כי היא בריה קטנה בלי דעת ושכל וחכמה, ותשמיע קול נעים.

כן האדם, הגם שיש להקב"ה כחות כתות אלפים ורבבות המרכבים ומשבחים ומפארים בשפה ברורה ובנעימה, בשיר ושבח הלל וזמרה לפניו, מקבל השי"ת תענוג מהאדם בריה שפלה בגוף עבור יותר ממלאכי מעלה.

178. *Emunah:* Hearing The Song of Creation

ר' שלום נח ברזובסקי, נתיבות שלום, שירת ההקדמה / *Shalom Noah Berezovsky (b. 1911*
Belarus), Netivot Shalom, Opening Poem

אמונת הזכה והטהורה, נותנת ליהודי
מבט מיוחד על כל בריאה. הוא רואה
את הבורא ית"ש מתוכה, מהשמים
ושמי השמים, ומן הארץ וכל אשר
עלי', מכולם ירגיש את כח הפועל
בנפעל, ואיך שאתה מחי' את כולם.
ובאור האמונה ישמע את שירת
הבריאה היוצאת מכל נברא.

A pure and unadulterated *emunah*
(belief or artistry) provides a Jew
with a unique perspective on all of
creation. Who can see the Creator,
of the blessed Name, from within it,
from within the innermost heavens,
from within the earth and all that
is on it. Who can sense the power
of the Cause in the effect, how You
infuse all with life. In the light of
this *emunah*, she can hear the song
of creation that emanates from each
created thing.

179. The Piezetzner's Essay on *nigun*

בני מחשבה טובה, ר' קלונימוס קלמיש שפירא אות יח / *Kalonymus Kalman Shapira, B'nei Mahshavah Tovah, Number 18*

The Piezetzener Rebbe, the famous Rabbi of Warsaw who died shortly after the Warsaw uprising in 1943, left behind a trove of teachings, stashed in between the walls of a home, that were discovered by a carpenter who was repairing the same house many years later. His teachings explicate various paths to deepening one's Jewish experience of the spiritual, and he often wrote about music. This essay, in particular, captures a full description of the power of the nigun in his world.

The great Rabbi Aaron of Karlin (d. 1872) in the collection entitled House of Aaron comments on the verse: "Sing from the heights of Amana" (Song of Songs 4:8). These are his profound insights: "A Jew expresses his faith (*emunah*) most fully and most joyfully when he sings out unreservedly (*lit.* 'sings his head off')." We cannot address the whole area of music, pitch, and so on at this point. We merely want to state that anyone, at any level, can reach into the living waters of his soul and pour forth the living voice within him.

איתא בספר "בית אהרן" על הפסוק תשורי מראש אמנה (שה"ש ד' ח') וזלה"ק: די גרעסטע אמונה וויפיל א ייד האט, איז זינגען דער ראש דערפון (תרגום), עכלה"ק. אין כוונתינו לברר את ענין הנגינה ועולם הנגינה בזה, כי דיברנו עתה רק איך ידלה כל איש באיזה מצב שהוא, מים חיים ממקור נשמתו, ויגלה את הקול החי אשר בקרבו.

Don't pose for yourself this doubt: don't we see cantors and great musicians whose hearts are far from God, they have no faith and no heart, God save us.   (*continued*)

אל יקשה לך הלא רואים אנו חזנים ומנגנים גדולים שלבם רחוק מד' אין אמונה ואין לב רח"ל

There are even musicians amongst the idolaters, for a melody, ultimately, is only a kind of exposure of the spirit and its feelings, which are revealed in speech, as when one speaks with a friend of their thoughts and feelings of pain or joy, but this is even more true with the [timbre of] the voice. As it is brought in our holy books: when one's sorrows are overwhelming, God forbid, and one can no longer find the words to speak, then one will break down into crying and weeping, using only his voice, no words.

ואפילו בין העכו"ם יש מנגנים, כי הניגון הוא רק מין גילוי הנפש והרגשותיה, ומתגלה בדיבור שמדבר האיש אל חבירו את מחשבותיו והרגשותיו של צער ושל שמחה ועוד יותר בקולו. וכמו שאיתא בספה"ק ראיה על זה שכאשר תתגבר צערו של האדם ח"ו, אי אפשר לו כבר לדבר רק צועק ובוכה בקולו לבד.

Therefore, the *nigun*, which comprises the sounds of the joy or bitterness that wakes a person's passions, through which the holy sparks and the limbs of the spirit are revealed. There is no guarantee as to what a person will do when their feelings are awoken or how the revealed part of their spirit will actualize.

לכן הניגון שהוא קולות שמחים או מרירים מעורר את הרגשות האדם, שבהם ניצוצי ואברי הנפש מתגלים, אבל אין עוד הכרע מה יעשה האיש בשעה שמתרגש ומה יפעל בחלק נפשו שהתגלה,

(continued)

וכמו שישנם שני אנשים שמחים, זה
מוסיף בשמחתו לעבוד את ד', וזה
שמח בשמחה של הוללות, כן גם
הניגון שהוא אחד מן מפתחות הנפש
שמעורר אותה ואת הרגשותיה, יכול
להיות איש שפותח את נפשו, וחלק
ממנה יוצא לחוץ, ומ"מ לא לבד
שאינו עושה בו מאומה אלא עוד
פוגם בחלק נפשו זה, אם בשמחה של
הוללות, או בשבירת הלב של עצבות
ויאוש, עד שנופל מן בטחונו ואמונתו
ועושה גם מעשים אשר לא יעשו
רח"ל.

וכיון שאנו חברתנו לשם ד' היא,
ורוצים אנו להוציא את נפשותנו
להמשילה על גופנו, לקשרה
בקדושתו ולבטל אותה ואת עצמותנו
בנשמת שד"י, לכן נרגיל את עצמנו
ברינה ונגינה של עבודה לשמים,

Let us suppose there are two people
who are experiencing joy. One
may direct his feelings of joy into a
deepening commitment to serve God;
the other may be totally frivolous.
Similarly with music, which is one
of the keys of the soul, waking it
and its passions. But it is possible to
open our soul, to release some of our
spiritual essence and then do nothing
at all with it—or possibly damage
it! If his joy is vacuous, if his angst
leads to nervousness and despair, he
will wound that portion of his soul
that is exposed. When he falls from
such a height, there will be enormous
damage to his faith and foundations.
The misuse of spiritual power can
lead us to deeply improper actions,
God help us!

Is not our *havurah* (group) devoted
to God, and don't we want to bring
our spirits to the fore to help direct
our bodies, connecting them in
God's holiness, nullifying it and
its [independent] essence in the
soul of God? Thus, we must train
ourselves in [the spiritual practices
of] celebration and song for the sake
of divine service.   (continued)

We don't necessarily need to compose new melodies, just as you would not prescribe to someone who wants to gladden himself through drink to press his own wine, or one who wants to awaken themselves or another through words, that they must compose a new discourse.

לא שנצטרך לחבר נגונים חדשים, כמו שלא נאמר שמי שרוצה לשמח את עצמו ביין צריך לעשות יין מגתו דוקא, ומי שרוצה לעורר את עצמו או זולתו בדבורים צריך לחדש שפה חדשה.

[Here is an exercise:] Take a musical phrase, turn your face to the wall, or simply close your eyes and remind yourself that you stand in the presence of God. With your heart breaking open, you are here to pour out your soul to God with music and melody, emerging from the depths of your heart. Inevitably, you will begin to feel the emergence of your spirit in great joy and delight. At first it was you singing to your soul, to wake her up, but slowly you will feel your soul singing her own song.

קח לך איזה תנועה של ניגון, הסב פניך אל הקיר, או רק תסגור את עיניך ותחשוב שוב, שאתה עומד לפני כסא הכבוד, ובשבירת לבך באת לשפוך את נפשך לד' בשירה וניגון היוצאים מקרב לבך, ואז מעצמך תרגיש שנפשך יוצאת ברננה. אם מתחילה היית אתה המנגן לפני נפשך לעוררה מתרדמתה, מעט מעט תרגיש שנפשך התחילה כבר לנגן בעצמה.

Each song is always a riddle; its voices, what are they, its rises and falls, what are they? Why is it sometimes long and sometimes short in coming?

חידה היתה לך תמיד הנגינה, הקולות מה המה, עליות וירידות מה הן, ולמה זה פעמים שבה בארוכה ופעמים שבא בקצרה,

(continued)

ואת הכל אתה רואה כבר, בקולה
בוקעת לך נפשך דרך עד למרום,
ובשמים כאילו אחזו בהמייתה
ומשכוה בלשונה. ליבה, מעיה וכל
פנימיותה עם נגינתה יוצאים, ודרך
הקולות עולים, ועליותיה נפילותיה
וכל גלגולי דרכה בקולה נחקקים,
ותנועא דמנגנא בו נחרתים, והניגון
נתרקם, את נפשך נושא הניגון במעיו
לשפכה ולקרבה לד'.

ויש לפעמים שבלא ידיעתך תדבר גם
דיבורים לפני המקום, אם בתחילתם
עוד את רצון גופך יודיעו, אבל כל
כמה שתתרגש, ויותר תצא נפשך
מנרתיקה לעוף אל על, במדה זו
תעזוב את העולם, ומעומק לבך
תצעק נפשך בתפילה טהורה תפילה
לה' כגון אלה: "רבונו של עולם אין
הימעל האב רחמנות אויף מיר, און
העלף מיר אין אלא עניינים, אוי
געוואלד און געשריגן ווי ליג איך
עפיס, רבונו של עולם ראטעווע מיך
ארויס".

All this has already been witnessed, with its voice your soul blazes a trail upward, up to the highest realms, grabbing it with its stirrings and drawing it with its tongue. Your heart, guts, and interior go out with your spirit's song, and the way of songs is upward, and its ascent and descent, all of its revolutions are carved, each movement of the musician is etched, and the melody is engraved in the timbre of the voice. The melody bears your spirit in its guts, pouring it out before the Divine.

Sometimes, unconsciously, one might say things to God, perhaps making known your body's desire, but as you continue and become impassioned, your soul will further come out of its hiding place to fly up above, leaving the bounds of the world. From the depths of your heart your spirit will cry out in pure prayer to the Divine, like so: "Master of the universe in Heaven, have mercy on me, and help me with these things, *oy gevald*, how I cry so long over this. Master of the universe, save me!"   (continued)

People begin with salvation in all matters and conclude with a cry to save them from where they've fallen. Do not diminish in your eyes these utterances, since they've been dug out of the soul.

Sometimes words will not awaken within you, and you will not feel any lack. Still, you should try to feel this feeling, since you cannot conjure up what you feel from a mere remembrance. This is like a child that messed up before their parent. The child does not want anything from their parent, they just moan and sigh, "Daddy, [Mommy]." The parent asks, "What do you want, my child?" "Nothing," they answer, further sighing and moaning, "Daddy, [Mommy...]"

This is an important principle. In the whole area of expressing the soul, we have much to learn from children. Children behave with a total absence of artifice and pretense.

(continued)

מתחיל בישועה בכל עניינים שלו ומסיים בצעקה להצילו ממקום נפילתו, וכן כיוצא באלו, ואל יקטונו בעיניך דיבורים כגון אלו כי מחצב הנפש הם.

ויש לפעמים שלא יתעוררו בך דיבורים ולא תרגיש שום בקשה, ומ"מ תרגיש איזה הרגשה שאי אפשר לך לצייר מה אתה מרגיש, מן התרפקות היא, כילד שמתחטא (פיעשטעט זיך) לפני אביו, אינו רוצה מאומה מאביו, הומה ומתאנח "אבי, אבי". האב שואל "מה אתה רוצה בני?". "כלום", הוא משיבו, ושוב הומה ומתאנח "אבי, אבי".

כי דע לך שבענין דרכי התגלות הנפש יש הרבה פעמים ללמוד מן הילד, כל מעשיו אינם בכוונה,

The child's very soul is expressed in each of his activities. He is transparent. His soul shines through in everything he does, including this rapprochement we described, this flowing of soul from father to son. Sometimes, when you sing you will have this experience. There are no words, there is nothing to say, there is nothing that you need. Rather, the soul rejoices and pours out herself, softly chanting, "Oh God, oh God."

This does not need to be solely with a broken-hearted melody, but it can be one of [authentic] joy as well. In all [true feeling] one can actualize the revealing of the spirit. This is the way of the hasid, sometimes they cry during a joyous melody, or during its dance, and sometimes they even dance to the melody for Kol Nidrei!

When you are with your *havurah* when they sing along with prayer or a meal, or another occasion, make sure to sing with them, not just to make your voice heard, as described by Jeremiah, "She shouted out against me" (12:8).

(continued)

רק מעצמה נפשו מתגלה באופנים שונים ועושה תנועות ומעשים כפי תנועות נפשו, וגם חיטוי זה (פיעטשעןן) השתפכות נפשו אל נפש אביו הוא. וגם אתה לפעמים תרגיש בניגונך מן המיה וחיטוי, באין אומר ובאין דברים ובלא שום בקשה, רק נפשך מרננת ומשתפכת ומפלטת רק, "רבש"ע, רבש"ע".

ולאו דוקא בניגון של שבירת הלב, רק גם בניגון של שמחה, בכולם תוכל להשתמש לגילוי הנפש וכך דרכו של החסיד, הוא בוכה לפעמים בניגון שמח, וגם בשעת רקידתו, ולפעמים רוקד גם בניגון של "כל נדרי".

לכן כשתהיה בחברת חסידים בשעה שמנגנים אם בתפילה, בסעודה, או באופן אחר, תרנן גם אתה עמהם, לא רק להשמיע קול בחי' "נתנה עלי בקולה" (ירמיהו יב ח) וכו'

רק כדי להוציא את נפשך ולהעלותה בחי', "ויהי כנגן המנגן ותהי עליו רוח ד'", מן ניגון החופה שמזווג את החתן והכלה וד"ל. ולאו דוקא בשעה שאתה בחברת חסידים בשעה שמנגנים, רק גם בביתך בכל עת שתרגיש את עצמך מוכשר לזה תוכל לרנן כנ"ל. ואין אתה צריך לצעוק בקולות, כי יש מי שמנגן רק המיה בלחש וקולו נשמע במרום.

Rather, in order to raise up your soul. As in the verse, "When the musician played (*kenagen hamenagen*), the spirit [*sic*] of God came upon him" (2 Kings 3:15). Like the song of the *huppah*, which unites the bride and groom (and the wise understand). You do not need to be in a community to sing this way. Even when you are at home, any time you feel capable, you can sing as described above. And you do not need to scream and shout. There is music made even with a whisper or a breath that can still be heard in heaven.

Selected Bibliography

The following list of books and articles is far from comprehensive, but will provide a variety of different entry-points into the study of Jewish musical-spiritual traditions.

Adler, Israel. *Hebrew Writings Concerning Music, in Manuscripts and Printed Books from Geonic Times up to 1800.* München: G. Henle Verlag, 1975.

Avenary, Hanoch. "The Hasidic Nigun: Ethos and Melos of a Folk Liturgy." *Journal of the International Folk Music Council* 16 (1964): 60–63.

Baer, Abraham. *Baal t'fillah: oder der practische Vorbeter : vollstandige Sammlung der gottesdienstlichen Gesange und Recitativ der Israeliten nach polnischen, deutschen (aschk'nasischen) und portugiesischen (sephardischen) Weisen nebst allen den Gottesdienst betreffenden rituellen Vorschriften und Gebräuchen (dinim u-minhagim).* Frankfurt: J. Kauffmann, 1877.

Beck, Guy L., ed. *Sacred Sound: Experiencing Music in World Religions.* Waterloo, Ontario: Wilfrid Laurier University Press, 2006.

Bernard, Andrew. *The Sound of Sacred Time: A Basic Music Theory Textbook to Teach the Jewish Prayer Modes.* Charlotte, NC: Andrew Bernard, 2006.

Bialik, Hayyim Nahman, and Yehoshua Hana Ravnitzky, eds. *The Book of Legends/Sefer Ha-Aggadah: Legends from the Talmud and Midrash.* Translated by William G. Braude. New York: Schocken Books, 1992.

Bin Gorion, Micha Joseph. *Mimekor Yisrael: Classic Jewish Folk Tales.* Edited by Emanuel Bin Gorion. Translated by I. M. Lask. 3 vols. Bloomington: Indiana University Press, 1976.

Bodoff, Lippman. "Music for Jewish Liturgy: Art for Whose Sake?" *Judaism* 36 (Winter, 1987): 97–103.

Buxbaum, Yitzhak. *Jewish Spiritual Practices.* Northvale, N.J.: Jason Aronson, 1999.

Eisenstein, Judith. "Mystical Strain of Jewish Liturgical Music." *Journal of the American Academy of Religion Thematic Studies* 50, no. 1 (1983): 35–54.

————. "Tensions in the Music of Jewish Worship." In *Shiv'im: Essays and Studies in Honor of Ira Eisenstein*, edited by Ronald A. Brauner, 231–40. Philadelphia: Reconstructionist Rabbinical College Press, 1977.

Farmer, Henry George. "Maimonides on Listening to Music." *Journal of the Royal Asiatic Society* 45 (1933): 867–84.

Fenton, Paul. "A Jewish Sufi on the Influence of Music." *Yuval: Studies of the Jewish Music Research Centre* 4 (1982): 124–30.

Fishbane, Michael. *The JPS Bible Commentary: Song of Songs*. Philadelphia: Jewish Publication Society, 2015.

————. "To Jump for Joy: The Rites of Dance According to R. Nahman of Bratzlav." *The Journal of Jewish Thought and Philosophy* 6 (1997): 371–87.

Frankel, Ellen. *The Classic Tales: 4,000 Years of Jewish Lore*. Northvale, NJ: Jason Aronson, 1993.

Friedmann, Jonathan L. *Music in Jewish Thought: Selected Writings, 1890–1920*. Jefferson, N.C.: McFarland, 2009.

————. *Quotations on Jewish Sacred Music*. Lanham, MD: Hamilton Books, 2011.

Ginzberg, Louis. *Legends of the Jews*. Philadelphia: Jewish Publication Society, 1955.

Glazerson, Matityahu. *Music and Kabbalah*. Northvale, N.J: Jason Aronson, 1996.

Gold, Shefa. *The Magic of Hebrew Chant Companion: The Big Book of Musical Notations and Incantations*. Woodstock, VT: Jewish Lights, 2013.

————. *The Magic of Hebrew Chant: Healing the Spirit, Transforming the Mind, Deepening Love*. Woodstock, VT: Jewish Lights, 2013.

Goodrick, Mick. *The Advancing Guitarist*. Milwaukee: Hal Leonard, 1987.

Green, Arthur. *Radical Judaism: Rethinking God and Tradition*. New Haven; London: Yale University Press, 2010.

Hammer, Jill. *Sisters at Sinai*, Philadelphia: Jewish Publication Society, 2001.

Heskes, Irene. *Passport to Jewish Music: Its History, Tradition, and Culture*. Westport, CT; London: Greenwood Press, 1994.

Hoffman, Edward. "Returning to the Source - Dreams and Music." In *The Way of Splendor: Jewish Mysticism and Modern Psychology*. Updated 25th Anniversary Edition. New York: Rowman & Littlefield Publishers, 2006.

Hoffman, Shlomo. *Ha-Musikah ba-midrashim*. Tel-Aviv: Makhon le-Musikah Yisre'elit, 1985.

————. *Ha-Musikah ba-Talmud*. Tel-Aviv: Makhon le-Musikah Yisre'elit, 1989.

————. *Miḳra'e musiḳah: yalḳuṭ shel pesuḳim meha-Tanakh she-meḥutam musiḳah be-'Ivrit, Anglit, Tsarefatit, Sefaradit.* Tel-Aviv: Makhon le-Musiḳah Yisre'elit, 1974.

Idel, Moshe. "Conceptualizations of Music in Jewish Mysticism." In *Enchanting Powers: Music in the World's Religions,* edited by Lawrence E. Sullivan, 159–88. Cambridge, MA: Harvard University Press, 1997.

————. "Music and Ecstatic Kabbalah." In *The Mystical Experience in Abraham Abulafia,* 51–65. Albany: SUNY Press, 1988.

————. "Music and Prophetic Kabbalah." *Yuval: Studies of the Jewish Music Research Centre* 4 (1982): 150–69.

————. "Music in Sixteenth-Century Kabbalah in Northern Africa." *Yuval: Studies of the Jewish Music Research Centre* 7 (2002): 154–70.

————. "The Magical and Theurgical Interpretation of Music in Jewish Renaissance Texts: From the Renaissance to Hasidism." *Yuval: Studies of the Jewish Music Research Centre* 4 (1982): 33–63.

Idelsohn, Abraham Z. *Jewish Music: Its Historical Development.* Revised edition. New York: Dover Publications, 2011.

————. *Jewish Liturgy and Its Development.* New York: Dover Publications, 1932.

Imber, Naphtali Herz. "Ancient and Modern Music of the Jewish People." *Music: A Monthly Magazine, Devoted to the Art, Science, Technic and Literature of Music* 6:2 (1894): 496–98.

————. "The Music of the Psalms." *Music: A Monthly Magazine, Devoted to the Art, Science, Technic and Literature of Music* 6, no. 2 (1894): 568–88.

Kalib, Sholom. *The Musical Tradition of the Eastern European Synagogue, Vols. 1–2.* Syracuse, N.Y.: Syracuse University Press, 2002.

Kaplan, Aryeh. *Inner Space: Introduction to Kabbalah, Meditation and Prophecy.* 2nd edition. New York: Moznaim Publishing Corporation, 1991.

Katchko, Adolph. *A Thesaurus of Cantorial Liturgy, Vols. 1–3.* New York: Hebrew Union School of Education and Sacred Music, 1952.

Levin, Neil, ed. *Z'mirot Anthology: Traditional Sabbath Songs for the Home.* Owings Mills, MD: Tara Publications, 1981.

Lewandowski, Louis. *Todah W'Simrah.* 2 vols. Berlin: Ed. Bote & G. Bock, 1876.

Loeffler, James. *The Most Musical Nation: Jews and Culture in the Late Russian Empire.* New Haven; London: Yale University Press, 2010.

Malkah, Shai. *Shirat Kol Chai: Pirkei Nigun, Midrash v'Zicharon*. Beit Va'ad le-Torah Har Chevron, 2005.

Mark, Zvi. "Silence and Melody Facing the Void: On the Place of the Mystic Melody in the Confrontation with Heresy in the Writings of R. Nachman of Bratslav." In *Mysticism and Madness: The Religious Thought of Rabbi Nachman of Bratslav*, 155–72. London: Continuum, 2009.

Miletto, Gianfranco. "The Human Body as a Musical Instrument in the Sermons of Judah Moscato." In *The Jewish Body: Corporeality, Society, and Identity in the Renaissance and Early Modern Period*, edited by Maria Diemling and Giuseppe Veltri, 377–93. Leiden, Boston: Brill, 2008.

Moshe Yehi'el Elimelekh of Levertov. "Ma'amar ha-Nigun." In *Sefer Shemirat ha-Da'at: Ma'amar ha-Midot, Emet ve-Shalom, Machshavor Me'irot, Imrei Tal, Avodat ha-Lev, Heimah Divrei Elohim Chaim*, 3–25. Jerusalem: Machon Linzei Maharitz she-al-Yedei Chasidei Biale Be-Eretz ha-Kodesh, 1985.

Nathanson, Moshe. *Zamru Lo: Congregational Melodies, Prayers, Zemirot, Hymns*. 3 vols. New York: Cantors Assembly, 1960.

Newman, Louis I., and Samuel Spitz. *Hasidic Anthology: Tales and Teaching of the Hasidim*. New York: Schocken Books, 1963.

Orenstein, Walter. *The Cantor's Manual of Jewish Law*. Northvale, N.J: Jason Aronson, 1994.

Pasternak, Velvel. *Hasidic Music: An Annotated Overview*. Owings Mills, MD: Tara Publications, 1999.

——————. *Songs of the Chassidim: An Anthology*. 2 vols. New York: Bloch Publishing Company, 1968.

Pinson, DovBer. *Inner Rhythms: The Kabbalah of Music*. Northvale, N.J: Jason Aronson, 2000.

Reb Noson of Nemirov. *Rabbi Nachman's Wisdom*. Edited by Rabbi Zvi Aryeh Rosenfeld. Breslov Research Institute, 1973.

Rosenbaum, Samuel. *A Guide to Haftarah Chanting*. New York: Ktav Publishing House, 1973.

Rossi, Salamone. *Cantiques de Salamone de Rossi* [Sheet Music]. Edited by Samuel Naumbourg. Paris: Chez L'editeur, 1877.

——————. *Hashirim 'asher lishlomo*. 3 vols. Edited by Fritz Rikko and Hugo Weisgall. New York: Jewish Theological Seminary Press, 1967–1973.

Schall, Noah. *Hazzanic Thesaurus: Sabbath*. Cedarhurst, N.Y.: Tara Publications, 1990.

Schapira, Kalonymous Kalman. *A Student's Obligation: Advice from the Rebbe of the Warsaw Ghetto*. Translated by Micha Odenheimer. Northvale, N.J.: Jason Aronson, 1995.

—————. *Conscious Community: A Guide to Inner Work*. Translated by Andrea Cohen-Kiener. Northvale, NJ: Jason Aronson, 1996.

—————. *Benei Mahshavah Tovah*. Jerusalem: Va'ad Chaisdei Piaseczno, 1973.

Scherman, Nosson, ed. *Perek Shirah: The Song of the Universe*. Brooklyn: Mesorah Publications, 2005.

Schwartz, Howard. *Tree of Souls: The Mythology of Judaism*. Oxford; New York: Oxford University Press, 2007.

Shiloah, Amnon. "Musical Concepts in the Works of Saadia Gaon." *Aleph: Historical Studies in Science and Judaism* 4:1 (2004): 265–82.

Shiloah, Amnon, and Ruth Tene. *Music Subjects in the Zohar: Texts and Indices*. Jerusalem: Magnes Press, Hebrew University, 1977.

Shiovitz, Jeffrey. *Zamru Lo: The Next Generation* . 3 vols. New York: Cantors Assembly, 2004.

Slobin, Mark, and Moshe Beregovski. *Old Jewish Folk Music*. Syracuse, NY: Syracuse University Press, 2000.

Smith, Chani Haran. *Tuning the Soul: Music as a Spiritual Process in the Teachings of Rabbi Nahman of Bratzlav*. Leiden, Boston: Brill, 2010.

Trugman, Avraham Arieh. *The Mystical Power of Music*. Jerusalem: Targum Press, 2005.

Weisenberg, Joey. *Building Singing Communities: A Practical Guide to Unlocking the Power of Music in Jewish Prayer*. New York: Mechon Hadar, 2011.

—————. , ed. *Kane Street Synagogue Shabbat Songster*. New York: Kane Street Synagogue, 2011.

—————. *Nigunim: The Songbook*. New York: Mechon Hadar, 2014.

Wolfson, Elliot R. "Biblical Accentuation in a Mystical Key - Kabbalistic Interpretations of the Te'amim." *Journal of Jewish Music and Liturgy* 11 (1988): 1–16.

—————. "Biblical Accentuation in a Mystical Key - Kabbalistic Interpretations of the Te'amim II" *Journal of Jewish Music and Liturgy* 12 (1989): 1–13.

Wooten, Victor L. *The Music Lesson: A Spiritual Search for Growth Through Music*. New York: Berkley Books, 2008.